This work of art and science is a must read for seasoned executives and millennials alike. It simultaneously insulted me, made me laugh out loud, and made me agree and disagree with myself. Most importantly, it made me really think about leadership, strategy, corporate decision making and culture differently.

—Susan DeVore, CEO of Premier Inc.

Provocative, irreverent, brash—and very wise. Don't be fooled by the informal tone and levity. The ideas here are dead serious and immensely practical. Ben and Mark do a wonderful job of cutting through the clutter and challenging conventional thinking. Their message: Think clearly. Do things differently. And above all, think for yourself.

—Phil Rosenzweig Professor at IMD, Lausanne Switzerland
and author of The Halo Effect

If you like empty corporate slogans, PowerPoint templates, and boring compliance committees, this book is NOT for you. If you are obsessed by external competition, love true strategy debates, and are always ready to speak up when it matters, this book might become your survival kit to corporate BS.
Vive la difference!

—T. Philardeau, Senior Vice-President and Head of Nutrition SBU,
Societé des Produits Nestlé SA

Hilarious, sharp, and insightful. Ben and Mark deliver on the promise of giving us a spot-on understanding of the realities of today's corporate world. I have found new required reading for my graduate students.

—Jon Down, Associate Professor of Strategy & Entrepreneurship for
the Pamplin School of Business, University of Portland

Gilad and Chussil provide guidance for the newly-minted MBA to the wizened middle manager for how to become and remain a maverick. They do this by demonstrating that many of the slogans espoused by mythologized corporate titans and exalted business scholars are either false or irrelevant to what front-line leaders and employees experience each day. The constant challenge is to question assumptions and think critically, while also being a supportive contributor to the organization. With references to pop culture and management scholarship, Gilad and Chussil have written the rare business book that is highly-readable, actually funny, and practically useful."

—MICAH ZENKO, DIRECTOR OF RESEARCH AND LEARNING, McCHRYSTAL GROUP; AUTHOR OF RED TEAM: HOW TO SUCCEED BY THINKING LIKE THE ENEMY

A refreshing and honest perspective about surviving in Corporate America. In this great read, Ben and Mark use humor and candor to get beyond the politically driven business world we live in today and toward the key principles that will help guide leaders and businesses.

—PAUL AMOS, PARTNER IN JBA CAPITAL AND FORMER PRESIDENT OF AFLAC

As a young millennial woman, I face an uphill battle to create change in my work environment. Mark and Ben's book provides sage advice so I can be heard and challenge existing practices while avoiding a forced exit. Recent graduates and young professionals can benefit *greatly* from *The NEW Employee Manual.* I know I will!

—VICTORIA FREITAG, PROGRAM COORDINATOR, COMMUNITY INVESTMENT TRUST

the new employee manual

a no-holds-barred look at corporate life

Benjamin Gilad
Mark Chussil

Entrepreneur Press®

Entrepreneur Press, Publisher
Cover Design: Andrew Welyczko
Production and Composition: Eliot House Productions

This publication is designed to provide accurate and authoritative information
in regard to the subject matter covered. It is sold with the understanding that
the publisher is not engaged in rendering legal, accounting, or other professional
services. If legal advice or other expert assistance is required, the services of a
competent professional person should be sought.

Illustrations by: Rudall30 / Shutterstock and Andrew Welyczko

Library of Congress Cataloging-in-Publication Data
　　Names: Gilad, Benjamin, author. | Chussil, Mark, author.
　　Title: The new employee manual : a no-holds-barred look at corporate
　　life / by Benjamin Gilad, Ph.D. and Mark Chussil, M.B.A.
　　Description: Irvine, California: Entrepreneur Press, [2019]
　　Identifiers: LCCN 2018046450| ISBN 978-1-59918-642-9 (alk. paper) |
　　　　ISBN 1-59918-642-X (alk. paper)
　　Subjects: LCSH: Corporate culture. | Corporations.
　　Classification: LCC HM791 .G55 2019 | DDC 302.3/5—dc23
　　LC record available at https://lccn.loc.gov/2018046450

Printed in the United States of America

23 22 21 20 19　　　　　　　　　　　　　　10 9 8 7 6 5 4 3 2 1

contents

Part I

down the rabbit hole

Chapter 1

corporate dysfunction, competing as a skill, and you . .3

Chapter 2

how to identify a corporate oop (overconfident oblivious person) 21

Chapter 3

job descriptions vs. jobs. 39

Chapter 4

training to compete. 53

Part II
how corporate thinks

Chapter 5
the myth that customers matter **71**

Chapter 6
big numbers, wrong numbers, more numbers,
and sloppy thinking **87**

Chapter 7
benchmarking: be just like *them,* only better **107**

Chapter 8
the consequences of sloppy, lazy thinking **125**

Part III
how corporate communicates

Chapter 9
the negative side of being positive 139

Chapter 10
what corporate obsesses and obsesses about 153

Chapter 11
who said anything about chapter 11? 171

Chapter 12
does corporate mean what it says? 175

Part IV
what corporate does

Chapter 18

corporate believes in magic formulas 273

Chapter 19

corporate filters inconvenient information 287

Part V

we are with you, maverick

Chapter 20

can corporate heal itself? 303

Chapter 21

executive summary 319

the NEW employee manual

introduction

"If you don't stand for something, you will fall for anything."

—GORDON A. EADIE

We are mavericks. We know you are too, or you wouldn't be reading this line.

Who are we? Well, in short, we are two corporate renegades, two veterans who have seen it all—or, at least a lot. We are Mark and Ben, your guides through corporate life. For the past 30 years, each of us has run hundreds of strategy-testing simulations known as war games inside large and powerful corporations all over the globe. In these workshops, we dove deep into companies' cultures and their people's skill at competing. We are here to share with you our downright honest exposé of real life in the corporate world.

You can't find two more different people than us. Mark is a refined product of two of the best schools in the world, Yale and Harvard. He is a serious guy, a teacher, a creator of strategy simulations, reflective and considerate, polite, and a deep thinker. Ben is an unrefined product, despite (or because of) his Ph.D., who takes nothing seriously, expresses everything brilliantly, and is direct to a fault. He also loved teaching undergraduate business students at Rutgers for two decades because, as he says, "Where else can you find people who believe everything you tell them?"

Yet, despite our differences, writing this book was the most natural thing for us. After many decades of working with seasoned managers and senior executives on six continents as well as thousands of business students and young professionals, we share one passion: making companies and individuals more competitive. More competitive means less sloppy.

We also share one perspective: Many companies that *used to be* competitive have developed dysfunctions that are robbing them of their futures. The one to pay for their sloppy, or lazy, or ossified thinking will be you, the reader. And it makes us mad that *you* pay the price for *their* sloppy thinking.

This book is not your dad's or mom's employee manual. It's the *new* manual for corporate survival, fitting today's realities and the challenges facing employees who join or work in large, seemingly successful companies. Those companies already issued very specific and detailed employee manuals covering everything under the sun *except* how to compete well in our brave new world. Our manual will help you navigate the Corporate (with a capital C) labyrinth. Where Corporate's manual shapes you into a dutiful cog for the good of the machine, ours helps you enhance your career for the good of, well, you . . . *and* your company.

Our book should make you feel skeptical: skeptical of empty slogans, obsolete rituals, obsessive pursuits, and bigwigs' playbooks that no longer work. That alone should be worth this book's price. Skepticism, you see, is a good thing because it is only the skeptic, only the free-thinker, only the *maverick,* who asks new questions and finds useful answers.

WHO SHOULD READ THIS BOOK?

This book is for mavericks.

A *maverick* is an independent thinker, unorthodox by definition since orthodox thinking is group-think. Not all group-think is bad, but how do you distinguish the bad from the good? You have to be a maverick even to ask such a question.

Are you a maverick? Ask yourself:

- Do you look for the big picture? It's easy to focus on the here and now. What makes people strategic is that they never lose sight of the broader landscape. They see the here and now in the context of the big picture.

- Do you reckon with other players' perspectives—competitors, customers, regulators, suppliers, distributors, etc.—when you plan your moves?
- Do you lead with logic, as opposed to fables? Does everyone in your team/unit/organization understand what makes the organization succeed and how each person contributes to that success?

If you already suspect something's wrong with the orthodox thinking in your organization or in those you've heard about, we confirm your thoughts and we provide evidence and support. If you don't, we open your eyes.

In business terms, *maverick* translates into "managers and professionals who haven't drunk the Corporate Kool-Aid *yet*." We briefly contemplated using the classic acronym MPWHDCKY to refer to these readers, but it seemed a bit cumbersome and "maverick" is easier to work into good, solid grammar. Corporate, incidentally, would adopt the acronym MPWHDCKY in a heartbeat. Corporate *loves* acronyms. That, you will see, is part of what makes corporate Corporate.

In short, this book is about being or becoming a maverick. Mavericks know when to swim against the current and when to let the current carry them a distance. Mavericks are critical thinkers. We offer you the tools you need to swim, float, and—above all—survive as a maverick.

This book is a must-supplement to traditional textbooks you've read over the years. Textbooks focus on functions; we focus on dysfunctions. Someone has to prepare you for not-so-pretty reality, and you may already be stuck in one and think: What's wrong with me? We are here to help. There is nothing wrong with *you*!

We dedicate this book to all those mavericks—newly hired, seasoned but repressed, in the market for a new job—willing to commit to the *skill of competing* and keenly interested in keeping their organizations as sharp and alert as they were in the early days. We met a few of those over the years.

Now it's your turn. Welcome, maverick, to your NEW employee manual.

down the rabbit hole

corporate dysfunction, competing as a skill, and you

"Two things are infinite: the universe and human stupidity; and I'm not sure about the universe."

—Albert Einstein

Welcome to corporate life. Now throw away the handbook you received at orientation. Lesson 1 isn't about where to locate the cafeteria or how to contact human resources. It's about *you* and your ability to compete.

With that in mind, we apologize, but we're going to start on a negative note. After all, false positivity is sloppy thinking, and we've already told you that sloppy thinking makes us mad. So here goes: The golden age of Western corporations may be coming to an end. As negative notes go, that's a doozy. If you are about to enter or re-enter the professional/managerial job market in business, you should know this: Old-world Western companies are under pressure. Don't be fooled by their temporary high profits, due to luck, in the form of low interest and tax rates. The rise of China, the decline of innovation, the shrinking of free trade, and the aging of consumers put future profits at risk, and place entire industries under threat of permanent decline.

All companies *ostensibly* focus on being competitive. Even those that do not can still appear to outsiders as successful and powerful. The reality we witness in our practices can at times border on comic, defying gravity and reason, not to mention vision and market understanding. Quite often the companies cultivating sloppy thinking and behavior are relatively big (though we provide examples of uncompetitive behavior at companies of all sizes later in the book). We want to say there is karma, but we can't. The success of big companies–you know their names—is often the result of inertia and luck. Big brands take time to die, but when they do, it seems like "overnight." Think JCPenney, Netscape, Yahoo!, Borders, Lehman Brothers, General Motors, MCI, AOL, General Electric. Somewhere earlier, a founder, a visionary entrepreneur, had a fantastic competitive strategy, and the company grew like the Face of a Book. Then deep pockets replaced smarts.

So you might think corporate bigwigs will grab fresh thinkers by the shoulders, look deeply into their eyes, and whisper: Go forth and compete as hard as you can for us! We need your business skills, your up-to-date knowledge, and especially your unorthodox ideas about competing!

That may be true . . . unless you work for Corporate, that is. Corporate (with a capital C) is a term we use to indicate companies with Dilbert-like cultures. They have been successful in the past but have developed internal orthodoxies that replace the skill of competing with self-sabotaging rituals, taboos, conventions, habits, and processes that undermine their competitiveness. Dilbert is popular because it reflects more than a grain of truth about real Corporate life.

Are you working for a Dilbert-like Corporate company? Are you contemplating the false security and grandeur of joining one? Consider this: Once you enter this world, you are trapped. You can't exercise your skill at competing even though you, being a fresh thinker, are the company's first line of defense against competitive sclerosis. You can't even think because thinking takes time, time is money, and money worships action, not thinking. Yet there is growing evidence, reported in a 2018 *Harvard Business Review* article, that thinking is more important to competing. The big question is: Do you have what it takes to compete?

ARE YOU COMPETITIVE?

Business schools teach students how to solve problems. But competition is not a problem; it is the normal condition of business. How do you know you make good, competitive decisions? Many will fall into the trap of suggesting "results" as the ultimate measurement. As we show, though, results are both ambiguous and hard to interpret as their direct cause is confounded by so many variables that the ability to pinpoint what led to what is obscured.

We propose a different test. We say the correct indicator of your skill at competing is the quality of your decision-making process.

That's also the ultimate tool we recommend you use in a dysfunctional Corporate culture. Once you understand the symptoms of the dysfunctional culture, you can deploy your superior decision-making to make sure at least *your* decisions, within the constraints of the company and your non-CEO role, are competitively skillful. At the end, the skill of competing is a critical component of leadership development. It is as important for aspiring managers as preparing slides for their bosses' presentations or reading obsessively the biographies of Jobs, Buffett, Sandberg, and Branson.

our competitive elevator pitch

Who are we to question large and powerful companies' skill at competing? We specialize in developing competing *as a skill*. We've helped thousands of managers slow down, listen to multiple perspectives, see the big picture, and anticipate unintended consequences. We believe in role-playing and computer-based simulations as the ultimate safe environments to observe, learn, and (most important) exercise that skill. It is not something one acquires by marinating in business-school lectures. We know that because we've marinated, too. We've studied in business schools and taught in business schools. Our key observations, though, come from real life, not business school: We've run war games for major companies on six continents. War games simulate moves by opposing parties, allowing companies to pressure-test their strategies.

The Corporate dysfunctions detailed in this book are mental, not physical, so our approach is similar to psychotherapy. We identify the symptoms of decay, diagnose the causes, then prescribe behavioral, managerial solutions; that's why it's a business book. And unlike psychotherapy, we do not recommend years of weekly sessions lying on a couch. Customers don't wait patiently for you to solve your problems, and while making bad decisions is considered OK in Corporate, lying on the couch in the middle of the day is not. Nope—you've got to get in gear and compete like it's your job. (Spoiler alert: It is.) You do that by first rethinking competition as a skill.

COMPETING AS A SKILL

The ability to compete is at the core of the ability to survive and prosper, yet it is hardly ever clearly defined or even discussed in the context of business schools or corporate training programs. It is, instead, assumed. It is similar to the quality of "leading," which typically translates in the popular press to quoting Sir Richard Branson (Virgin's founder) or Sir Winston Churchill or both (they are both British, so it's OK). Sometimes Elon Musk, too.

As companies grow, the skill of competing is taken for granted, smart strategy is replaced with imitation and tradition, and thinking competitively is reduced to "that's the way we do things around here." A dysfunctional Corporate culture discourages aspiring managers from applying their own skill at competing.

Competing is a deliberate attempt to win or succeed. It's an effort directly geared to achieve one's goal when other players are involved, some of whom actively attempt to prevent that goal from being attained. So it is easy to define the opposite of skillful competing: Decision-making processes that produce decisions that so thoroughly ignore or discount any other player or high-impact agent in your market, they will inevitably lead to not succeeding.

Note that we did not use the word "losing." Losing is a negative word. In the world of Corporate, negativity is a no-no (yes-yes, we

meant the pun). Negativity hurts morale and causes you to lose...
to not succeed. In other words, it is a negative thing to be negative.
You'll read more about it in the chapter on Positivismitis.

If you are a chess player and make a hasty move that exposes
your king, you aren't competing well. If you run a marathon in
high heels, you are probably not going to win. Corporate behaviors
equivalent to exposing your king or racing in high heels—behaviors
that can be judged *a priori* (in advance) as contrary to the attempt to
win—are what you need to identify in order to improve your ability
to compete. And no one exhibits those behaviors better than COOCs
and OOPs.

KNOW YOUR COOCS AND OOPS

If you are a maverick by nature, chances are you'll run into a COOC
sooner or later.

COOCs—Corporate, Overconfident, Oblivious Cultures—are
universal. A COOC in the U.S. is the same as a COOC in France or in
Singapore—only the quality of the coffee differs. You see, Corporate
is truly global. Get used to the acronym. COOCs adore acronyms.
No one speaks English in COOCs, not even in England. Instead,
people exchange acronyms. It saves time, and in that time saved, you
can be expected to do more meaningless "busy work." Remember the
TPS reports in the movie *Office Space*? That acronym was brought to
you courtesy of the COOC of Initech.

The COOC environment produces the OOP: The Overconfident,
Oblivious Person (OOP), who you'll read more about in Chapter 2.
It's almost inevitable. You can't survive decades in a COOC without
adopting some OOP characteristics. But you must, repeat, *must* fight
it as hard as you can, or you are lost.

A list of prominent COOC characteristics should help a bit. It is
like eHarmony's list: A set of requirements you should keep in mind
when going on interviews, talking to recruiters, taking the tour, and
especially meeting with potential colleagues. Knowing if a company
has a COOC full of OOPs takes practice. The best way to get your

mind wrapped around the concept is to think of your relationship to Corporate as you would a personal relationship. Deciding on a company where you can build your career is not that different than deciding on a future spouse, after all.

BEHAVIORS LEADING TO CORPORATE DIVORCE (I.E., THE END OF YOUR DREAM JOB)

Once you enter Corporate, your life changes forever.

This is very similar to marriage. So what predicts a miserable marriage? A 2015 post in *Business Insider* reported on a 14-year longitudinal study of couples by John Gottman of Washington University and Robert Levenson of UC Berkeley that claims four behaviors can predict the occurrence of . . . *divorce*. The parallels with the way Corporate treats its mavericks are so convenient, we figured we'd borrow the results for pedagogical purposes. Both Corporate and marriage can involve disillusion and dissolution. But 14 years to wait for results? Wow. Corporate waits six months and then pulls the plug on most "strategic" initiatives. We won't keep you hanging like that.

If some behaviors harm relationships, might similar behaviors harm your career? Occasional dysfunctional *behavior* is normal for *all of us* and not necessarily an early warning sign. Some coasting, slacking, and sloppy thinking is expected in the frenzied pressure-cooker of modern life. Some rituals and traditions even save time and have some benefit. When a COOC cultivating OOPs is prevalent, though, the skill of competing atrophies and busy-work rituals take its place.

Let's take a quick spin through some of the behaviors that might indicate your relationship with Corporate is headed for the rocks or, at the very least, a counseling session or two.

Contempt

"Contempt, a virulent mix of anger and disgust," say the marital study's authors, "is far more toxic than simple frustration or negativity. It involves seeing your partner as beneath you, rather than as an equal."

We've known managers who were promoted to directors and overnight developed contempt for anyone who was not a director. Peers who were equal-thinkers yesterday became inferior-thinkers today, saboteurs in their slow and incompetent work, and just not up to par!

"If you constantly feel smarter than . . . [someone else]," says psychologist John Gottman of the University of Washington, "you're not only less likely to see his or her opinions as valid, but, more important, you're far less willing to try to put yourself in his or her shoes to try to see a situation from his or her perspective."

In marriage, that can cause tension. In Corporate, it causes executives to look down at competitors and employees alike. The feeling of superiority, though, has little to do with reality.

Here is one example for contempt toward competitors. In a war game Ben ran with a huge medical distributor, management insisted on importing a machine of inferior quality to compete against a superior machine that was the market leader. The unspoken assumption was that given its size (humungous) the client could not lose, and offering a complete product line was more important than offering quality products. That's a classic cultural dysfunction of large companies: Imperial, entitled Corporate not seeing it was blinding itself with hubris.

When Ben pointed out that this was perhaps misguided and predicted failure, he was sent into exile. The machine, by the way, failed. The company was later acquired. It is now a division in another, even bigger, Corporate.

Corporate contempt toward its own rank and file is even worse. The idea that strategy can be informed from the *bottom up* goes so much against the Corporate grain that when it happens, it's dismissed with disdain. Like this:

Presenter: "We were just informed that the Earth is not flat."

Executive: "Who says?"

Presenter: "Pythagoras from Finance and Aristotle from Business Development. They said the way a ship disappears over the horizon proves it."

Executive: "What are they, scientists? Mathematicians?"

Presenter: "No, philosophers."

Executive (relieved): "Well, if we believed everything our philosophy department tells us . . ."

(Presenter and Executive laugh heartily.)

Presenter: "We ran it by our consultants. They didn't love it. They said no one else believes it. HQ in Athens may be skeptical."

Executive (decisive): "OK. Forget it. I am not going to rely on some philosophers who think the Earth is not flat."

Our modern-day experience suggests that the *exceptions* to Corporate contempt for junior and middle management may be confined mostly to private companies. There, egos are less important than getting results. The message from the family- or entrepreneur-owner to the hired executive seems to be "When you play with someone else's money, you can develop an ego; when you play with my money, you better not. Treat newbies and middle managers with the utmost respect. They may be more competitive than you are."

One recent example involves Olive Garden (OG), whose parent company Darden was taken over by an activist investment firm (Starboard). A story in CNN's *Money* in 2015 reported that the investment firm mocked OG's strategy of unlimited breadsticks prior to dinner. Darden's top management naturally defended the practice since that formula worked for years. Once Starboard took over and stopped serving endless breadsticks, patrons spent more on alcohol and desserts since they didn't fill up on breadsticks. Sales and profit went up. When managers at lower levels in the company presented the same logic, they were ignored by top management who "knew better."

Criticism

In relationships, says the divorce study we are using as a template, criticism can add up, "feeding darker feelings of resentment and contempt." In Corporate, criticism is officially endorsed when it flows in the approved direction: from the top down. After all, if one allows for a free exchange of honest perspectives, one may get into heated debate that involves criticizing strategy or execution, and heated debate interferes with *do something* (also known as the Corporate cultural imperative). This is a huge no-no in Corporate. Middle management is not to question top management's strategic thinking, and newbies are told by their middle-manager bosses to "shut up and go back to work; this is how things are done here." That trickle-down conformity kills independent thinking.

In a strategy workshop at a famous consumer products company, a group of idealistic, company-minded young managers made a damning presentation of the division's strategy. The three executives in the room ordered them, in so many words, to shut up. In itself, that order is not uncommon. In some Asian cultures, less-senior managers will not speak at all before the more-senior ones do, let alone disagree with them. But the famous company's problem was that the role of the younger managers was to play devil's advocate and *point to* potential blindspots in the division's strategy.

The division's performance continued to slide against the competition. A year later, the senior executives who ordered the warnings to stop were themselves ordered to go. Sometimes the karma works.

Sometimes executives run business war games expecting (or even *demanding*) the games to confirm their strategies and thereby end criticism. In one case, a company was second in its market. The company president said being number two was the worst place of all. Mark pointed out that the president's strategy would most likely not result in being number one, so if the president dislikes being number two so much, perhaps he ought to try being number three. He practically threw Mark out of the room.[1] Oh, by the way, the president's strategy did not work and he no longer works at that company.

---

[1] That story demonstrates maverickness at its best and worst. Let Mark's tale reinforce reality: having a different perspective is not always welcomed, so try to be diplomatic.

Defensiveness

In the study on failing relationships, "taking responsibility for your role in a tough situation can be uncomfortable, but it's often what keeps a bad situation from escalating," says Gottman.

The Corporate corollary here is the Cover Your Ass (CYA) routine familiar to every employee and manager (except first-day novices). The whole idea behind CYA is practicing the art of defensiveness. In some cultures, especially those with a strong class status, CYA is pronounced as bosses abhor admitting errors in judgment to their (inferior in status) subordinates and will "kiss up" by shifting the blame downward to them at a drop of a hat.

In theory, the ability to admit a mistake is one of the most-admired leadership qualities, but if it is practiced anywhere it's the best-hidden secret on Earth. In an often-quoted 2014 study from Jeanine Prime and Elizabeth Salib of the Catalyst Research Center, humility is hailed as the quintessential trait of good leadership. Humility creates the right nurturing environment for innovation and inclusiveness. Alas, the examples mentioned such as—who else, Google—do not match reality.

There is a reason why "managing up" with defensiveness—the CYA mentality—is so prevalent. It's a chain reaction: If your boss' boss uses CYA to protect their job, your boss is all but forced to do the same to protect their own job. You may find it hard to break this cycle, but it doesn't mean you have to join the party yourself. Owning your mistakes may leave you vulnerable but will save your integrity, and in the long run, you will win respect.

The vicious cycle of "kissing up" and managing downward reaches its ultimate conclusion in a Mao-style educational camp wherein lower-ranked employees take the blame for sunspots, frogs, locusts, and everything bad happening to the stock price. The confessional takes place in a weekly ritual, formally and euphemistically known as the *management meeting*.

While CYA classically characterizes defensive culture, it's also often accompanied by . . .

Stonewalling

The relationship study found that "blocking off conversation can be just as toxic for a relationship as contempt because it keeps you from addressing an underlying issue."

According to a 2015 *Harvard Business Review* article by Donald Sull, Rebecca Homkes, and Charles Sull titled "Why Strategy Execution Unravels," which reports on a survey of 8,000 executives and managers in 250 firms worldwide, *less than one third* of those surveyed reported they could have an open and honest discussion about sensitive issues. Read that again: *less than one third*. In his 1994 book *Business Blindspots*, Ben called this "Corporate Taboos." Corporate taboos are well-known issues associated with strong top-executive beliefs, and everyone knows they are too sensitive to be mentioned or discussed. IBM's famous taboo in the '80s kept anyone from daring to challenge the thinking that IBM's future profits were in mainframes only. At General Motors under Roger Smith, advocating Japanese human-based quality-control methods was "dangerous," as Mr. Smith believed strongly in using robots to win the race even as evidence from a joint venture with Toyota showed otherwise. In a world moving at warp speed, it is comforting to know that *nothing has changed* in the two decades since *Business Blindspots* released. Blocking off conversations is management's red line in the sand: Cross it and you are fried.

As the Avon example shows (see "A Case Study in Corporate Divorce" on page 16) companies whose skill at competing has atrophied love taboos. General Motors' strategic plans didn't mention the Japanese competition until 1985. Kodak refused to acknowledge the rise of online digital photo sharing. Intel's focus on PCs led it to abandon smartphone chips.

COOCs (Corporate, Overconfident, Oblivious Culture—this is the LAST time we'll tell you!) love and cherish taboos. Good executives fight dysfunctional culture. Bad executives think it keeps them safe. They might be right for a while. But under the hot lights of the marketplace, even concealers melt.

a case study in corporate divorce

The stunning decline of Avon, a 126-year-old cosmetics empire built on the direct-sales model, offers a bare-faced example of every factor mentioned in the divorce study: Contempt and criticism (from the top), defensiveness from everyone else, and stonewalling from the leader.

Many market shifts can explain Avon's decline, from slowing growth in emerging markets (especially Brazil and China) to rising competition from retailers and online sales. Recruiting and retaining Avon's sales reps has declined badly in North America, from a force of 470,000 in 2009 to approximately 285,000 in 2014. The decline in Brazil and Asia was more moderate. In 2015, rumors swirled that Avon was about to sell its North American business.

But Avon's trouble seems more internally created than externally forced. Under Andrea Jung, then Avon's CEO, the company's growth stalled in 2005. Profits began to decline, with its last profitable year in 2011. Growing losses led its stock price to plummet in 2014.

Avon entered the game of restructuring with gusto. It restructured, then re-restructured, then de-structured, starting in 2005 when Jung cut 30 percent of managers and chopped 15 layers down to eight. As a 2012 article in *Fortune* magazine reported, another restructuring in 2009 created "a revolving door at Avon that left employees demoralized and uncertain about who was in charge." And then again, under a new CEO, Avon reorganized its sales force in Q2 2013, which resulted in the disruption of its sales representatives' pool.

a case study in corporate divorce, continued

Avon followed every step in setting goals as described in Chapter 10. As *Fortune* reported, in 2010, Avon announced a target of $20 billion in sales, which was double its revenues then. "Less than a year later, after a bad quarter, the company cut off funding for most of the initiatives. Executives communicated a new directive: Avon would eventually hit $20 billion but not by 2015."

And naturally, as trouble mounted, consultants galore were called in. The result, among other changes, was acquisitions. (Ben and Mark have independently found that war-game teams immediately and invariably want to acquire some poor company.) In 2010 Avon acquired Silpada, a direct seller of silver jewelry, for $650 million. It runs it as a separate business. In 2011, the company had to take a $263 million write-down on Silpada.

The problems with Avon's strategy were deep, representing Jung's blindspot about Avon positioning and strengths. Jung acted as if she didn't actually like the direct-sales model. Her sales reps, especially in South America, didn't match Jung's own glitzy persona. Her attempts to open kiosks in malls and market higher-end lines backfired, as did her attempt at joint ventures with Sears (they balked at the last minute) and JCPenney (cancelled after two years). How did it backfire? It alienated the sales reps by competing with them for the same customers. It's not that direct sales in general has gone to the dogs; total direct sales in emerging markets grew by 30 percent between 2006 and 2011. Avon's share grew by only 1.1 percentage points.

---

a case study in corporate divorce, continued

Avon's response? Spend more on advertising, *of course.*

You'd expect that with so many mounting challenges, Jung would be a bit humbled. You'd be wrong. When it came to stonewalling, Jung was the master.

"At Avon, when something doesn't go right, just put some concealer on it," says a former communications manager. When questions about the logic of the acquisition price and management structure arose, Jung told analysts, "You guys are going to love this like we do."

We?

A damning statement later came from a former Avon CEO, Jim Preston. In a *Fortune* interview he said, "How could you go through five or six years of the performance that they've had and not begin to ask serious questions, and say our hires are not right, and our operating systems are not right?"

Mavericks have two choices if they find themselves dealing with COOC dysfunction: They can shrivel in their cubicles and find life miserable, or they can diagnose the dysfunction, file it away under the right category (we offer about 20), carefully pretend to drink the Kool-Aid so as not to raise the wrath of their OOP bosses, and find clever ways to offer fresh, unorthodox strategic thinking at every job they do. In the next chapters, we will sketch the principles of fresh, unorthodox, maverick thinking.

advice to the maverick

If you want us to play the role of Corporate coaches, we constructively and nondefensively say forget it. We do not use concealers. We refuse to tell you the obvious ("think twice about your emails"), the trite ("dress professionally to make a fine first impression"), and the vague ("pick the right time to ask for a raise").

The best advice we can provide mavericks who are about to join a company is to make sure it's not a Corporate company. That means you've got to know how to look past the grand lobby, the portraits of CEOs stretching back centuries, and the excellent health benefits. Those trappings are about the company's past, but you care about its future. You know how they ask you "Do you have any questions for us?" during interviews? Tell them, "Oh, yeah, I do," *and then ask them*.

Come prepared. Be respectful, but tell them you've read about their competitors and you are worried about Competitor X, which seems to be making headway against them. Ask them the equivalent of the question they'll surely ask you: "What do you see as the company's biggest weakness?" *Watch how they respond.*

Just make sure you have enough cash for the cab back home.

how to identify a corporate oop (overconfident oblivious person)

"The reason I talk to myself
is because I'm the only one
whose answers I accept."

—GEORGE CARLIN

In the previous chapter, we told you to look for signs of Corporate behavior that will inevitably lead to you divorcing it (or it divorcing *you*). In this chapter, we will zoom further inside the inner workings of your potential employer. We will provide you with quick, telltale signs of OOPs (Overconfident Oblivious Person): Bosses and colleagues who lack your skill at competing but who can still make your life miserable.

It can take time to detect managers who lack skill at competing. They may hide their uncompetitive mentality under a rational exterior.[1] They may appear to be respectable small-c corporate citizens, even statesman-like. They may impress and charm their way into your heart.

To tell mere charm from genuine interest in competing, you may need to ask penetrating questions, such as "What is our competitive position?" or "How are we different than competitors in the eyes of the customers?" But such inquiry takes effort and research, and it can be dangerous politically. You need portable OOP *radar*.

Our combined experience, of course, enables us to recognize OOPs quickly, but then we invested a lot of effort and training into

---

[1] They don't think they're hiding anything. They might sincerely believe they *are* skilled at competing. They might even be right, if they judge their skill as Corporate does.

that skill. For us, tagging an executive as an OOP takes no time. It's hard to hide orthodox, formulaic thinking and empty slogans.

For the sake of our loyal readers, we would like to offer you an opposite-of-competing dashboard (everyone loves "dashboards" in Corporate), which will make your lives easier. In other words, there are some behaviors that automatically mark their owner as an OOP. Knowing them will save you a lot of heartache.

OOPs are everywhere. In this section, we're going to identify the most-likely OOP sites in your office. Later, we'll go hunting out in the wild, in the world of conferences and conventions.

The first place to look for invasive OOPs is your overflowing, never-ending source of missed meanings, jargon, and general lack of clarity: your inbox.

YOU'VE GOT OOP MAIL

Much of your email comes from OOPs outside your company. They tempt you with offers of insight, bargains, almost-free demos of useless software, and career opportunities.

Here's how to tell that OOP mail has come for you:

- Anyone who sends a professional, work-related email that begins "Hello! My name is Olga."
- Anyone who sends email with the recipient's name in the subject ["Ben, deals chosen just for you!"], which is a dead give-away that it is not personal at all. It advertises that the email comes from a mailing list, right, Ben? "Ben, join countless [we haven't counted] others [other what? Males? Floridians? Libertarians? Ph.D.'s?] who have saved money by spending it with us! We look forward, Ben, to having you, Ben, join us. We need a Ben. Some of my best friends are Ben." When your name appears three times as often as the word "the," you have a good clue. Beep! You've got spam from an OOP vendor!
- Anyone who sends an email whose subject is a command. "Drive more website traffic from Twitter!" What if I don't

want to? Or what if I am a stickler for the English language and interpret it correctly as hurting Twitter's traffic?

- Anyone on group email chains who refers to other discussants with a punctuation mark. "I agree with @Mark." Pretty soon: "@I agree with @Mark." @Oy.
- Anyone who offers a link labeled "unsubscribe" (instead of "make us stop") on emails to which you didn't subscribe in the first place, @Ben.

The OOP Mail Coming from Inside the House

OOPs inside your company love sending email, too. They love showing you how much they know, who they know, how much they know about who they know, and how much they can improve the company with their strategic ideas. They love even more showing you how much they think they are being competitive, when they're really just stringing together word salad that has no real competitive drive. Let's take a look at these inside-the-house offenders:

- Anyone who sends an email with the subject line "Market Analysis: 2050–2060," 17 attachments, and an introduction that begins with "To: Distribution List."
- Anyone who sends an email saying, "Here's how we can save money for our company!" with ideas such as "recharge your phone at home." You'll know it's an uber-OOP if the CEO is cc'd.
- Anyone whose emails state, "I'd like to start our next meeting on time" and then shows up half an hour late and explains they had an important phone call.
- Anyone who in 2018 shares widely a 2003 article from a famous consulting firm and adds: "Ideas that never go out of fashion."
- Anyone who asks for "all the information we have on Company X" without specifying why.
- Anyone who sends an email proclaiming "competitive pressures have risen significantly in the past few decades" unless

they are 70 years old and actually remember the pressures decades earlier. When CEOs send this message, they are uber OOPs.

You've Got OOPdates

LinkedIn is a wonderful professional network, or at least it used to be. Aimed at professionals only, it started with a few thousand gainfully employed managers exchanging perspectives, experiences, and virtual brain power. Over the years it morphed into a 400-million-member monster—399,999,995 of them trying to sell something to the five who are still employed.

You will meet quite a few OOPs on LinkedIn. Here are some telltale signs of LinkedIn's atrophied professional value:

- *Influencers.* LinkedIn recognizes a class of bestselling bloggers/ authors/speakers/pain-in-the-neck/goody-two-shoes "mentors" and pushes their posts to millions. The Influencers are prolific publishers, coming up with new variations on their incredible wisdom every week. Or twice a week. Who can keep up? If we do, we'll be unemployed. Their advice always concerns how to behave, so we assume most of them are unemployed wanna-be bestselling authors, keynote speakers, etc., masquerading as bestselling bloggers/authors/speakers, etc. The heading is always in the form of a list: "10 Ways Remarkably Polite People Are More Successful," "Seven Habits of People with Remarkable Mental Toughness," "The Five Things You Should Never Say in an Interview," and "The Five Things You Should Always Say in an Interview." The lists are often the same, but from warring authors/bloggers/ emotionally high speakers. (Talk about skill at competing! They've covered the market.) Their advice is earth-shattering. Like this gem: *Polite people, for example, don't touch unless they are touched first.* Does it make the person who touched them first impolite? Oh, never mind, logic is not the strength of those incredible thinkers. From the same influencer: *Polite people never gossip, and never . . . wait for it . . . never stop being polite.* Yes, the last point means they are probably all on Prozac or are the veddy proper product of British boys' schools. In short, the summary of this wisdom is they are successful because they are polite, and they are polite because they never stop being polite. (We need to sit. This is overwhelming.) Of course, another Influenzer (no, this is not a typo) on the same day publishes a list of "Three reasons passionate and assertive people are more successful," which advises the opposite.

- *Influencers' followers.* The influenzers[2] have many fans. Hundreds of thousands of eyes look at their formulaic essays. Out of those hundreds of thousands, at least a few thousand go to the extreme of expressing that they "like" the essay. And then there are a few hundred *dedicated* commentators.

The comment section for LinkedIn posts is where you'll find OOPs without end. Here are the dominant species:

- Those who just shriek with delight at the repetitious, trite, absurdly trivial, repetitious advice/point/suggestions made by the blogger/author/keynote speaker/self-proclaimed guru. "Wonderful!" "I love this. Another great article, Travis!"
- Then there are those who have a bit of perspective on the trite, absurdly trivial points: "Great ten tips, number five is by far the most difficult and arguably the most important." In other words, Don't think I am a dumb fan; I have my own dumb opinion on the dumb advice."
- And then there are those who must add with authority, "Gone are the days when the screaming lone wolf used to get all the attention! Politeness holds the key to positive influence." Hmmm . . . We want what this person smokes. On second thought, maybe not.

---

[2] From the root Influenza, as in spreading like an epidemic. You got it, right?

- Lastly, there are the self-proclaimed authorities in their own minds. One of us has been flamed and downright stalked by one such commentator, who disputed that one of us, with an MBA from Harvard Business School, studied under HBS Professor Michael Porter. He (the commentator, not the one of us) might have confused Porter with Potter, as in Harry?

LinkedIn offers interest groups. At the beginning, people posting in the groups were interested in *discussions*. These were fun, especially when they veered into political fights in groups that had only a marginal connection to politics. The participation was a sign of the vitality of the community. Slowly but surely, as the space filled up with the 399,999,995 unemployed advisors, consultants, and change agents, real discussions died out. In their place came important posts, such as "What the Beatles Can Teach Entrepreneurs about Success," "Four Reasons Why Content Marketing Drives Traffic (and Revenue)," "Antibody Drug Conjugate and Big Pharmaceutical Companies," and "Put the 'R' Back in Your CRM." All those titles are real, taken from the group of some competitive-intelligence vendor. None has anything to do with competitive intelligence. None received any comments, elicited any discussion, or added anything to anyone. Such irrelevancies now represent 99 percent of the posting in groups. The number of posts is approaching the videos of kittens and puppies on YouTube but without the redeeming social value. The number of group members keeps growing. It is proof of entropy.

No one is *discussing* anything. Everyone is a blogger, everyone is an authority, and everyone sells something or another. *No one is buying anything, ever*, but the number of posts desperately trying to generate leads and income based on the "Four Reasons Why Content Marketing Drives Traffic (and Revenue)" keeps growing. If this isn't a sure sign of OOPs in action, we don't know what is. Just call them what they are: Noodleheads. "Excellent point, @Ben and @Mark! You did it again!"

Spokespeople

Spokespeople are a special class of Corporate OOPs since their task is to cover up the screwups of their bosses. They are not to be blamed for uncompetitive thinking; they are just uncompetitive by association. We call them OOP derivatives, or OOPD for short. At times, OOPDs must wonder about the absurdity of their task. Here are a couple of examples.

In May 2015, an oil spill in Santa Barbara dumped about 100,000 gallons of crude onto Southern California beaches. According to CNN, in response to the spill, Pat Hutchins, Plains All American Pipeline's director of safety, said the company has been committing money to safety improvements for the past seven years.

How is this relevant? It is . . . if you subscribe to the "I do my best" non-sequitur line of defense.

Also in May 2015, JPMorgan Chase and several other too-big-to-fail banks were found guilty of foreign-exchange rate rigging and fined $5.6 billion. Can you count how many times since the financial collapse that banks have been fined for violations of rules or laws? We lost count. So how do banks react? JPMorgan simply released this statement: "We have strengthened our controls over the past several years." Antony Jenkins, Barclays' CEO, said in a letter to Barclay's shareholders: "This demonstrates again the importance of our continuing work to build a values-based culture and strengthen our control." No kidding, *really?*

The reader may note our sarcastic tone. Sarcasm is a defense mechanism against evildoers, responsibility-shirkers, or just OOPs. We highly recommend retaining a sense of straight-faced sarcasm, or you will find yourself using in-your-face profanity instead. Corporate doesn't understand sarcasm, so it is safe. Corporate doesn't allow profanity, so be darn careful.

OOPS IN THE WILD

Now let's move out of the office and into the wide world of conferences. As you'll see, it's a veritable buffet of OOPs, from the conference keynote to the requisite cocktail hour. (Don't forget your drink tickets!) At times, it is easy to detect Corporate OOPs' declining competitive skill by asking them a simple question: Which conference did you go to lately?

Most rational managers realize that keeping a relatively objective and insightful perspective on what's happening "out there" (in their various markets and in the larger business environment) is a smart thing to do for a practicing manager. It may even be essential for competing. Competing, you recall, involves out-thinking your competitors, which in turn, requires that you look for new ideas and perspectives, not ones already widely shared by everyone else in your segment. Thus, an important way managers develop external perspective is by attending conferences where they can meet people with *different* perspectives and hear a variety of *different* views, some controversial, some less.

That's what you want. Alas, that's not what you get. As a 2015 article in *USA Today* showed, the conference business has gone to the dogs. No, worse: It's gone to the vendors. In "Tina Brown Now in the Conference Business," Michael Wolff, a seasoned commentator, discusses a new venture by former *Newsweek* editor Tina Brown. With backing from *The New York Times*, Brown was set to offer general-interest conferences on women's issues. In the article, Wolff revealed a secret many of us already knew: Conferences today are organized by commercial vendors who have turned them into shameless "pay to play" meetings. Speakers are not invited because of their quality but because they pay for access to the attendees or throw back cash to the organizer. Conferences have become more about entertainment than learning. Think "Playing Invisible Turntables," an actual TED talk.

So why do people pay for, at best, a stream of infomercials in PowerPoint? Is there a connection between insular management and the tendency of companies to finance conference-going without asking for value in return? "For one thing, there are so many conferences," says Wolff. "It is rather a disappointment, when you hope to meet the high and mighty, to show up and find a sparsely populated room with people *just like yourself.*" (Emphasis added.)

Touted as great opportunities for "networking," what many vendor-organized conferences deliver is nothing more than a meeting (and at times commiserating) with same-same people and predictable, comfortable, meaningless speeches by recycled keynote "celebrities." When managers insulate themselves from high-quality, diverse perspectives and find comfort in those who are *just like them*, they are seeding their own failure. This is how one develops CCH: Chronic Conference Hopping (CCH).

CHRONIC CONFERENCE HOPPING

So who cares that conferences have become big business with little value? If you believe in early detection, you should. The smallest mole can be an early sign of skin cancer, and looking forward to conferences *to see friends* can be an early sign of CCH. That's why you need the OOP radar. Or maybe an OOP MRI.

You, the reader, may face great temptation to join the CCH crowd. It's fun. It's in fun cities (Atlanta—it's almost always Atlanta). You can bring your spouse. Yet our carefully constructed, double-blind and triple-washed studies suggest that it is time for Corporate leaders to pay attention to CCH. The three-martini lunch from the good old days, when American companies didn't have to compete and the world was their oyster, has turned into full-scale, endless "networking."

a case study in cch

Let us demonstrate the CCH disorder with a case study from the field of competitive intelligence (CI). Each of us has spent 30 years in or around this field. It is a *relatively* young field (compared with, say, agriculture), with just a few thousand professionals worldwide. The vast majority of these managers work in Fortune 500 firms. So our experience is by no means representative of other important business fields, like finance,

a case study in cch, continued

accounting, and human resources. Or maybe it is, and we just don't know. Actually, we suspect that in these *other* fields, the CCH syndrome is much *worse:* The bigger the conference-pot, the more opportunities for Corporate to meet and remember, reconfirm, and *reinforce* the same old stuff. Or, as one of us—the unrefined co-author referred to in the introduction—indelicately prefers: to regurgitate.

Keep in mind, there are numerous and much more ostentatious demonstrations of dysfunctional cultures. But this is a classic case for quick detection with your OOP radar, and most people who are asked "Which conference did you go to lately?" don't suspect you are trying to detect a COOC company.

In the '80s and '90s, when the CI field was growing fast, there was only one conference to attend. Today, when the field has matured, there are at least five annual vendor-organized conferences that we know of and probably 20 we never heard of.

Then, of course, there is also an event called the "CI Summit," which, it turns out, is from the Construction Institute. We wonder how many competitive intelligence managers ended up there and *didn't even notice*.

In short, there may be more conferences on competitive intelligence than there are competitive-intelligence managers. That's because CCHers go to *multiple* regurgitation events.

CAUSES OF CCH

Since conferences are basically alike—despite the hype from the organizers—and the subjects (and often the speakers) are reprocessed, exchangeable, and recyclable (the blue bin, please!), we are facing a socio-medical phenomenon that requires some analysis. Since no rational person soaks up a slideshow or voiced-over webinar and thinks, "Now I have an MBA from Harvard!" or goes to a doctor who's a de facto employee of a pharmaceuticals company, we don't expect those CCHers to learn anything in a conference from pay-to-play speakers. We know it, they know it, and yet they keep crowding the halls. For those new to the scene, the best explanation is simply "Suckers never die; they just get replaced.[3]" But what about repeat offenders? Assuming some people keep going from one conference to the next (we know several who fit this category) or keep attending the same conference year after year (we know even more who fit this mode), there are only three possibilities:

1. They don't learn anything, so they keep going hoping one day to learn *something*, or
2. They keep going (and their employers keep paying) to kill time until retirement or layoff, or
3. There is a deep, existential explanation for this dysfunctional behavior.

The first two possibilities are cynical and, obviously, we are not cynical. We are deep, existential people, and we have three deep, existential explanations for the dysfunction. They are not mutually exclusive. Here they are.

A Psychological Model of CCH

A psychological explanation must look at the root of CCH. One possibility is that many professionals harbor subconscious fears that their work is not truly appreciated and that they may be laid off at the first cost-cutting. Their conference-going is a manifestation of the biblical "cast your bread on the waters" type behavior (a.k.a.

---

[3] Yes we know, the saying is actually "There's a sucker born every minute." Everyone knows P.T. Barnum said that . . . except there's no evidence he did. Proof of suckers? https://quoteinvestigator.com/2014/04/11/fool-born/

you never know where your next job's coming from). In short, their employers *pay* them to look for their next job—very generous of them. Also, that generosity might comfort the employers who feel guilty when they do lay them off.

A Behavioral Economic Model of CCH

A more cognitive model of CCH maintains that conferences have become a form of social entertainment paid for by employers. As long as conference-going doesn't have to show any real changes in behavior or improvements in productivity, the incentive is:

- A free bar in the reception (sponsored by . . .), or
- A mug taken home to the kids (courtesy of . . .), or
- A weekend at the Magic Kingdom (a fitting place for Mickey Mouse conferences).

The incentive is self-reinforcing, so it invariably leads to more conference-going. This explanation, however, can't explain all conferences, as some take place in Wisconsin or New Jersey. Go figure.

A "Lazy Manager" Model of CCH

A more-recent research approach using MRI studies of CCH reveals a surprising source for the behavior: A lack of serious investment in updating one's skills. The theory, advanced by some CCH survivors, suggests that instead of in-depth training, which actually upgrades one's skills, lazy managers may prefer to conference-hop for the purpose of identifying *vendors* to whom they will outsource their own work.

Evidence for this model is the phenomenon, observed in several controlled studies at conference halls—*triple*-blind studies, as *we* haven't even looked at them, and neither should you—of lonely managers with a small budget surrounded by armies of vendors fluttering about them in a feeding frenzy. Bolstered by feeling like a king or queen for a day, these managers face the shock of reality upon returning to cubicle 34/2638-D at their companies. Some actually require therapy sessions. (HR leaders should be aware of the added cost, discussed by HR-service vendors in several *HR conferences*.)

You may question our focus on conference hopping. Aren't there fishier, shadier OOP behaviors? There are. But our experience shows those hopping also tend to engage in other OOP behaviors. CCH is the symptom, not the disease.

AVOID BECOMING AN OOP

There is a common theme to those who write annoying emails, follow false messiahs on LinkedIn, believe spokespeople, and attend conferences where they gain no value: They are sloppy thinkers. They are not bad people; they work hard; they take their jobs seriously. They are just not skilled at competing.

You are a maverick, so we know you do not fall for trite advice, join herd behavior, and applaud OOP thinking. Still, how do you keep thinking independently when the Corporate pressure to conform to COOC is so high? After all, you must keep getting fresh perspectives from the external environment, even from LinkedIn or conferences.

You start by systematically deleting all Influencers' banal posts in your LinkedIn feed as well as disconnecting those members of your network who pile on most of these posts. You may lose some "My Network" count, but you will gain respect from us (if you join our networks, of course). Then, you carefully select which conferences to attend. Going to conferences, trade shows, and external events is *in principle* a very worthwhile activity. Worthwhile, that is, as long as you are careful and diligent about where you go. It is unbecoming for a maverick to fade into CCH with a finger calloused from "liking" LinkedIn's Influencers' banal clichés.

Watch out for buzz areas, such as "Technology and Innovation," "Social Marketing in the 22nd Century," and "Big Data and Small Questions." If everyone goes to those "hot" events or joins those LinkedIn groups, you already know there is little to gain by joining.

That's the herd enticing you. Just remember that we are on your side and remember our advice: If you want to outperform the herd, you've got to do something the herd isn't doing. That includes creating two internal email folders titled OOPs and NON-OOPs. If anyone asks, just say it means Optimal Operational Pointers. It sounds almost as good as the last email from an in-house OOP who urged people to watch a "Body Language for Leaders" video that puts the viewers to sleep within two minutes of watching the speaker's body language. Put all OOP emails in the OOP folder and never ever read them. Bleach the folder periodically by clicking "Delete All." Trust us, if an OOP who emailed 17,329 colleagues notices *you* haven't replied, you have proof the person is an OOP.

From a 30,000-foot view, companies should continually look for opportunities to expand their managers' perspectives genuinely and meaningfully because that is one of the most effective ways to compete successfully. Companies whose managers and executives lose the finger on the market's pulse and listen only to the voices in their heads turn out, over time, to lose their pulses. Competing well *requires* understanding the perspectives of third parties: Customers, competitors, disruptors, regulators, distributors, suppliers, even potential customers. Tunnel vision enables and empowers "disruptors," and offers them the company's lunch. Think of it this way: There's nothing, literally nothing, that a disruptor can do that well-heeled, well-established incumbents cannot do first. Disruptors don't know more than incumbents because they have magic disruptor DNA. They know more because they *look for* more.

While looking for fresh ideas outside the industry's confines and the business' walls is a logical move for companies wishing to stay competitive, trust Corporate to turn it into conference hopping for OOPs. We do not claim that conference hopping is the most egregious symptom of a dysfunctional culture (nor are @lousy emails or paying attention to Influencer posts on social media). It is not even the most conspicuous one. It is just a suspicious dot on the radar screen. However, our double-blind annual survey of CEOs, cafeteria workers, and ourselves showed 78 percent regarded conference hopping as highly correlated with losing focus on competing. Another 20 percent didn't see the correlation as they were away at conferences and couldn't reply to the survey, and the final 3 percent couldn't do the arithmetic.

advice to the maverick

This chapter is full of silliness, and we had a great time writing it (don't worry, we wouldn't give up our day jobs, if we had any), but its message is serious. We aim to help you identify an OOP boss or colleague quickly using *tiny* behavioral signs or confirm your suspicions using our vast experience. As you stand on the side of a cavernous hall filled with merry conference goers networking furiously, you may experience the side effects of being a maverick: Isolation, a sense of rejection, and baffled wonderment at the world's happiness with sloppy thinking. Make this chapter your friend: You are not alone, and you are not wrong. The desperate Dear-Maverick emailers, the liking-LinkedIn sycophants, and the ritualistic conference hoppers are by definition OOPs. They are not bad people; they are just the definition of conformity and orthodoxy.

But you are human, so you crave acceptance and team hugs. Even though respect is what most mavericks actually need, social urges can be fierce. Therefore, we—the maverick's only true friends in the world—aim to help mavericks sucked into the CCH sinkhole to start the painful rehabilitation process. Luckily, sufferers don't have to master 12 steps when they join Conference Hoppers Anonymous. Just a few:

- *Stop the hop*. Cancel all plans to attend conferences to meet the same people and hear the same spiels over and over again. The first week is going to be rough. Consider secluding yourself in your cubicle until the physical tremors subside.

advice to the maverick, continued

- *Take your budget dedicated to the socializing-entertainment-cum-"learning" and split it among the following:* Attend skills training with any serious and accredited venue in anything remotely connected to competing; travel to your competitors' important markets and take a tour with your salespeople to understand market realities; take a course in internet security or geriatric nursing . . . *just in case.* You know these are growth areas for the next 40 years or so.

Similarly, kicking the habit of reading all emails and all LinkedIn popular posts is hard. We recommend this remedy:

- If you feel the urge to read the email with the cute heading "Is Quantum Computing an Opportunity for Us or Not?" remember it's from a technical, pain-in-the-neck, know-it-all, expert-in-their-own-mind who has to show deep understanding regardless of the relevance to your job. You don't need to read the email. Here's what it surely concludes: "Only the future will tell, but we have to stay vigilant." Now ask Alexa to stay vigilant for you so you can keep reading our book.

- If you feel the posts from the LinkedIn Influencers calling themselves "Number 1 Leadership Thinker" and showing photos of motivated attendees in their Bangalore seminars are calling your name, change your name.

You can never let your guard down. Vendors will send you a million emails with glitzy reminders of the wonders of their gathering, the beauty of the hotel food, keynote speakers just short of obscurity, and spouses' city tours. They'll call you "leader," "game changer," and "innovator." Resist the temptation! You know the truth. If necessary, call the 1-800-NoFreeLunch hotline and get help. Or a free lunch. (This free lunch was sponsored by . . .)

job descriptions vs. jobs

"Just believe everything I tell you, and it will all be very, very simple."

"Ah, well, I'm not sure I believe that."

—DOUGLAS ADAMS,

LIFE, THE UNIVERSE AND EVERYTHING

Now that we've stepped into the capital-C Corporate land and you've got a feel for the potential COOCs and OOPs that could be in your future, let's talk about how you can navigate them early and effectively. You do that by paying close attention before you even get hired. "But," you ask, "isn't this the New *Employee* Manual? Which implies that I am an employee?" No. It's the *NEW* Employee Manual (emphasis on New), and it replaces the one they gave you during orientation. So if you read this book and realize, *I am about to join Corporate*, you can still bolt. Our goal here is to help you find your way from the first handshake to the exit interview, whether those events are days or decades apart.

Let's start with the job description that lured you in. Even mavericks can fall prey to job descriptions. In this chapter, we expose the myth that job descriptions actually tell you what you'll be doing on the job. We choose an example of a corporate market analyst in charge—presumably—of keeping the company competitive by keeping management informed about market and competitive developments of significance. We know this space intimately as we have trained thousands of analysts, and most new hires start as professionals in support roles, not as managers. The description below, however, applies *equally well* to every job in Corporate whether in marketing, sales, product management, business development, or the mailroom. The job description is always carefully crafted to sound sexy while committing to nothing.

The job descriptions we've seen for such positions dangle alluring assignments before you, such as briefing top management on strategic issues, compiling intelligence reports of utmost importance that will affect huge decisions, and generally letting you shine. To an independent thinker, this sounds like a dream job. If you are a recent MBA and spent $200,000 or more on an Ivy League degree, this will be an unbelievably good starting point. Alas, the operative word is "unbelievable."

VENI, VIDI, VICI[1]: YOUR FIRST DAY, FANTASY VERSION

Here is a "before" and "after" reality check for you, maverick reader, as you shop around for the right job that will use your skill at competing. First, the "before" (what you think your days will look like):

8:00 A.M.   You arrive. Meet the executive team at 10:00. Need to finalize your presentation on early signals of change in the market. Decide to use only four slides.

12:00 P.M.   Fantastic meeting. The CEO asked you to meet her later for a special assignment to assess the intelligence around an acquisition prospect. She will want your perspective on the candidate's relative competitive positioning. May recommend a war game on that market segment to role-play how competitors will react to your company's entry. Expect a month of hard work, so you plan not to accept other assignments for now. You are excited, though, to have impact. Great impact.

6:00 P.M.   Just finished reading your last seven issues of *The Economist*. Found an intriguing article on new technology applied in a different industry. Looked at your updated organizational network graph to see who in

---

[1] "I came, I saw, I conquered." Latin, popularly attributed to Julius Caesar, but he might have heard it from Elon Musk.

your community of practice is best to tap for more insight. Found two people. Scheduled virtual conferences with them. You will tap their brains and maybe get them excited about exploring the application of this new technology in-house.

6:30 P.M.   Someone called from a vendor selling something on the tradecraft of trolling social media using APIs. Promised they can also get you copies of the strategic plans of every competitor. Newly worldly in your Corporate post, you ask them why you would want to know that since strategic plans never get implemented anyway. They stammer. You hang up. You have no time for GIGO (garbage in, garbage out) junkies. You want to deliver value. You know you can deliver value. You are the embodiment of the skill of competing.

Wake up! Wake up! We hate to be the bearer of bad news, but someone has to shake you free of this delusion.

---

is your job bs?

What *should* you expect when you join a large company? According to a new book, *Bullshit Jobs: A Theory* (Simon & Schuster, 2018) by anthropologist David Graeber, only 37 to 40 percent of employees in Britain and the Netherlands felt their jobs were meaningful. The rest filled their days with "bullshit jobs" defined by the author as pointless tasks that employers pretend to believe in. A 2016 paper by Gary Hamel and Michele Zanini estimated the number of corporate bureaucrats in the U.S. to be about 24 million, or 1 for every 4.7 workers. As *The Economist* observes wryly, "Executives may know that half of their workers' time is wasted, but not which half."

VENI, VICI, SEDI[2]: A DAY IN THE *REAL*-LIFE JOB

Buckle up. Here is how it *truly* happens in Corporate:

8:00 A.M.   Left home at 5:30 A.M. to beat traffic. Didn't beat traffic. Meeting in 20 minutes in room 304D for the X-T54 (code name) product team's market review. Need to skim the 700-page report from the consultant at Snow and White Research Company on the new ingredient evolution in South Asia's special mineral market with focus on western Cambodia's emerging growth with projections. Cost $7,500 and says nothing interesting. You know their projections are fantasy, anyway, but the product director knows their project leader. She has been buying their horrible reports for a year now. You break down on page 548 and start watching a Netflix movie instead. Something about a woman named Bridget who married the perfect man after a 12-year courtship. You are married but you don't remember your spouse's name at this point. Saw said spouse for 40 minutes last week.

9:20 A.M.   Meeting started 30 minutes late. The product manager was flustered because her VP chewed her ear off about a new ad run by your competitor in the NCBXX TV channel in a suburb of Buenos Aires showing a price that was two whole pesos lower than yours. She ripped the BlueChipRedCharge agency for not informing her. Their rep promised that, from now on, she will get all 10,886 pages of media spending and ad scanning (with share-of-voice charts in the Southern hemisphere) every Monday at 5:00 A.M. (that's when *she* comes to the office).

---

[2] I came, I saw, I sat. Latin. Commonly done but not popularly attributed.

9:45 A.M.   Got a call from the amped-up brand manager of your company's soon-to-be launched new product. He wanted a price comparison of the new product with every product available in the stores in the U.S. Called your kids and told them to keep the Sunday inserts in your hometown's paper so that you can get the latest deals offered in your area and summarize them in a chart for this guy. Called your information vendor to gather circulars from all major metro areas and cut out the coupons and send you a report. The account guy said it will cost $25,000. He promised to check with his boss if the scissors can be bought from the current budget.

11:00 A.M. Just finished listening to a webinar by a company talking about Searching Beyond Google. Apparently, you can find the name of the supplier of the printing promotion material for a local Indonesian competitor. They use a shade of blue your agency doesn't on their packaging. You sense a breakthrough.

1:00 P.M.   Lunch. Lousy sandwich at your desk. No time to waste. Need to read another 500 pages from Snow and White on the emerging online market in widgets in Uzbekistan. Not sure why. Also, you have 145 emails to answer. What's the market share of General General, your main competitor, in eastern Russia's modern trade stores? Better call the vendor. Must remain on top of this important factor for your company's competitive-positioning PowerPoint slide.

4:00 P.M.   Had a meeting with your boss. Asked her if you can go for training in market analysis since you are truly not sure why you are doing what you are doing. She says don't worry, she wasn't trained either; she just went to a conference in Las Vegas, and it's not rocket science. She said you can watch some slides online instead.

6:00 P.M.   Your boss called. A private-equity company made a bid for your company. There will be job cuts. She was told the entire operation is under review. She doesn't understand why. She always gets great compliments from the sales and product teams on the news clips she sends them every Monday.

You need to brush up on your Hindi. There is a rumor the company has big plans to expand in New Delhi. How far is New Delhi from Miami? Maybe the commute won't be that bad.

QUESTION ASSUMPTIONS LIKE A PRO

Let's assume you take this job. You soon find out the real life of corporate analysts and others—in marketing, business development, strategy, or other departments—differs greatly from the job description. Your reasonable expectations of being able to affect the company's competitive strategy is shattered.

Please remember: Not every corporation is capital-C Corporate, and even though capital-C Corporate may be bonkers, it is not evil. Corporate does not set out to shatter your expectations. It sets out to achieve the company's prosperity, including yours, and it may genuinely believe its job description is *accurate*. It *is* accurate, if you think like Corporate.

Corporate thinks all those tasks, reports, and analyses are helpful, even necessary, and that's why your real-life days on the job don't match your fantasy. Corporate thinks lots of "actions" mean an effective job. Not even we, Ben and Mark, are safe. Our clients have shown us PowerPoint presentations as thick as encyclopedias—an ancient, pre-Google collection of knowledge—and containing numbers without end. You think we were kidding about western

Cambodia's special mineral market? Well, we were, but we've seen the real-life equivalent.

But Corporate doesn't have to be evil to cause trouble for itself, and you. Merely being bonkers is quite enough to corrode its skill at competing, like dimming a searchlight. If you can identify the causes behind Corporate's assumptions and beliefs about what needs to be done, you may be able to gain some maverick insight into what lies ahead for you, and how to make it work.

Corporate-with-a-capital-C turns the skill of competing into the science of burning cash in endless, aimless, ritualistic activities. An overwhelming portion of junior/middle managers' time in Corporate is spent executing tactical tasks of dubious but unquestioned (as in ritualistic) value. For example, researching every statement in a document to ensure accuracy even if it will never be read, attending unproductive meetings, reading distribution lists irrelevant to you but on which there may be a quiz in the unproductive meetings, and spellchecking bosses' slides.

To question the underlying value of those activities, you have to question some fundamental beliefs of what "works." Corporate strongly believes in "benchmarking"—the incessant comparison of how it does things with how others do those things (see more about this in Chapter 7). Questioning beliefs in "what works" is often considered sacrilege—"but the best companies do it that way!"—and results in excommunication *or worse.*

Galileo questioned the assumption that the sun circled the earth. You know how that ended for him. Similarly, questioning executives' assumptions is a tall task.

This topic comes up often in our speaking engagements. Ben once led a webinar for a strategy forum on the topic of the skill of competing. One of the participants, a strategic planner for a major Corporate, asked "How do you change management's deeply held beliefs?"

Our short answer was, "You don't," at least, not on your own. Life will do the work for you. A steep drop in Corporate earnings can encourage people to question assumptions once they stop trembling. And as we claim later, simulations (such as war games) are amazingly effective depending on who is in them and how they are structured.

Sloppy or outdated assumptions held by senior executives will dictate whether or not your analyses will be taken seriously. As a maverick, you don't attack each and every assumption. You choose your battles. To do that, distinguish between assumptions management is open to questioning (if presented with a convincing case) and those carved in stone. The latter should be left alone, as your head meeting the stone will be painful.

Which assumptions are carved in stone? Often those that are closely related to a CEO's big strategic initiatives.

Richard Fuld, CEO of Lehman Brothers, the 158-year-old investment bank that he drove to bankruptcy in 2008 with reckless derivatives-investment strategies, had this to say according to a report by Bloomberg in 2015: "Regardless of what you heard about Lehman Brothers' risk management, I had 27,000 risk managers because they all owned a piece of the firm."

Were the 27,000 "risk managers" responsible for the acquisition of five subprime mortgage lenders? Were they the ones to look over the massive leverage of 30 to 1 or even 100 to 1 in debt over equity? Was John in cubicle 245/23 in Annex A responsible? The Corporate Overconfident, Oblivious Culture at the late Lehman Brothers was clearly the result of Fuld's management style, his assumptions about where growth was to be had, and his core belief that investment advice was too limited a scope for Lehman Brothers. It was not his risk managers' core belief; they followed *his*.

BUST ASSUMPTIONS EARLY

Since all jobs involving or supporting decision-making involve, or at least should involve, continually *questioning* assumptions, you must first *uncover* Corporate's assumptions. This simple rule applies to all employees and managers whose performance evaluation depends on their ability to compete against other market players even though Corporate never says anything about competing. Of course, the job description doesn't include references to management's assumptions being off by a mile or a decade. The beliefs that drive management's competitive strategy come out like flowers after the rain in informal discussions and executive meetings. But what if you are not there? What if you are there, but you don't know how to uncover the assumptions *because no one showed you how*?

Follow the Analogy: Executives' Favorite Tool

An easier strategy to discern what management thinks is to follow executives' use of analogies and metaphors. Executives *adore* analogies and metaphors: They see them as the quickest, hippest way to make a point. American executives love to liken business to sports, even as their European visitors stare blankly at baseball stories. (The Americans enjoy both the instant replay and the European strikeout. It's a double play!) But listen closely, and you'll see a Corporate-atrophied competing culture.

Giovanni Gaveti and Jan Rivkin, of the Harvard Business School, suggest that "it is extremely easy to reason poorly through analogies, and strategists rarely consider how to use them well." In their 2005 article, they described analogies used to apply retail principles from supermarkets to the likes of Toys "R" Us, Circuit City, and CarMax. While analogies often rely on cross-industry insights—a solution from one industry is applied to a similar industry—the resemblance can be superficial and misleading. Moreover, in competitive analysis, a neat, attractive, compelling analogy can make deeper thought seem unnecessary. Finding just the right analogy makes it feel as though you've solved the problem and know what to do! Best of all (or so it seems), it frees you from worrying about details such as what other parties may do as you implement your solution.

cautionary analogy tale

A case in point: IBM and HP.

Leo Apotheker, once the CEO of HP, convinced HP's board to buy Autonomy, a software company with a one-trick pony—searching unstructured databases—for a price that reflected not Autonomy's record but Apotheker's obsession with IBM. His analogy centered on the way IBM transformed itself from a seller of hardware to a seller of software and services. Following this analogy, Autonomy was supposed to transform HP into an enterprise service/solution giant.

The problem was, IBM had always dealt with high-level IT executives (selling them its mainframes) and jettisoned its consumer business in 2004. HP had been selling printers and PCs to consumers and deriving most of its cash from that business, which dominated its management hierarchy. The two markets are so different that under the next CEO, Meg Whitman, HP *split* its business.

Apotheker's Autonomy transaction became infamous for accounting irregularities. The root problem, though, was not Autonomy's inflated revenue; it was what *led* to the need for inflation. Apotheker's incorrect analogy about HP and IBM led him, seemingly rationally, to an inflated evaluation, and hence an inflated acquisition price for Autonomy.

Ill-considered "hub" beliefs—fundamental core assumptions—give credence to false analogies. When they take root at the top of the Corporate pyramid, false analogies can lead to disastrous decisions. If you happen to work for a company where analogies fly freely at every meeting, examine the analogies critically. Mavericks never take anything for granted—not even at IBM.

advice to the maverick

What's the practical takeaway for you from this chapter? It's natural to shoot for an exciting Corporate job. But wait! Be skeptical of recruiters' too-good-to-be-true ads. They are always, but always, too good to be true. Ask specific questions:

- Will I be expected to follow certain templates in my analysis/tasks, or can I employ whatever frameworks work best?

- Will I get face-to-face time with executives?

- Am I expected only to collect, collate, and distribute raw information, or is there scope for my recommendations and insights?

- Will I be given a uniform like in the post office?

If you suspect the answers are too vague, it is better to wait for the next opportunity, even if at the moment all you manage is a McDonald's afternoon shift. At least there, you are in charge of something real.

A bad start to your career is not easy to fix. And while you can't assess COOC before setting foot in the company, you may find some clues on Glassdoor.com. This site includes reviews of companies' cultures by current (or former) employees. It can give you a sense of culture if you filter petty grudges from worrisome signs.

However, if you already accepted that wonderful, dreamy Corporate job, our advice is to remain skeptical. Be skeptical of facile, ego-boosting analogies thrown around by management. They are as bad as football metaphors. *Football metaphors, bad?* Yes. You are a team, but you are not bound to a set of simple fixed rules regarding who you can knock down as you run around.

advice to the maverick, continued

In short, being skeptical is not a sign of a negative personality, a bad team player, or a cynical misfit. It is a sign of unorthodox, independent thinking. It's a sign you are a positive maverick.

training to compete

"If you want to know what
a man's like, take a good look
at how he treats his inferiors,
not his equals."

—J.K. ROWLING,

HARRY POTTER AND THE GOBLET OF FIRE

Competing is a human activity, not yet outsourced to Siri, so employees who are skilled at competing should, in principle, make a company competitive. We think most reasonable people see the truth in this statement. You'd think Corporate does, too, and would, therefore, train and test its people for skill at competing. The military does it all the time: They have their commanders face opponents' maneuvers in war games and field exercises. They brief and debrief missions and exercises. They learn from mistakes and they build on success to help them outsmart real-life opponents.

It's easy for the military because the skill of competing teams can be assessed quickly and unequivocally. Did you surprise the other side? Did you take the hill? Did you steal the other team's flag?

In this chapter we will look at how companies should train their people to compete. We will compare *effective* training to Corporate's use of empty slogans as substitutes for serious skill enhancement. To the maverick, that means learning to recognize and look past the Corporate platitudes.

HOW DO YOU TRAIN TO COMPETE?

In business, training and testing the skill of competing is subtler and significantly more complicated than for the military. Companies aren't allowed to drop bombs, for example, and outcomes of decisions can take years to materialize. Competing skillfully involves integrating three elements:

1. *Strategic mindset.* The ability to see the big picture, which includes seeing *other market-players' perspectives* and identifying opportunities and risks that others *don't yet see.*
2. *Leadership.* The ability to lead a team in the desired direction, which involves the ability to show the internal logic of your strategy. You persuade your team to follow; you don't have to order them to do so.
3. *Management.* The ability to plan and execute a superior strategy while being alert (i.e., agile) to other market-players' moves and countermoves.[1]

We believe that the key to training managers to compete is by extensively and intensively using strategy *simulations* throughout their careers (including creating action plans and testing them against other players' potential responses). We've seen it work in hundreds of engagements involving thousands of managers. The most effective simulations are war games, like the ones we've mentioned before, that pit teams who are role-playing the company against teams who are role-playing their competitors. Some war games use technology, quantifying outcomes using competitive-strategy models. Other war games use referees, letting senior executives judge which outcome is more robust.

If war gaming works so well, though, why doesn't everyone do it? Why is it considered revolutionary rather than obvious? Because Corporate-with-a-capital-C thinks it's *already* training and assessing managers' skill at competing.

HOW CORPORATE *THINKS* IT TRAINS TO COMPETE

Corporate's idea of training to compete applies the osmosis process: Shuffle people from assignment to assignment, from function to function, from country to country, all so those people can accumulate experience and absorb wisdom. Then Corporate assumes

---

[1] Brightline Consulting surveyed 500 senior executives regarding implementation of their strategies. Fifty-three percent stated that their strategic initiative failed to reach its goal because of competitive moves. www.brightline.org/eiu-report.

haphazard trial and error can separate the competitively skilled from the unskilled. This awfully long and expensive process requires management to claim it "celebrates failures."

When's the last time you saw a failure party? How many people can you name who were promoted because they failed?

Failure is not the objective. The objective is to learn how *not* to fail. That's why we appreciate the military's approach with war games and why we conduct our own. *Simulated* failure is cheap. The title of a chapter that Mark co-wrote in *Wharton on Dynamic Competitive Strategy* (Simon & Schuster, 1997) expressed it well: "Putting the Lesson before the Test." Learn the lesson before you take real-life risks.

And that's why we agree with Dr. David KrU.S.uer, president of the Santa Fe Institute's, statement: "Everyone says failure is a wonderful thing. I totally disagree."

For Corporate, however, it is cheaper to use platitudes than use strategy simulations to test and upgrade its managers' skills.

---

a note on war games

The issue of routinely, extensively, and wisely using simulations to train and sharpen management's skill at competing will naturally come up throughout this book. This is our expertise. We expect companies to adopt simulations (e.g., qualitative and quantitative war gaming) as a regular part of their managerial cadre's development. Just as an athlete trains before *every* competition, companies in the future will adopt simulation tests before *every* major competitive-strategy decision. If we may toot our horns, a good place to start for companies will be Mark's stunning Top Pricer Tournament™ (https://whatifyourstrategy.com/services/tournaments/) and war games (https://whatifyourstrategy.com/services/war-games/), and Ben's eye-opening war games (www.giladwargames.com).

Beware the Platitudes

Corporate-with-a-capital-C has its own method to increase its skill of competing. Instead of routinely training using a variety of simulations and selecting its leaders from among those showing high skill, it uses platitudes *equally* applied to all, such as "People Are Our Number-One Asset!"

We understand the need for uplifting proclamations on special occasions. We realize a lot of those "feel good" statements are customary responses to predictable situations, such as the company's annual cheerleading meeting or the departure of a beloved executive. The mantras and clichés save time and effort compared with genuine and authentic statements, not to mention being much cheaper than actually training and selecting people based on their ability to compete. In economics, using platitudes is understood as "saving on cognitive-processing resources," which are always in tight supply. Sometimes in *very* tight supply.

Generic statements, such as "people are our number-one asset," are seen as encouraging and affirmative, or at least harmless. On the contrary, if they're not backed by clear, consistent action, they create a cynical workforce that knows executives and big shareholders are way *more* equal, external consultants are way more influential on management thinking, and employees often come last, especially during financial distress. Some "niceties" are so obviously wrong or empty they are laughable.

Take, for example, Walmart raising its hourly wage in February 2015 because it was good business. As Doug McMillon, Walmart's CEO, said in various public forums and on Walmart's site, the decision was based on the premise that happier employees will raise the level of customer service. In his message to Walmart's 1.3 million employees, reported on Walmart's blog, he said, "You've heard us say things like 'our secret to success is that we're all working together and our people make the difference.' While that phrase started as a meeting theme in 1979, it became a way of thinking. It's what we believe. It's what I believe. Our actions must match our beliefs."

McMillon himself rose through the ranks of Walmart, from an hourly associate with low wages to its highly paid CEO. According to the website, Salary.com, he earned $22.2 million in total compensation in the 2018 fiscal year. If McMillon figured higher pay can improve Walmart's service and it's just "good business," he should/would have done that or fought for that many years earlier, not suspiciously close to the rising public and political pressure. Clearly, if he believed 1) higher wages make employees happier, 2) happier employees improve service, *and* 3) *service is a critical element in the success of Walmart's strategy* (which was true long before 2015), then he or his predecessors could have acted on that belief. As the ACSI.org site reports, Walmart has been among the lowest-rated department or discount stores in the nation on customer service satisfaction. But Walmart prospered *despite* lousy customer service. Its strategy of everyday low prices paid off handsomely—even with unhappy employees. Its statement that "our employees make the difference" has been mostly a platitude, not a pillar of its strategy.

Walmart's *real* attitude toward motivating employees vs. reducing costs is not unique. Our next example is even more familiar to the managerial cadre.

Open Space, Empty Promises

Corporate's lack of sincerity when saying, "We are all in it together!" manifests itself in countless ways. One egregious way that interferes with even the most competitively skilled people is the "open space" floorplan.

Anthonia Akitunde's report on American Express Open Forum details study after study about the lack of any evidence whatsoever that cubicles improve productivity or creativity or anything ending with "vity" (and, by this point, certainly not brevity), yet the move is not "let's go back to privacy, quiet, and concentration," but to *completely* open space. You wanted an office? You won't even get a cubicle! Who would ever have thought that Pink Floyd's immortal words "Tear down this wall!" would so inspire big, beige corporations? You can't make this stuff up.

Now that's dysfunctional culture at its best (that is, its worst). If the first move failed, ramp it up. It's equivalent to launching globally a product that failed locally. We're not supposed to be afraid of failure, right? So the bigger the failure, the less we're afraid.

Videos posted on Inc.com in 2016 of halls filled with desks seating clones, many with headphones to block out noise, suggest Corporate is trying to adapt coach—excuse us, "main cabin"—airline seats to the office. The greater the density, the greater the profitability. The idea that collaboration is *improved* with people desperately trying to insulate themselves with headphones is as logical as the idea that prison improves social skills because it brings people kind of close together. So why do companies insist on the crazy idea that hurts the ability of their best people to exercise their skills? Our hypotheses[2]:

- Open-space furniture vendors and architectural designers take executives to better lunches than traditional office space designers, probably in restaurants with *private booths*. By the way, in what sense is the space "open" if it's teeming with people? The wild prairies of Wyoming are open space. Google's offices, not so much. As the *Washington Post* reported in 2014, the open space at Google was actually killing productivity.
- Repeating the phrase "office of the future" on 129 slides has a hypnotic power that puts otherwise smart executives in a semi-comatose state, preventing them from making informed decisions.
- Many executives grew up in the horrible cubicle system and feel it is needed to "build character." They also walked four miles to school, uphill both ways, carrying a sibling and/or a neighbor, in the snow, barefoot, and without an iPhone. If I survived it, so can they! So *should* they!
- Benchmarking Google has become a status symbol regardless of relevance.

---

[2] Write to us if you have more hypotheses! We're all in this together. You are our number-one reader!

- Open space saves money on facilities and furniture.

We vote for the last reason, but no HR executive will ever admit that this lowly goal is the real and only motivation. It is almost as if Walmart said, "We pay low wages because it lowers our costs." Duh!

Some Silicon Valley CEOs, in an attempt to demonstrate their shared-fate philosophy, place their desks in the open space together with their employees. We admire these people.

First, they know everyone is looking at them and they might have a zit. That shows solidarity with the commoners.

Second, they make billion-dollar decisions amid so much noise that they can hardly hear the other side's lawyer on the phone. It is more dangerous not to hear the other side's lawyer than it is to hear your own. That takes guts.

Third, the elevator music filling the open space numbs the cortex as well as the soul. That's Corporate evolution at work: Only the toughest can make it through the day.

If we may suggest, it seems to us an alternative policy would be to invite employees randomly into executives' plush offices on the 27th floor for a day to let them taste success. The American dream rests on the idea that upward mobility comes from skill and merit, not from a relationship with a ruling family or a duke of some hazard. One of us came to this country with no money and little English. Now he is at the top of his field, with no money and little English but *with a great co-author who edits his writing.* [Co-author's note to editor: That "great co-author" phrase, which I *swear* I didn't write, stays in the book no matter what.] [Editor's note: Your modesty is well-earned, but you did have a comma splice on page 17. Do better.] [The first co-author's note to editor: What's a comma splice?]

No great thinker said, "Please, surround me with noise and distraction; how can I get any work done when I can hear myself think?" Low cost is not, in itself, high productivity. Give us some privacy, please. Bring back our walls!

HAPPINESS IS NOT NECESSARY

We've seen that Corporate excels in discouraging employees from competing by packing them into "open spaces," speaking to them like a motivational poster, or paying them badly. Is the opposite necessary for skillful competing? In other words, if you pay well, speak honestly, and provide plush offices, does that improve how well you compete in the marketplace? Not so much. What raises employees' skill at competing is training employees to compete.

We don't intend to disparage HR's functions. We don't have much expertise in organizational-psychology science. That said, we are somewhat skeptical of the value of "change consultants," motivational speakers, and other modern shamans selling such *profound* wisdom as "make sure employees are satisfied, and they will stick around longer." They may stick around longer, but that doesn't mean the company will succeed.

The most famous "let's make them happy" experiment was the so-called Hawthorne study where Western Electric employees improved productivity when lighting in the factory was changed, whether brighter or dimmer. Researchers concluded it wasn't the lighting but the attention—whether paternalistic or Big Brotherly—given to the employees. That, they announced, caused spikes in productivity. The problem with their conclusions was that there was no control group, and the employees were worried about being fired (it was during the Depression). *Jobs are vanishing fast . . . people with pens and notepads are watching and measuring . . . hmm, how should I behave?*

Employees skilled in competing raise the odds of success. (Luck plays a part, too, but it's not always good luck.) But *happy* employees?

Maybe.

Find Your Superior, Not Perfect, Strategy

If you say, "the two—happy and skilled—are not mutually exclusive," you are a kind spirit but not an empiricist. The biggest flaw in the wildly popular concept that happy employees will make a company compete better is that it is not necessary for a company to reach its goals. Competitive strategy is *necessary* for reaching one's goals as long as there are other players vying for the same goals.[3] That's because "competitive" implies your strategy can lead to reaching your goals *despite* other players' strategies. Your strategy doesn't have to be perfect, if there even is such a thing. Your strategy doesn't have to be sophisticated, complicated, or best-ever. It's competitive as long as it reckons with competitors and other interested parties in reaching your goals.

Competitive strategy that incorporates competitors' moves or countermoves can lead to reaching your goals even if execution is very nonperfect (i.e., lousy). Example? Netflix. Ranked low on customer service and satisfaction in a *USA Today* report from 2013, its strategy nonetheless filled a real need. Remember, "competitive" is relative: Netflix is superior as long as the alternatives (expensive bundled packages from cable companies and over-the-air broadcasts) are seen by customers as inferior. Another example is airlines. You may question how long a company can ignore customers' complaints and still prosper, but as airlines proved, the answer is, "Quite long, thank you, please stay on the line, all our representatives are busy due to an unexpected heavy volume of calls since 1766." Orville Wright flew the world's first heavier-than-air powered flight. Alas, his brother Wilbur was bumped due to overbooking.

Decoupling Happiness from Competing

We will say this again later, but you might be unhappy now, and we do not want an unhappy reader. We are not Grinches. We are not against happy employees or happy readers. Being happy is one of

---

[3] Alternative: *lots* of good, long-term luck. Note that, by definition, you're about as likely to have lots of bad, long-term luck. We recommend a competitive strategy.

case study: strategic cause and effect

Sometimes a strategy that was necessary for success starts to fail, but the decline is hardly ever caused by unhappy employees or even unhappy customers. A failing strategy will make people unhappy, but unhappy people do not necessarily make a strategy fail. In other words, watch out for cause and effect. Example: Dell. The strategic concept of Dell was ingenious in the '80s when its direct-sale model and built-to-order machines propelled it to the top of the PC market. One of Dell's early pillars of success was its fantastic customer support, which was based on the *enormous* amount of data on the performance of its machines collected via Dell.com. Dell used Big Data when all others used small data. Then Dell moved its support to India to save money, and the service deteriorated severely. *You* try to support an annoying customer who is looking for his control panel on the back of the monitor at 5 P.M. U.S. time when it is 3 A.M. *India time.* Loyal customers (such as Ben) were appalled. But even so, the decline of Dell was not due to its unhappy customers; it was due to the introduction of tablets and smartphones. Many customers loved the simplicity and portability of those new technologies. For them, the new technologies changed the reference point for what qualified as "superior." Happy employees and happy customers are not necessary to the performance of the strategy, but superiority to alternatives *is.*

our happiest occasions. All we're saying is that happy employees are not necessary for a company to succeed. They can't save bad strategy and, as the examples above suggest, they are not always necessary for a good strategy to succeed. (Note, too, that unhappy employees are not necessary for a company to fail.)

McDonald's and the other giant fast-food chains are testaments to that. Anyone who goes through a drive-in window at rush hour can attest that a smile and a happy face are in short supply, and yet we all still go there because its costs only $20 to feed a family of seven, including Buddy the Rottweiler. While a happy work force is *probably* more loyal, and a sour-faced employee is not a great inducement to come back and shop, the ultimate factor in performance is the strategy itself, not the people. Even executives, charmingly naive and spiritual as they are, know that. So their claim that "people are our number-one asset!" is just their imitation of motivational speakers.

Instead of focusing on those empty platitudes and slogans you read about earlier in this chapter, companies should train, test, and deploy their people in improving strategy. The best mechanism is to run war-game simulations, with mavericks, before important strategy decisions. The second-best mechanism is to identify mavericks and promote them. The third-best mechanism is to allow for strategic ideas to bubble to the top with little filtering. Not all ideas are good, not all employees are strategy-minded, but just repeating the orthodox formula over and over is a recipe for decline, and only mavericks are capable of changing the course.

We are not against happy employees. Au contraire. We are against empty hype. So let's stop with the insincere hyperbole. The truth might hurt and platitudes might soothe, but "necessary adjustments to our global work force brought about by difficult demand conditions" puts the lie in "we are all in this together." Improving a company and its employees' *skill in competing* is a better strategy than syrupy slogans and will more likely result in improved performance. And now, everyone's happy.

advice to the maverick

Fighting the dysfunctional culture of hyperboles and empty slogans starts with you!

Corporate, being supportive but Corporate nonetheless, will encourage you to be a good team player. (Not a *great* team player, which would make you stand out from the team and thus undermine the team.) But even the greatest team in the world can't succeed with sloppy strategic thinking. Slogans like, "People are our number-one asset!" mean little if Corporate actually pays no attention to fresh-thinkers' ideas.

If you cave to the rituals of the company or if you, too, spout empty slogans and hyperbole, your maverick days are over (or at least on hiatus). Some smart people choose this route. We don't blame them. Unorthodox thinking takes effort and courage, and success is not assured.

Staying a maverick means entering a quiet struggle against powerful rituals and traditions. "Kissing up" is not just occasional, shall we say, diplomacy; it is also staying silent in tedious forums even when you know openness and "no BS" rules could have much more impact on the company and your own success. And some smart people choose this route. Why? Because it's easy.

If you are an independent thinker, however, how can you overcome the empty-platitude-loving, happy-employee veneer of Corporate culture? You can't wait for top management to come down from Mount Olympus and adopt straight talk, but you can agree with your peers and underlings that you are all going to be better off speaking your minds and sharing lessons. You can start by arranging *one meeting a week* in which real discussions take place, blinders are put aside, and no records are kept. The intent of these meetings should not be a "whining session" but a discussion where all perspectives are welcome, and the goal is small-c corporate improvement.

advice to the maverick, continued

Incidentally, that's the purpose, in some cultures, of going out drinking with the boss. Alcohol, whether or not the actual cause of loosened tongues, gives a kind of permission to get real and "apologize" the next day (after the message was delivered). Do be careful, though, that you've properly identified the culture you're in. Get it wrong and you could end up in Scotch and hot water.

You'd be amazed how much more can be accomplished (and even better, how much you and your company can compete) when you do not succumb to the hype.

how corporate thinks

the
myth
that
customers
matter

CHAPTER 5

"I love mankind . . . it's
people I can't stand!!"

—CHARLES M. SCHULZ,

THE COMPLETE PEANUTS,

VOL. 5: 1959–1960

A t the receiving end of every competitive strategy are the customers. Their decision to buy or not buy determines the success or not-success of a company's effort.

As a maverick, your role is to question constantly your company's *stated* dedication to satisfying customers while *actually* tormenting them in every possible way.

Companies must put their best feet forward whenever they interact with customers. Always greet the customer with a smile! (And non-smelly feet.) After all, the customer is always right, and if that's too much to swallow, just remember that the customer is the one with the money.

In this chapter, we explore the conventional wisdom that Corporate cares deeply about its customers and the equally funny hypothesis that it matters. We also explore the new myth that Big Data makes Corporate more customer-centric. While unhappy customers might not cause a strategy to fail as long as the alternatives are worse,[1] the question every maverick should ask is, "What's the breaking point for customers?" We think the examples below might help point that out.

---

[1] That includes what is known as "switching costs." How difficult it is to switch from your current bank, for example.

HOW NOT TO TALK TO THE CUSTOMER

Everyone, even executives, knows that we love, love, love our customers! That's why Corporate invests so much in the latest technology and highly trained call centers to provide warm, personal customer service. Just like this:

Your Call is Very Important to Us

Thank you for calling Fungibull.

Your call is very important to us. That's why we haven't hired enough people to answer it right away.

Please listen carefully to the following 18 menu options, as the options have changed.

At any point, you may hang up and dial again. To keep this message useful, we will repeat this information. At any point, you may hang up and dial again.

Here are the 18 menu options, which have changed. At any point, you may hang up and dial again.

Option 1. To continue this message in Spanish, press 1 to call our Spanish line. International rates and a hefty profit surcharge may apply.

Option 2. To continue this message in Swedish, press 2 to call our Swedish line. International rates and a hefty profit surcharge may apply.

Option 3. To continue this message in Aramaic, press 3 to call our Aramaic line. Inter-temporal rates and a hefty profit surcharge may apply. We are experiencing heavy volume on this line as everyone wants to talk to Moses. Please be patient.

Option 4. To leave a message for a customer service representative, press 4. Please leave your name, your phone number, your political affiliation, your hair color, the serial number of the product or service you are calling about, the exact nature of the problem and its unknown causes, and the longitude, latitude, and elevation where the problem occurred. To keep costs low so we can delight you with lower prices, your message is limited to 12 seconds. You must provide all information so we can serve you better. Please speak slowly and clearly, because to keep our costs low so we can delight you with lower prices, your message will be heard by a person in a low-cost country where English, Spanish, Swedish, and Aramaic are not spoken.

Option 5. To select from a list of our 200 most popular complaints, press 5 at the end of this greeting. Your selection may be recorded for quality assurance, but we can assure you it probably won't.

Option 6. To speak with a shipping and handling engineer about an order you have not received, press 6.

Option 7. To speak with a catalog engineer about a catalog you have not received, press 7.

Option 8. To speak with a catalog engineer about a catalog you would prefer not to receive, press 8.

Option 9. To speak with a message engineer about this message, press 8. Just kidding, we said to press 8 for option 8. Press 9 to speak with the message engineer. Remember, humor in your life is like a flower in the carburetor.

Option 10. To speak with a billing engineer about your bill, hang up and dial again.

Option 11. To be reminded by a call engineer that your call is very important to us, press 11. You will hear a soothing message and then have the opportunity to select another option.

Option 12. To hear the multiplication table in English, press the product of 3 times 4.

Option 13. To hear the multiplication table recited by R2D2, make a funny electronic noise.

Option 14. Sorry, I've lost count. Hold on a second. Please keep holding. Please keep holding. Your call is very important to us. Please keep holding. Oh, there is no option 14. Do not press 14.

Option 15. If you have forgotten the reason for your call and would merely like to tell us off, press 15. To enable this option after you press 15, enter the password, which is the exact population of Mauritania at the time this greeting ends.

Option 16. This option is intentionally left blank. To select it anyway, press 16, then hang up and dial again.

Option 17. To treat your helpless sputtering rage by speaking with a counselor-engineer, press 17. Additional undisclosed charges will be added to your bill.

Option 18. To speak to Ralph, press 18. Ralph does not work here.

At any point, you may hang up and dial again.

You have 0.3 seconds from the word "now" to press your desired menu option. Now.

You have not entered a menu option in the time allowed. We will connect you to the first available operator. At any point, you may hang up and dial again.

Thank you for calling Fungibull. All operators are busy with valued customers like you, but not you. We know your time is valuable, and we apologize for the delay. We will play soothing, uninterrupted music while you wait.

Dum de dum de ba dum

All operators are still busy with valued customers like you, but not you. Your estimated wait time is *<sound of static>*. We will play soothing, uninterrupted music while you wait.

Ooooh la de dum dum

At any point, you may hang up and dial again.

Ba dum ba dum

Thank you for continuing to hold. At any point, you may hang up and dial again. All operators are still busy with valued customers like you, but not you.

Zumm de lum zumm

Your cursing has been monitored by a propriety engineer. Your call has been pushed back in line by 84 callers. Your new estimated wait time is *<sound of static>*.

La de la de THUMP

Your call is very important to us. At any point, you may hang up and dial again.

BRACK THUMP BRACK SCREEEEECH la de ba la dum zumm

Are you still here? Thank you for continuing to hold. All operators are wondering why you don't hang up and dial again.

< SLAM >

Thank you for calling Fungibull. Your call was unexpectedly interrupted. As a convenience to valued customers like you, we have called you back.

Your call is very important to us. Please listen carefully to the following 23 menu options, as the options have changed. At any point, you may hang up and dial again.

That's never happened to you, has it?

When Corporate sets up these hard-to-navigate, customer-unfriendly phone trees, we have to wonder: Have they called the number themselves? Have they experienced the horror of never being able to talk to an actual human being? Food for thought: Airline

CEOs fly on their own airlines, sometimes even in coach. (Yes, really, but not on long flights.) Two gave interviews while sitting in coach seats in aircraft on the ground. *The Wall Street Journal* interviewed American and Delta CEOs in "When Airline CEOs Try the Cheap Seats" (United's CEO declined the invitation) and their message was "if you want more space, buy it."

As a business strategy it's sensible, or at least defensible. The even better news is that it's honest. What's galling about the phone menus is that they're dishonest, from the hypocrisy of "valued customer" to the utter inflexibility of the system. They make customers dread contacting a company that wants the customer's business . . . and they hand an opportunity to any competitor who's willing to make the process painless. We want to kiss the hands of the human beings at companies who answer their phones.[2]

INSTRUCTIONS: HOW NOT TO HELP THE CUSTOMER

There's a simple, huge, one-word difference between the airlines and phone menus.

Phone menus are the result of cost analysis. Companies using automated menus save on hiring humans. The airlines' strategies are the result of cost-*benefit* analysis. As long as the benefits of cheap travel to the vacation paradise outweigh the cattle-car space saving, passengers will keep flying in cheap seats. Keeping benefits in mind keeps cost-cutting from getting out of hand.

At times, you can spot out-of-control cost-cutting with another single word. The word commonly appears in the assembly instructions for many products. You will find it a few lines from now. Do not overlook it.

Many modern products require some assembly. Some need nothing more than inserting a battery. Some, like the ultimate build-your-own furniture kits, consist of an oak-tree seed and a bottle of

---

[2] We also thank the companies that enable quick and easy online interactions, but we're not yet ready to kiss the screen.

water. Most instructions are clear, such as *battery not included*. But some are not, like this: *Do not overtighten*.

As we home-improve our homes, we come across products whose directions warn us not to "overtighten" something. This confuses us. How are we supposed to know how much tightening is too much? If something shatters, cracks, or crumbles, we figure we've overtightened it, but that information is tardy and not helpful. Remember, we don't want to under-tighten it, either. We don't want it to fall apart and spill a *Caution! Awfully Hot!* liquid on us. Customers may sue. (More about that when we get to Corporate's great agricultural achievement, the Denial Tree.)

A pleasant alternative would be, "Go ahead and tighten until you reach the limits of your strength." To do that, the item being tightened would have to be strong enough to withstand our formidable strength, and we all know that sturdy is out in these cost-conscious times (which apparently have been in effect for 30 years or so, based on how often we are warned of the delicacy of items about to be tightened).

We think the elegant beauty of "do not overtighten" can only be understood from the perspective of a lawyer. (*Your Honors, we hereby state for the record that we are not, have not been, and expect never to be against lawyers. One of us almost became one ourselves. Ipso facto. Habeas corpus. De minimis non curat praetor.*) "Do not overtighten" may also be understood from the perspective of folks in customer support who, in turn, are dealing with a situation created by cost accountants (against whom we also have nothing).

Let's replay the conversation between the customer and customer support:

Customer (C): "I was putting the product together and it broke."

Support (S): "When did it break?"

C: "Sunday."

S: "No, at what point in the assembly process? Were you tightening something?"

C: "Yes."

S: "You must have overtightened it. The instructions specifically state not to overtighten it. Bad customer. There is no warranty, express or implied, on overtightened items. We would be happy to sell you a replacement. Want my advice?"

C: "Yes, please."

S: "Do not overtighten it."

All businesses tighten; it's called efficiency and productivity. Tightening does for the business what tightening does for the product: Prevent it from falling apart because of loose assembly. But Corporate *overtightens*, cutting costs—budgets, materials, personnel—wherever costs are found, even if those costs generate benefits. They do it because they're led there by simple, persuasive logic, which we can boil down to this: It is cheaper to print "do not overtighten" on the instructions than it is to supply products that can withstand formidable strength. It is even virtuous to do so because driving out excess costs permits lower prices, which makes customers happy. That's true . . . until we overtighten. Unfortunately, the dividing line between nice-and-tight and overtight is as hard to discern in business as it is in home improvement.

Overtightening in business leads to being thrown off your flight (or dragged off) when an airline overbooks and to being unable to get an airline seat for days if your flight is canceled. Notice that the airline blames the weather, not overtightening, for stranding you for a week in Manitoba. Overtightening leads to being put on hold for hours with 35 options (the menu has changed). Overtightening leads to being vulnerable to hiccups anywhere in a long supply chain. Overtightening leads to nutritional quality gradually being subtracted from food, unless it is organic, and then it overtightens your wallet.

The first question, of course, is: When does tightening become overtightening? How can you tell the difference?

The second question is: So what? Is overtightening bad?

Nobody intentionally overtightens. Probably nobody thinks they overtighten at all. The relentless pressure of Wall Street to increase profit, though, favors tightening costs over increasing revenue. Increasing revenue can be hard. Tightening costs, on the other hand, is easy. All you need is a CEO who doesn't like costs.

Tightening is the first reaction of Corporate when performance goes down. It seems natural because it's something we can do *right now* to bring profits up. It seems necessary, too. After all, making money for shareholders is a key goal for CEOs who are employed on their behalf.

Cost-cutting can become a self-inflicted Corporate problem in three ways:

1. Cutting costs across the board—that is, equally across all functions—feels equitable, but it is rarely a skillful way to compete. It says we're as willing to cut development of our next generation of products as we are to cut conference-hopping.
2. Cutting costs to maintain profits *now* can reduce our long-term competitiveness. Ironically, the cheapest time to spend money is when the market as a whole turns down. That's because your competitors are reflexively cutting. If you can resist your own cut-costs reflex, you can out-invest them at a bargain price.
3. Tightening costs lets you compete on price, but competing on price is the most-dangerous, least-profitable way to compete. It is the blunt object, the brute force, of competitive strategy, and lower-cost nations will win that game.

You will notice that this chapter is not titled "In Defense of Wasteful Practices." We are not defending waste; we are in favor of efficiency and productivity. All we're saying is that cost analysis at many companies makes an implicit assumption: If saving $1 is good, then saving $2 is twice as good. It makes the implicit assumption that saving the next dollar is equally as good as saving the previous dollar. In other words, the tools we use to gauge the goodness of tightening make it hard to tell the difference between nice-and-tight and overtight.

There's even an opportunity to create (inadvertently?) a vested interest in overtightening. If people are paid a percentage of a company's profits or cost savings, for example, then they have an incentive to err on the side of tightening too much rather than too little. That's especially true for people who don't plan to stay long at the company. We might get the same effect when executives get much compensation in the form of stock options because the "benefits" of overtightening (profits are up!) are evident before the downsides kick in (sales and market share are down). Customers pay the price of cost-cutting—phone menus (now with 42 options, the menu has changed again), marooned in Manitoba, flimsy products, data breaches, etc.—but by then the executives are sailing their yachts in Florida, tightening the ropes ("lines" to those who understand sailing) and hoping they don't snap.

ARE YOU SATISFIED NOW? NOW? NOW?

Corporate is a great fan of customer-satisfaction surveys for much the same reason Corporate sings "people are our number-one asset." Its affection for those surveys is surprising at first blush. Corporate likes to control everything, after all, so one would expect it to do customer surveys with fake or dead customers. If dead people can vote, surely they can take five minutes to answer a short survey. But courageously enough, Corporate hires companies to survey real, breathing customers. Who hasn't spent two hours with a tech-support agent, who couldn't solve the problem, just to receive an email with a quick customer-satisfaction survey?

We said Corporate is a great fan of conducting customer-satisfaction surveys. We didn't say Corporate is a great fan of *acting* on them. COOCs carry out surveys as part of the routine, the "busy work," the rituals. The statistics are collected automatically by a service like Survey Monkey and once a year presented in an annual retreat to get: 1) righteous indignation, 2) stern-but-toothless demands for improvement, and/or 3) a good laugh. It's cheaper than getting Beyoncé to that retreat and arguably more relevant.

But let's not be too cynical. Let's assume Corporate actually tries to learn something from these surveys of customer satisfaction. Then, Corporate has a real problem.

Customer-satisfaction surveys can provide tremendously valuable insight into people's experiences with a product or service. They don't say much, though, about what made a person become a customer in the first place. To learn *that*, you need to contrast what was different about people who became customers (what did they want, what did they believe, what experience did they have when they visited the site or store, etc.) from people who decided not to become customers. Ideally, you'd split the latter group into those who decided to buy from your competitors and those who decided not to buy at all.

Here's another way to think about it: Customer satisfaction concerns the *previous* purchase, and for strategy and forecasting, you need to worry about the *next* purchase. We were very happy with our trusty, powerful HP calculators (does that make us old?), and we'd give HP fabulous customer-satisfaction scores. That said, we will not buy another calculator from them or from anyone. We've got calculators in our computers, iPads, smartphones, and with the Internet of Things, probably in our toothbrushes. *Hey Siri, brush my teeth, and while you're at it, warn me if you see any heteroskedasticity near the gum line.*

is overtightening bad?

Examples from industries like airlines, cable TV, retailing, and many others suggest that bad service born of overtightening is not actually a hindrance to profitability. But this is true only as long as everyone provides similarly bad service or the costs of switching to better alternatives are prohibitive. The problem for companies is that bad service practically begs *new entrants* to offer those alternatives or offer as bad a service but at even lower cost. Overtightening is profitable for Corporate until the new entrants swoop in and offer a better alternative.

---

is overtightening bad?, continued

Even if the new entrants do not offer superior service, it's easier for them to compete with bad service than good. At least, the customer can hope, it will be variety. Uber had an easy time competing with notoriously bad taxi service. In free markets, the lifecycle of industries is actually an inevitable invitation to innovation (a Schumpeterian view, as Ben likes to say). We could even say that there *is* a lifecycle in some industries *because* Corporate overtightening opens the door to competitors.

Races to the bottom on costs are not logically inevitable. They seem inevitable and are *made* inevitable by several Corporate rituals. One of them is the nature of market research.

Market researchers are awesome folks. They can actually explain to you the difference between logistic regression and factor analysis. Can you spell "heteroskedasticity"? Market researchers can! What they can't do is answer some very simple questions directly related to the skill of competing. Exhibit A: Customer-satisfaction surveys.

So when "customer focus" means focusing on current customers, mining data on millions of transactions, or using digital marketing's hocus pocus to target you down to your DNA, Corporate is actually looking at the rear-view mirror. That's not competing, that's nostalgia.

advice to the maverick

Customers pay your salary. That makes them interesting by itself. But Corporate has made a science of measuring customers at the molecular level without actually understanding them. It keeps testing the hypothesis that you can *abuse* customers and they still stay with you. As science goes, this is a testable hypothesis. The problem is the results of this test come too late for Corporate to recover if it missed the mark.

Cost-cutting that results in savings to the customers, not only to the company, is smart strategy. Cost-cutting that results in some inconvenience to customers but doesn't turn them off completely can still be smart if it allows a company to compete more effectively. But cost-cutting becomes a bad idea when it enrages customers enough to overcome switching costs or opens the door to new entrants with a better strategy (including a lower cost/price). Some of Blockbuster's policies, such as fines for not returning videos after only two days, sent customers to the budding Netflix with its mail-in discs with no return-by date and, ultimately, its streaming service. You may think this is common sense, but to an executive with short-term incentives to cut costs, it is not.

As a maverick you should not be a naive advocate for customers. Strategy is not about making all customers happy. Not all customers are good customers for the business. Competing skillfully means balancing costs and service to retain the desired customers and attain profitability at some point in time. Technology helps a lot in reaching this balance. Amazon, for example, forewent profitability for years while investing in technology and incurring costs with phenomenal service until it gained enough market power to raise prices and maintain the loyal Prime customers.

advice to the maverick, continued

As a maverick your unorthodox thinking should go here: At what point do our cost-cuts turn off customers? This breaking point is an important part of the concept of "customer experience." Monitor your company's churn rates; that is, not only how many new customers you gain, but also how many old customers you lose. Consider an index of suffering, not only an index of delight. Think we're making that up? Check out Hipmunk, a website for booking flights. Hipmunk came late to this game, but by creating a misery index (under a tab called Agony), it stood apart and thrived. It was later acquired by SAP based on its consumer-oriented approach.

big numbers, wrong numbers, more numbers, and sloppy thinking

"Those are my ~~principles~~ numbers, and if you don't like them . . . well, I have others."

—VARIATION ON GROUCHO MARX

Most of the world's religions are ancient. Judeo-Christianity, Islam, and Buddhism are thousands of years old. There are newer religions like Mormonism and pseudo-religions like Scientology, but being relatively recent, they have limited membership. It takes time for a religion to take root.

It is, therefore, surprising how quickly the religion of Numerology has taken hold in Corporate. Worshiping numbers based on the holy script of Excel has become a universal, unifying element of all top executives from New York to Timbuktu. They say the world is a small village. That's a myth. It still takes a day to fly from the U.S. to Europe and two days to get to Hong Kong. Planes fly slower now than in the '70s to save fuel. But it is a small world when it comes to the type of presentations one makes to top executives, no matter where they are. If you don't have the numbers, don't show up. If you have numbers, *any* numbers, complete fantasy numbers, welcome, welcome, our friend! Come in! Here is the projector!

Now let's be clear. We love numbers. Mark wrote a pricing-strategy simulator that calculates and analyzes tens of billions of numbers in billions of scenarios. (No joke.) Ben taught statistics for 17.9 years at a major university. (Also no joke.)

But you know and we know that there are meaningful, useful numbers and nonmeaningful, nonuseful numbers. The trick is to tell the meaningful from the nonmeaningful. We don't know about the

COOC's culinary palate, but we fear the COOC's indiscriminate taste for numbers.

In this chapter, we look at Corporate's use of numbers, executives' addiction to Excel, and the effect of a dysfunction we label Numerology on the ability to compete effectively. We also clear up the myth that quantitative analysis is always superior to qualitative insight . . . and the reverse, that qualitative has some ineffable virtue that beats bytes. The problem is in worshipping either over the other. Working *together*, the qualitative and the quantitative allow the maverick to be a super maverick.

DEATH BY SHARK

The core, classic dysfunction with numbers centers on using wrong or misleading numbers. A critical thinker will spot and dispel the spell speedily, but most of us fall prey at times to the allure of numbers thrown at us. It's natural. Thinking critically is exhausting and it *takes time*. Worse, your colleagues will roll their eyes and mutter words like "perfectionist" as though it's negative.[1] Worst of all, Corporate values action over *everything* else. Stop fiddling with those numbers, and *do* something!

We will illustrate.

Your odds of dying as the result of an unprovoked shark attack are roughly 1 in 300 million in the U.S. The odds are more than 20 times higher in Australia. Therefore, if you don't want to be killed by a shark, you should flee Australia immediately for the U.S. It's safer here, except maybe for the politics.

The numbers and arithmetic are correct. The analysis and conclusion are silly. Yet that's the kind of reasoning CBC News used and Premier Traveler's April 22, 2013, newsletter reproduced.

---

[1] One of us has heard "perfectionist" before. What are the odds that it might be the one who's got the billions of scenarios? The other one of us was the one throwing that word at him and in return got a billion more scenarios and gave up.

In "Scary Flights with Happy Endings," the Canadian Broadcasting Corporation (CBC) said:

"Statistics from the United States Department of Transportation suggest that the odds for the general population of dying in:

- A car crash: 1 in 7,700
- A motorcycle accident: 1 in 91,500
- A railroad accident: 1 in 306,000
- A bicycle accident: 1 in 410,000
- An airplane accident: 1 in 2,067,000"

You should see, instantly, that those numbers don't pass the sniff test. Your odds of dying in a motorcycle accident are less than one-tenth what they are for dying in a car crash? Really? That doesn't sound right. And it's not. It's because the CBC didn't compare the *risks* of traveling on two wheels or four. It compared the annual *rates* of motorcycle fatalities and automobile fatalities per 100,000 people. Just like the shark-attack rates with which we began.

Your odds of dying while doing something are zero if you don't do that thing. As you relax at home in Melbourne, Florida, your odds of a fatal shark encounter are zero. The same zero as when you relax at home in Melbourne, New South Wales. You'll enjoy the same serene sense of shark-free safety in southern North Dakota as you would in the southern Northern Territory.

It makes sense to talk about the rate of shark-attack deaths as among the causes of human expiration. Very, very few people in the world die by shark. But it doesn't make sense to use the same rate to talk about the *risk* of death by shark when very, very few people go into waters with sharks.

The CBC apparently took the rate of motorcycle deaths in the U.S. per 100,000 people and re-stated it. That's fine: 1.09 per 100,000 is the same as 1 in 91,500. But the number doesn't express the risk of taking a motorcycle out for a ride.

The rate of motorcycle deaths per 100,000 people combines: 1) the rate of motorcycle deaths among the people in the 100,000 who get onto motorcycles, and 2) the rate of motorcycle deaths—zero—among the people in the 100,000 who don't get onto motorcycles. Combining the two rates dilutes the risk of motorcycling. The nonmotorcyclists arithmetically become safe and/or lucky motorcyclists, leading us to underestimate the risk. (Practically everyone travels by car, which avoids the dilution problem above.)

We can better measure your risk of death on two wheels if we state it per hour or per mile you travel on a motorcycle. Ideally, we'd also adjust for weather conditions, speed, and whether you're wearing a helmet.

Ideally, comparing the risks of motorcycles and cars, as the CBC did, would take a little more data. For one thing, people drive cars under almost all weather conditions. If cars were driven only under conditions conducive to motorcycling, we'd probably find cars even safer than the existing statistics.

The CBC's article focused on airline safety relative to other methods of transportation. As before: If you don't get in an airplane, you won't die in an airplane accident.[2] In addition, airplane accidents happen mostly at the start or the end of a flight. (You could argue they *all* happen at the end of a flight.) Cruising at 35,000 feet isn't the same as landing at a busy airport. One four-hour flight carries much less risk than four one-hour flights.

What you really want to know are the odds that you will arrive safely *on a specific trip*. We used statistics from *The New York Times* and the National Highway Traffic Safety Administration (NHTSA) to compare taking a car or an airplane. The *Times* quotes an MIT statistician saying that, based on the safety record of the last five years, "the death risk for passengers in the United States has been 1 in 45 million flights." The NHTSA says the car fatality rate is 1.11 per 100 million vehicle miles traveled. Based on those numbers, you should drive for any roundtrip shorter than 4½ miles. (Actually,

---

[2] Strictly speaking, it's still possible you'll die under an airplane accident, especially if you live in St. Maarten. See www.youtube.com/watch?v=4jW9wk_g9QY.

shorter than 4½ miles, plus the distance you'd have to drive to and from airports. Adjust for taxi drivers in certain cities.) For distances longer than that, take a plane.

We heroically slay all those stats so we can arrive (safely) at our final (*final?*) destination: These noble truths.

Imprecision or Garbage

We talk about garbage in, garbage out. We almost always mean imprecision when we say garbage. But the 1 in 91,500 statistic would be garbage no matter how accurately we measured it. It's garbage not because the number is wrong but because it is the wrong number to gauge risks. You don't have to be an expert in transportation safety to know that; all you have to do is think about whether it makes sense in its context.

A Flaw in the Foundation

Using a wrong (not imprecise) number is not a detail, a nicety, or an inconvenience. It is a flaw in the foundation on which we build decisions that affect money, careers, and lives. In this case, motorcycles falsely appearing safer than cars—forget about the airplane part—could wrongly encourage people to switch from cars to motorcycles for safety reasons. Wrong numbers can even affect crime and punishment. See the prosecutor's fallacy.[3]

Thinking about Systems

When we spoke about factors such as weather conditions, wearing helmets, numbers of takeoffs, and so on, we were actually constructing models of how a system works. And we were finding it useful, not frightening or technical! Even that brief exercise in systems thinking gave us a richer understanding of the problem and helps us defend ourselves against being deceived, intentionally or not, by others who cite wrong numbers at us. Keep at it. It's a skill you can practice and develop while entertaining your management the way we have for years.

---

[3] http://www.conceptstew.co.uk/pages/prosecutors_fallacy.html.

case study: feel-good numbers

"Our Feel-Good War on Breast Cancer," by Peggy Orenstein in *The New York Times*, describes consequences of numerical problems like those above.

Five-year survival rates for breast cancer go from 23 percent when discovered late to 98 percent when found early. That's a lot of lives saved and suffering avoided. But mammography "finds many cancers that never need treating and that are, by definition, survivable." They're akin to the people who don't ride motorcycles getting counted as people who survived riding motorcycles.

The article quoted Professor Steven Woloshin of the Geisel School of Medicine at Dartmouth. He posits a group of women diagnosed with breast cancer at 67 and who died at 70. Five-year survival? Zero percent. "Now imagine the same women were screened, given their diagnosis three years earlier, at age 64, but treatment doesn't work, and they still die at age 70. Five-year survival is now 100 percent, even though no one lived a second longer."

The point is not that mammography doesn't work. (Likewise, for prostate exams for men.) The point is that simplistic use of the metric—five-year survival—can exaggerate benefits.

Not surprisingly, Numerology problems show up in business, too.

"Our projections show a gain of 5.5 points of market share," says the analysis. That's nice. But from whom are you going to gain that 5.5 points, and why are they going to let you have it? In every market, there is always, always, exactly 100 percent market share. If you gain 5.5 points, someone(s) else must lose 5.5 points. But don't worry, your competitors will be happy to correct your analysis. In other words, they will fight back.

THE BIGGER PROBLEM: NUMEROLOGY ADDICTION

Quoting questionable numbers is widespread in Corporate and among the various consultants who want to satisfy their customers. In some industries, it has actually reached the status of *raison d'être* (a reason to exist): One doesn't question the premise (that numbers are holy) because without them there is no source of Truth (or "credibility," another Corporate cliché).

The vendor/consultant looking for business in such industries dumps as many numbers as possible on slides and hopes for the best. If Corporate executives don't think logically about possibilities, cause-effect chains, and results, why should the consultant?

Here is an example. In a post on LinkedIn, Ben described Walgreens's acquisition of Alliance Boots, the UK retailer known more for its beauty products than prescription-filling, as a desperate (though correct) move aimed at diversifying away from its reliance on declining margins in fulfilling prescriptions, a once-profitable business now being squeezed by PBMs (Pharmacy Benefit Management companies). The market for prescriptions in the U.S. has changed dramatically in the past two decades as these PBMs, working on behalf of large corporations, placed significant pressure on the margins of companies such as CVS and Walgreens.

CVS responded by buying a large PBM and has been weathering the storm relatively well. Walgreens entered the PBM business reluctantly and hesitantly, then sold its small PBM business for peanuts (or maybe we should say, for a bottle of generic ibuprofen) and has seen its profits from fulfilling prescriptions decline for over a decade.

In the LinkedIn discussion on the post, a market consultant commented on Ben's post with 291 words, too long to reproduce here verbatim. Let us instead sum up his points. He claimed Ben's analysis was not credible because:

- Walgreens operates the largest network of over 8,000 locations across the U.S., with over 75 percent of the U.S. population living within a five-mile radius of a typical retail store.

- At around $800 in sales per square foot, Walgreens has higher average sales than a Walmart that also sells drugs (~$400).
- You can't label Walgreens as "bleeding" because its pharmacy sales in the month of December 2014 increased by 15.7 percent overall and 14.2 percent in comparable stores.
- Walgreens' stock was up 12.2 percent in the month of December 2014. ROE (return on equity) was 9.68 percent in 2014.
- Walgreens is a $72 billion retail behemoth, so it is impossible to know if it should be in the PBM business.

We don't know if you got through all the numbers this consultant quoted. Part of the consultant's strategy might be to tire the audience with irrelevant numbers until they lose consciousness. But let's dissect this reply piece by piece. Small bites make it easier to swallow all the OOP jargon.

First, how is operating a network of stores in 8,000 locations (remember, numbers are essential!) relevant to the claim that filling prescriptions is no longer enough to maintain profitability? And was 75 percent of the population living within five miles of a Walgreens an asset when the giant PBM Express Scripts dropped Walgreens from its approved list of pharmacies in 2012 and customers just *crossed the street* to CVS (and Walgreens' CEO lost his job)? Notice the smokescreen: accurate numbers—75 percent and five miles, not 74 percent and six miles. *Very important.*

Next: How is it relevant to compare Walgreens' retail sales per square foot to Walmart's? For that matter, how is *any* revenue volume relevant to margins (profit, not sales) on the pharmaceutical side, which accounted for 60 percent of Walgreens' business?

And finally, stock price and ROI, the magical numbers one throws when all else fails. The beauty of short-term numbers when discussing long-term prospects is that they distract the audience from the real issue. According to Nasdaq.com's statistics, Walgreens' stock has known much higher volatility than CVS' stock over *five years* prior to the above LinkedIn debate, as CVS' health care model seems to be superior. Quoting an unsourced number for one year (2014) is a common error . . . or a rhetorical deception. Is 9.68 percent ROI better than others? Worse? Not that it matters, but CVS' numbers are better. Marginally. However, with ROE for Walgreens going down continually since 2010, and net margins in the 2 to 3 percent range and declining, should anyone point to a one-time number and expect "credibility"?

Yes . . . if you are a Corporate consultant, and your executive audience believes motorcycles are safer than cars and competitors want to share their market shares.

Numerology is a wonderful way of life for those who substitute data-worship for common sense, logic, and clear thinking. Skill at competing, it is not.

Amen.

IF NUMBERS ARE GOOD, BIG NUMBERS MUST BE BETTER

In recent years, Corporate Numerology has gone off the deep end with the frenzy around trillions of numbers contained in the term Big Data.

Google (verb) "Big Data" and you get 3.68 billion results (as of June 8, 2018).[4] Look at the top entries (first ten plus paid ads) and see who's on the first page: Oracle, IBM, SAS (a partner of IBM), McKinsey, Informatica. Big Data is Big Business. Is that expense justified?

Definitely, and not at all, depending on what you expect of it.

Definitely because of common sense. Big Data, along with the analytics to process it, means better, faster, more-accurate forecasts and, therefore better, faster, more-accurate decisions. The business press (and Oracle, IBM, et al.) can provide Big Stories, Big Anecdotes, and Big Case Studies to show how Big Data allowed companies to more precisely target advertising

---

[4] Oddly enough, when we Binged (Bing, verb, past tense) "Big Data" 20 seconds later, we got 15.70 million results. Does that mean that the internet's knowledge fell by 99.573 percent during those 20 seconds? We don't know. But if it did, it's a world record in *something*.

and promotion, segment the customer base, plan production and inventory, and a horde of other applications across all internal operations from HR to marketing to R&D. Just think about it: Which management will be more effective at competing, one using guesses and intuition or one using millions of numbers to back its decisions?

The answer should be simple, but it is not. Ironically, there is little data on the value of Big Data. We don't know whether the emperor is wearing new clothes or sharing a little too much data in the open office. In a 2012 *Harvard Business Review* article by Andrew McAfee of MIT, titled "Big Data: The Management Revolution," the author admits the scarcity of good measurements about the revolution of better management. He reports the results of a survey done by his team and McKinsey that shows those companies who reported using Big Data performed better. Yet he also revealed that too many executives are "pretending to be more data-driven than they actually are." This supports Phil Rosenzweig's conclusion in his book, *The Halo Effect*, about similar studies suffering from the effect of the dependent variable (performance) on the independent variable (use of Big Data), making the results quite useless. As Rosenzweig demonstrates, several very well-known studies of corporate "success formulas" resulted in spurious conclusions based on this bias.

So even though there is no data on the value of Big Data, we can declare that using more data and better statistical techniques can only improve management. And that is actually the problem as much as the solution. The use of Big Data and analytics has been almost completely restricted to internal data or social media's tactical information. Both belong to what Michael Porter called "operational effectiveness," but they have little or no effect on competing.[5]

---

[5] Quantitative tools that *do* have an effect on competing include some simulations and analytic paradigms such as game theory. These do not rely on Big Humungous Data.

big data hype

Using more data can improve internal operations, but it can be easily abused.

Big Data is wonderful. It puts small data to shame. "Look at you," says the Big Data bully to the small data, "You are too small to be significant."

In statistics, just 30 observations can support what's called statistically significant conclusions. However, small to tiny differences in means, proportions, or standard deviations that are not statistically significant with small samples may become significant with millions of observations. That doesn't make the differences useful; it just makes them statistically significant. Statisticians know that. Corporate doesn't.

But wait, there's more! The millions of data points are all from the past. All, as in 100 percent. Of course they are; there is no such thing as data from the future unless you are a fan of the *Back to the Future* movies. There are forecasts and predictions and stories and crystal balls and psychics, but no data. That's fine if you expect the future to look like the past, although if you expect the future to look like the past, then you don't need data from the future anyway. That's not fine if you expect the future not to look like the past . . . or if you want to do something dramatic and glorious that *causes* the future not to look like the past.

But wait, there's still more! There is the problem that correlation, no matter how huge and accurate the data sets, is not causation. There is a very strong correlation between youth and going to school, but the numbers don't tell us why. Understanding the process (a.k.a. the system

---

big data hype, continued

or the model) tells us that going to school does not cause youth; youth causes going to school.

So now market researchers can have the wrong numbers at a much more impressive scale, creating the dangerous impression that we know more than we do, and we can act with confidence. And amazingly, when the numbers don't "work" . . . we demand better numbers!

BIG DATA DOESN'T HELP STRATEGY

Managing better should be, and is, on every executive's mind. But this is a race with no winners and no *sustainable* competitive advantage. As one Fortune 500 company uses Big Data and analytics, another will rush to do the same. At that point, other companies will fear falling behind (consultants will spread the rumor that *everyone else* is already using Big Data), and these platform providers/consultants will perpetuate the expenditure until the next productivity improvement comes along. The race will continue as every one of the Big Data *vendors* becomes very rich, just as happened with investments in information technology. It's exactly how capitalism is supposed to work, but it does nothing for strategic thinking . . . or competing.

The difference between using Big Data and analytics for improving the current execution of existing strategy vs. improving the strategy itself (i.e., competing better) can be made crystal-clear using an example given (ironically) by McAfee to demonstrate the value of Big Data. The article tells about how a large company improved its marketing promotion for its various brands by using Big Data. The speed of the promotion cycle went down from eight weeks to one! The company? Sears.

Need we say more?

In fairness, the author at McAfee acknowledges that Big Data is not a substitute for the right vision and strategy (i.e., competing), but his caveats are naturally kind of an afterthought. They shouldn't be. Replacing good tactical decisions with excellent tactical decisions doesn't change the core of companies' problems one iota. Speeding up the promotion cycle is nice, but it won't stop the ship from sinking. Identifying strategic risks and strategic opportunities *early*, and acting on them before performance suffers, is what matters. That's what it means to practice the skill of competing.

To address this core problem, Big Data (and the analytics to convert it to intelligence) need to migrate to the competitive environment with its multitude of high-impact players, thus helping the leader skilled in competing to outsmart other players. Razor-sharp superhuman segmenting of one's existing hapless customer base to micro-target ads won't help one bit in understanding the effect of third parties on your performance and future prospects.

Case in point: Procter & Gamble. A 2016 article in *Harvard Business Review* breathlessly praised the P&G innovation machine. A report by McKinsey hailed its digital revolution. Yet P&G, the King of Consumer Understanding, has become a shadow of its former self. There is more to competing than throwing millions at Big Data. Competing means taking in the big picture.

The issue of applying Big Data to competition and others in the market devolves into two simple questions:

1. What are the important questions that affect how you compete well in your market?
2. Do the exabytes, zettabytes, or haveanotherabytes help you answer those questions?

Numbers do not speak for themselves. Data is not wisdom; it is not even analysis. It is data. *You,* the maverick, the independent, critical thinker, must find the appropriate numbers, apply the appropriate analysis, and reach the appropriate conclusions.

The first step, at the very core of building your skill in competing, is *learning to ask the right questions.*

The second step is to convince others, including your boss, that those questions have merit.

The third step is to back your answers with a *few relevant* numbers and meaningful insights from the quantitative analysis—not detailed Excel fantasy sheets.

advice to the maverick

Corporate often operates on an unspoken assumption: If one decimal place is good, then two is better; it is more accurate. We are not against decimal places or accuracy. On the other hand, as a maverick you can question the *need* for more, more, and even more accuracy.

You will hear people argue about whether a number is 3.2 or 3.3. Ask this key, big-picture question (and push back that "perfectionist" thing): "Will we make a different decision if we learn it's 3.3 and not 3.2?" If the answer is no, you've saved a lot of time and you've shown managerial savvy. If the answer is yes, you've focused the discussion. And if the answer is you don't know, you've opened a new option: Continue the analysis with 3.2, repeat the analysis with 3.3, and see how much difference it makes.[6]

You will see people draw trend lines. You will hear how excited they are that their Big Data allow greater precision for better forecasts and predictions. Greater precision, yes. But ask this key, big-picture question: "Why do we expect the future to look like the past?" That question means you've noticed an assumption—maybe right, but often wrong—that could come from the we-always-do-it-this-way tradition. What if we expect new technology in the market? What if demographics are going to change? What could cause the future *not* to look like an extrapolation from the past? Congratulations! You are introducing early-warning thinking.

---

[6] That sensitivity analysis focuses on a concept called "the value of information." You can even calculate how much it's worth to get more accurate information.

advice to the maverick, continued

It is easy to get bogged down in numbers. Market research companies and marketing advertising agencies have smart and sophisticated people who can *overwhelm* even the most ardent maverick with facts and data, and charts. They're not necessarily evil; they drink the same Kool-Aid they want you to sample. There is only one thing they cannot do for you: Compete. You've got to do that on your own. So after listening carefully to everything they have to say, get out of the room, breathe deeply, go back, and ask a simple question: So what?

Big Data can help you know tactical stuff: What packaging works, whether people who buy product A also buy product B so you should put them together on the shelves, and so on. In effect, Big Data is a huge, continuous, powerful, and useful test market. In that regard, it can even help you find the line between tightening and overtightening costs.

But Big Data misses the big picture. For example, it does not predict a competitor's behavior and how customers, your beloved salary-paying customers, will react to a competitor's move. Don't believe that? Think of it this way: Would Big Data predict *your* behavior?

We have seen Corporate presentations with 100-plus slides, each crowded with tables and lists and graphs and forecasts, amounting to thousands if not millions of data points on customers, costs, and trends. No one can possibly keep all that information in their heads, let alone make internally consistent sense of it. In fact, we have been called in *to cut through the mess,* like Alexander the Great cutting the Gordian knot.[7] We do that not by prioritizing or using a bold font on the most-important half-a-zillion bullet points (out of the entire zillion) on PowerPoint slides. We do that not by trotting out the

---

[7] If you are unfamiliar with the Gordian knot, read about it here: www.history.com/news/what-was-the-gordian-knot

advice to the maverick, continued

sharp-looking preference map from the marketing agency. We do it by refocusing on a few competitive principles—that is, on how to compete.

What you, the maverick, must do is zoom back from Big Data and orthodoxy-marketing thinking and ask: What's the big picture here? What are customers really buying (or trying to buy)? What are the change drivers that are not yet clear to everyone but may turn out to greatly affect the industry? How do competitors see the customers' needs, and are we at all different in perceiving what makes a difference there?

Pay attention to market research and the voice of the customer, but *do not* become their slave. Pick and choose the most intriguing findings; that is, intriguing *to you* as the herd can't distinguish between strategic and tactical findings. Focus on the few strategic insights that can help you and your company stand out in some way. If you are lucky enough to organize or participate in a war game, always look for the difference between how your company looks at customers' needs and how competitors do. It is in these differences that competing is paramount. Big Data can help only if you extract big insights from them, not if you simply flood customers with targeted advertising. Think about it: Amazon transformed customer experience with a simple idea of "recommended for you" based on Big Data. The true strategic insight was that customers will enjoy and use the "recommended" feature, not the Big Data behind it.

Steve Jobs' remarkable success was based not on *asking* customers what they wanted but on figuring out what they needed, what they would actually use, and what would make them look cool. Measuring does not substitute for listening, observing, and most important, imagining. More data is not "So what?"

advice to the maverick, continued

"So what?" is critical thinking applied to Big Data. By delivering a good "so what?" at the right moment, you repay the trust placed in you.

Before the Numerologists recover and snow you with more data, move to the questions that matter. Where is the market going? What can't we see with this data? What's around the corner that current customers can't tell us? What strategic opportunities are out there because others don't yet see them?

If they can answer you, great! Now you have moved the conversation and the analysis from decimals to decisions, from trends to thinking, from calculating to competing.

And if the Numerologists cannot answer you, let them leave the room in a huff taking their 234 slides with them. But don't let down your guard. They'll be back. Top executives in COOC companies love them.

benchmarking: be just like *them,* only better

"Only when the tide goes out
do you discover who's been
swimming naked."

—WARREN BUFFETT

L earning from the best, not reinventing the wheel, and striving always to improve operations are three reasons that make *benchmarking* a logical addition to companies' arsenal of tools in competing. Benchmarking does not mean tagging benches. It means finding opportunities to improve your business by comparing how your business does things to how purported best-in-class companies do those same things.

Benchmarking is a logical addition to companies' tools, until you realize benchmarking has gone from conscious, careful, and judicious comparisons to the Corporate zone of un-competitive wholesale rejection of anything *unique.*

It starts small, like Chronic Conference Hopping, open-space floorplans, and the shrine to Big Data, all of which you read about earlier. Some top executive decides it's time to compare their company with the industry, the same risk-class companies on the S&P 500, the global economy, or companies in the Milky Way galaxy. The scope of benchmarking is limited only by that executive's imagination and the persuasive arguments of the partner at the prestigious consulting firm selling benchmarking as a panacea to executives who are always looking over their shoulders. Since partners know executives from their days together at the consulting firm, the sale is easy.

You think we exaggerate? Read Duff McDonald's 2013 article in *The Observer*, "The CEO Factory: Ex-McKinsey Consultants Get Hired to Run the Biggest Companies (even some they couldn't fix in the first place.)" COOCs love other COOCs and circulate the same consultants among themselves.

Benchmarking is surely not limited by budget because the big consulting practices know how to play this game. We aren't trying to mock the large consulting firms. We are actually admiring their ability to reduce cash reserves at Corporate (the most eloquent analogy would be liposuction).

Developing BBP—benchmarking best practices—is not cheap. Oh, no. The money spent on the process can build a small navy for the country of Togo. That in itself suggests BBP has run amok, but it is not the real problem. As long as the logic behind the BBP is sound, one can at least weigh its cost vs. its benefit. As long as Corporate has money to burn (see Body Mass Index in Chapter 13), then *why not*? It's the Circle of Life: Corporate spends, consultants collect, consultants spend, and by the multiplier effect and trickle-down economics, we get the cost of a good school's MBA to top $200,000. Everyone wins.

The problem is when Corporate starts benchmarking everything that moves and some things that don't.

In this chapter, we expose the rampant use of mindless benchmarking to hide lazy strategic thinking. We also debunk once and for all a myth about what the great maverick Peter Drucker said about measuring and managing.

Let's start with a quick history lesson.

BENCHMARKING HISTORY

The company credited with bringing benchmarking to life is Xerox. (How appropriate, since Xerox was famous for making machines that made copies!) Depending on which source you read, it was David Kearns, Xerox's CEO, who in 1982 initiated a companywide benchmarking program to restore Xerox's quality and cost-competitiveness against its Japanese rivals, which were eating its lunch one sashimi at a time because Xerox forgot how to compete. According to a case study by the Indian Business School research center, "These initiatives played a major role in pulling Xerox out of trouble in the years to come. The company even went on to become one of the best examples of the successful implementation of benchmarking."

The problem is that by 2001, Xerox was close to bankruptcy, and in 2018, Xerox declared it would sell a controlling stake to the Japanese company, Fujifilm. Benchmarking is not a panacea. Worse. It can lead a company down the road to ruin.

Benchmarking didn't lead Xerox to ruin. Management did. But benchmarking *helped*. How? Well, benchmarking masks the real problems, allowing Corporate to substitute mindless imitation for strategic early warning. Imitating other companies couldn't solve Xerox's failure to see and act early on huge changes in the market for documents. It took two women, COO Ann Mulcahy and CEO Ursula Burns, to pull Xerox back from the brink by switching from manufacturing copiers to providing services. That was a change in strategic direction, a *big* change, and it has nothing to do with benchmarking.

BENCHMARK YOUR WAY TO THE BOTTOM

We tried to find out which companies over the past 25 years were the most "benchmarked." We couldn't. We remember in the '90s that the typical suspects were The Gap, Eddie Bauer, Corning, and Toyota, until these companies' operations came to screeching halts as mobs of benchmarking visitors posed safety risks and they had to stop the tours. These days it is probably Amazon, Google, and Apple, and you can see the benchmarking crowds gathering outside their gates from the International Space Station. We suspect, though, that just like the famous lists of companies in *Good to Great* (to nada) and *In Search of Excellence* (in royalties), many of those earlier icons are no longer shining stars. Some can actually be classified as red giants (as in dead, dying, or resuscitated), such as Amdahl, Data General, Delta Airlines, Digital Equipment Corp., Kmart, Kodak, Raychem, Citicorp, Sony, Wang Labs, Circuit City, Xerox, Fannie

Mae, and Pitney Bowes, among many others. Actually, twice as many companies stumbled after the previously mentioned books were published than continued to shine. That's the nature of these lists, and more generally, that's the nature of *benchmarks*. One never knows if what one is benchmarking is truly benchmarking-worthy or merely easy to benchmark. The difference between worthy and easy is a striking 12.5 percent (see Chapter 6 on Numerology).

Twelve and a half percent of what?

Exactly. *Excellent question*, folks. Moving on to slide 152, our double-blind study shows clearly in this histogram that . . . . Given COOC habits, we can probably pass that number by a few top executives without being challenged.

BENCHMARKING WHERE THE LIGHT SHINES

A drunkard is searching intently under a streetlight. A police officer comes up and asks the drunkard what he's looking for. "I'm looking for my keys," says the drunkard. "Did you lose them near here?" asks the cop. "No." "Then why are you looking here?" "Because," the drunkard says, "the light is better here."

Benchmarking happens where the light is (metaphorically) shining. That's by definition because you can only benchmark what you can measure and compare. But that may not be where you'll find your keys. Your keys—to your apartment or to your business—may be someplace new where no one has shone a light before.

In the field of competitive intelligence (CI), benchmarking existing programs is rife.

First, you go to a conference (see CCH syndrome in Chapter 2). Then you realize you haven't learned anything useful, and you are desperate. So you decide to benchmark best practices in CI across the globe because, well, why reinvent the wheel?

What wheels are reinvented is never clear. The fact that it is called "reinventing the wheel" is an admission of guilt to begin with, as it means the manager or executive has given up on doing something original and perhaps superior to the elusive existing "best practice."

We remember the days *inventing* was considered an achievement. Reinventing, by definition, is, of course, wasteful, and Corporate abhors waste. So *let's copy!*

What we can't understand for the life of us is this: If the process/activity is essential, and you benchmark how other companies are carrying it out, how can you ever outsmart the others? As an article in *Businessweek* in 2001 showed, Xerox's rampant benchmarking in the 1980s simply allowed it to (temporarily) catch up to Canon, Ricoh, Brothers, and others. It never made Xerox different in any way, so why would businesses prefer Xerox over the Japanese competitors? The essence of superior strategy with superior returns—the goal of competing skillfully—is to do the same things *differently* or to do *different* things altogether! Just doing "better" for a short while isn't enough, unless the CEO is near retirement, and then the incentive is clear.

Second, if the benchmarked process is *not* essential, so "why reinvent the wheel" may *conceivably* apply, then why bother benchmarking it with other companies at all? How much of a difference would it make?

In the publishing business, agents and editors understand this point perfectly. In every proposal, they ask prospective authors to detail what other books exist in the same competitive space and how theirs will be different. They do not ask how they are better. You don't benchmark yourself against other books—you *stand out*. You learn about other books to do something *different*.

BENCHMARKING MYTHS

Let's assume you ignore the illogic behind benchmarking. There are additional problems to consider.

One, those who provide the benchmark consulting often have no idea what a "best practice" actually looks like. So they go to Mountain View and join the crowd outside Google's gates. You can't go wrong with Google, can you? People used to say, "Nobody gets fired for buying IBM." Same idea here: Nobody gets fired for emulating Google.

Two, the most important qualities of some of the most important corporate processes and activities—especially the higher cortical functions, such as formulating strategy and adjusting it to changing reality—are nonbenchmarkable. But that has never deterred the benchmarking crowd. Consultants need to make a living, too, folks. When you poke consultants, do they not bleed? When you trip consultants, do they not stumble? No, that is a bad example. They never stumble. It's part of the practice of talking fast and confusing the buyer with irrelevant numbers. Consultants are Ivy League graduates, as sharp as they come. But that's a different issue altogether.

In the field of CI, the ambiguity of "best practices" implies that you might benchmark mediocre CI programs because you don't know what's actually "best." Instead, you use the company's "halo" as a proxy for the quality of its CI. In other words, if a company is famous, then its CI process must be excellent. The book, *The Halo Effect* (Free Press, 2014), by Phil Rosenzweig, suggests companies make that misinference more often than most executives care to admit. That means a company trips itself by joining the lemmings.

Without knowing what "best practices" really are, benchmarking is like searching under the streetlight because you can see better there. What you find are not your keys but *whatever is under the light*. It will most likely be an empty beer can.

case study: benchmarking ci programs

"There is nothing so useless as doing efficiently that which should not be done at all," said the great Peter Drucker. Introducing systematic, analytic, and sophisticated intelligence processes to corporate America in the mid-1980s was one of the most significant improvements to competing as a skill since Drucker's model of management.

case study: benchmarking ci programs, continued

Once it became clear CI is a strategic capability with bottom-line benefits, the Corporate crowd rushed to benchmark whatever CI functions were considered "hot" at the time. The leading intelligence program in the '90s was at an energy company that will remain nameless to assure continued fuel supply to the West. The reason it was the leading program was simple: Its people were the brightest bunch you'd ever encounter. They were all highly trained and certified in CI (yes, by Ben), and they produced such high-quality intelligence analysis that the company promoted the hell out of them. The head of the program later became one of the senior leaders of that energy giant.

Alas, that was also its downfall.

The brightest were snatched by other functions, promoted to leadership positions, or hired away. Their replacements were not as good. The new head of the program was a political operative with no experience and no training in CI. He decimated the program. For a few years, CI at that company was utterly nonexistent. Then a third VP was brought in. He vowed to return the program to its former glory. He proceeded immediately to hire a vendor to do . . . benchmarking.

People have often asked Ben: *What is the best intelligence program on the planet?* He'd say: *This and that.* Then they would run and benchmark the things they could benchmark easily from that intelligence program, such as budget, number of analysts, procedures, and "deliverables." COOCs adore "deliverables." (What you deliver and at what quality are less important.) Once the benchmarking study is completed (deliverables are delivered), the company then replicates whatever it can.

---

case study: benchmarking ci programs, continued

But benchmarking has little to do with the competing skill of the bench-marked company. In this case, the skill was in the way the benchmarked company *used* intelligence, the credibility of its analysts based on their brilliance, etc. It wasn't about the frequency of meetings, how long they spent SWOTing[1] the competition, and so on. Replicating process, as opposed to learning skill, is like thinking "If I put on Charlize Theron's perfume, I'll be Charlize Theron." Sorry, you are *not,* but you smell nice.

---

[1] SWOT means strengths, weaknesses, opportunities, and threats. It's an extremely popular framework for assessing, well, strengths, weaknesses . . .

WHAT IS "BEST" IN "BEST PRACTICES"?

Benchmarking addicts never figure out where they failed. *Our process was an exact replica of Kodak! OK, not Kodak, Merck! OK, not Merck, Vodafone, Pfizer, P&G, you name it, we benchmarked and replicated them all! Why did we fail?*

So here is a sacrilegious question: Does it matter how the famous retailer or the infamous pharmaceutical firm organizes its intelligence activities? Does it matter how much money they spend? Pharma spends a fortune on information and gets *bupkes* (Google it) in return; the retailer has no competitors to benchmark, only substitutes like an online merchant of galactic size. That's why it is *still* a leader but maybe not for long. And finally, the consulting vendor hired to lead the benchmarking study is a *former* director at a large company but won't tell you why he is a *former* director if the process was such a success. See the point? No? Go benchmark other points.

Since you are a maverick, we know you get the picture: Mediocre managers imitate other mediocre managers and replicate mostly the easy-to-see process (a.k.a. the "busy" work). They then get the mediocre results expected when imitating mediocre others. If they are unlucky, they get laid off after a while. And they can't figure out why. "We learned from the best!" they wail. Their successors promptly call in the benchmarking consultants. After all, their predecessors failed, so let's learn from the *best* instead. Mediocre lather, mediocre rinse, mediocre repeat.

Benchmarking the best is not bad in itself if you know what "best" looks like . . . and if you know how to distinguish analysis, decisions, and thinking from process, mechanics, and results. Cause and effect are hardly ever clear-cut. And when you see books about the secrets of someone's success, don't get too excited. Here's what J. Paul Getty had to say: "Formula for success: Rise early, work hard, strike oil." If only we could benchmark best practices for blind luck.

A TYPICAL APPLICATION OF BENCHMARKING

So how would you benchmark making decisions for your business' strategy? Strategy is the most important element in the skill of competing. A company will live and die by the superiority of its strategy relative to its competitors and relative to alternative offerings (substitutes). Nothing else matters if the strategy is wrong. All the implementation gurus, change agents, organization-behavior practitioners, motivational speakers, and armies of MBAs can't help a company if the strategy is ineffective.

Executing the wrong strategy perfectly is like riding a stationary bike *truly fast* to get to where you are going earlier.

To illustrate that point, let's imagine a COOC's top-executive meeting, following the completion of a benchmarking study by the famous consulting group's senior partner.

> *CEO*: OK, people, settle down. We need to discuss what to do given the announcement by the regulatory agency that the amount of fat, sugar, taste, unnatural substances, and calories in our foods will not be allowed to exceed 0 percent starting in 2019. Any suggestions?
>
> Silence.

CEO: OK, let's table that and move to our reaction to competitor OldHat increasing its market share in Tbilisi by 3/10 of 1 percent last week. That was a surprise! It caught us completely unprepared.

Consultant (senior partner): Jack, hold on for just a second. As we saw in the benchmark report on Amazon's strategy-deliberation process, they never spend less than 12 minutes on a subject in their Monday morning meeting with Bezos. It gives credence to the debate.

CEO: Oh, OK. Sorry. So any suggestions on the approaching regulatory disaster?

11 minutes of silence.

Consultant: OK, now we can move to the next topic. Let's increase the use of visuals by 15 percent to match Google's presentation process.

CEO: Excellent idea. Anyone want to draw something?

Consultant: When you draw, use the blue marker. That's how they do it at Zynga.

Yes, benchmarking can be that ridiculous. Reinventing the wheel can be a better idea than adopting the square wheel used by a famous retailer or world-renown (another COOC buzzword) high-tech giant. Keep Rosenzweig's *The Halo Effect* by your bed. Anytime you are tempted to "learn from the best," remind yourself to ask whether what you're about to learn is what made them the best.

IF NOT BENCHMARKING, THEN WHAT?

It is 2014. The screens for OLED TVs (the "panels") are very expensive to produce. Factory yields are low.[2]

---

[2] Much of the information in this section comes from "Is Samsung Giving Up on OLED TV?" by Scott Wilkinson, in the AVS Forum published on May 5, 2014. http://www.avsforum.com/forum/286-latest-industry-news/1530505-samsung-giving-up-oled-tv.html

Both LG and Samsung had invested in OLED panel technology. Each faced a big decision: Take the plunge and commit to making OLEDs in commercial quantities, or retreat from OLEDs, at least for a while, and see whether further R&D might drive down costs.

In many new technologies, manufacturers face a chicken-and-egg problem. They need volume to drive costs down to competitive levels, but they won't get that volume at anything close to their current prices. And in 2014, prices for OLED were high indeed: $9,000 for a 55-inch TV.

If you were LG or Samsung, you might have considered benchmarking other landmark TV technologies. In 2008, Pioneer plasma TVs had the best picture quality on the market, but plasma costs were still high while competitors' LCD TVs were driving prices down. Pioneer quit the plasma market in 2008 after big losses. The remaining plasma makers, including LG and Samsung, were out by 2014. On the other hand, LCD technologies were thriving. LCD's large sales volume and factory improvements might portend similar breakthroughs for OLED. Moreover, it seemed the demand would be there. OLED picture quality was unsurpassed, and movie buffs (like Mark) *wanted* OLED.

But was there money in OLED? Samsung pulled back. LG forged ahead. The same question faced by similarly huge companies with access to similar data. Different answers.

Who was right?

That simple question gives us a crystal-clear, ultra-high-definition picture of the difference between benchmarking and the skill of competing.

Benchmarking, market analysis, and more could do a lot to tell LG and Samsung about likely costs and demand, what each other's costs would be, etc. But the biggest and most important uncertainty for LG and Samsung was probably not manufacturing yields. For each of them, the key uncertainty was whether *the other one* would be in the market. That's how the skillful competitor would see the problem.

We can summarize the decision in a simple matrix, as seen in Figure 7.1 on page 120.

1 LG in Samsung in	3 LG in Samsung out
2 LG out Samsung in	4 LG out Samsung out

Quadrant 1. Both stay. They split the market demand and, due to the other's presence, likely feel considerable pressure to cut prices. This presents potential disaster for both.

Quadrant 2. LG exits, Samsung stays. Samsung has a good shot at OLED. LG pursues other opportunities.

Quadrant 3. LG stays, Samsung exits. LG gets the good shot while Samsung looks elsewhere.

Quadrant 4. Both exit. Both miss the OLED opportunity.

FIGURE 7.1

So both LG and Samsung could be right even if they made different decisions. It's likely they could only be right if they made different decisions.

Notice that it doesn't matter who makes the first decision. It doesn't even matter what the first-decider decides. What matters is whether the second-decider pays attention to the first . . . and that the second-decider *does not* imitate the first.

Fast forward from 2014 to 2017. Sony is making OLED TVs (and Mark bought one). A foolish move for Sony? A disaster brewing for LG? No. Sony uses LG panels in its TVs.

That's what competing as a skill looks like.

benchmark this

Sometimes, benchmarking leads to an unintended result. A few years back, when the FTC required companies to publish their top executives' compensation in order to shame those who robbed their shareholders blind with enormous compensation packages, everyone thought that type of data would allow for good benchmarking and would reduce flagrant pay to executives who provide little long-term value to share-holders.

Indeed it did, for about two years. Then the data showed compensation amounts increased even faster than before. Seeing what others were earning, executives shamelessly asked to either top it or at least meet it. Boards, the friends of the top executives (they were once top executives themselves), immediately declared that they had to top the competitors' packages in order to *retain talent.* "Talent" is one of those wonderful COOC terms, like "team." There is no "I" in "team," COOC says, and we notice there is also no "I" in "talent." On the other hand, you can get "me" from "team" . . . and "ale" from "talent." Ale for me? Thank you! And there are *three* "I's" in "incentivize."

They said *retain talent* with straight faces. So how about benchmarking the income differential between the CEOs and the average worker in Japan or Germany?

Germany and Japan must be untalented nations. They compete like skillful fiends, but they don't understand anything about robbing shareholders.

A DIFFERENT KIND OF BENCHMARKING

Corporate consultants and coaches will advise you to "learn from the best!" They will urge you to use benchmarking to improve operations.

We, on the other hand, being mavericks, tell you to question mindless benchmarking and, if relevant, to propose competitive benchmarking instead.

Best-practice benchmarking learns from companies inside or outside your industry (typically outside, as those inside will not cooperate with you) on processes that can improve your operations: Best inventory system, best IT infrastructure, etc. Competitive benchmarking compares strategies.

Competitive failure is about competitors' strategies vs. yours. Learning from the competitive failures of your own company, for example, involves understanding how competitors might have had more effective strategies than yours because of what they do differently. A technique called win-loss analysis is a specialty within the field of CI. It is especially popular with defense contractors, where a single lost bid can cost billions of dollars . . . billions *gained* by a competitor. So defense contractors spend days analyzing (benchmarking) bids once the winner is declared not only to understand their strategy vs. the winning bid but, as important, to understand the mindset of the customer/decision-maker. That understanding *may* serve to win the next one, assuming the same decision-makers are in place. Defense contractors also spend time war-gaming the next contract, as the past is never a foolproof predictor of the future.

Studying failure is depressing. You probably think, "Well, Steve Jobs didn't fail (oh, OK, maybe once when he was kicked out of Apple). Warren Buffett didn't fail (oh, well, several times as in Goldman Sachs and Wells Fargo). Don't dwell on failure, say the Corporate consultants, move on. We say, dwell, dwell."

Nature abhors failure and Corporate's consultants don't want to depress their paying clients. But failure teaches us a lot if we objectively ask, "Why did we fail? What did competitors do that we didn't?" In the Israeli military, every operation is followed by a debrief where failure is analyzed to bits without pointing fingers but without covering up, either. If an operation goes badly, it is always the commander's responsibility, not the soldiers'.

Similarly, strategic failure that goes without insightful analysis is bound to repeat itself, only on a larger scale. Even if failure is just bad luck, can you plan, the next time, for the contingency? Worst-case scenarios in war games are one approach mavericks can take to incorporate low-probability events with high impact into the strategy testing.

Competitive benchmarking supplants "best practices" with a focus on strategy, not operations, and *if done right*, calls for *magnifying* differences, not eliminating them. A technique called relative cost analysis (RCA), described in a *Harvard Business Review* case study by Jan Rivkin and Hanna Halaburda, compares your costs with competitors', focusing on what competitors *do differently*. It does not mean you should imitate the competitor (or they should imitate you). It means you should understand the reasons for their or your success or failure, and you should find ways to make the difference work for you. For example, Dell's cost structure in its early days was far cheaper than its competitors' because it sold direct to its customers and didn't have to keep inventory (i.e., different activities). Compaq couldn't imitate Dell because it had commitments to third-party sellers. But if it had understood the magnitude of Dell's advantage, claims a 1999 case study out of Harvard Business School by Jan Rivkin et al., it would have never started a price war (which it did and lost). Instead, it could have gone for differentiation.

advice to the maverick

If the best-practices benchmarking cult has taken root at your company, don't despair. The exercise will be forgotten quickly as implementing *process* benchmarks deteriorates into setting goals to achieve *financial* benchmarks. Welcome to Corporate.

If you just graduated from business school, one thing you can do in the spirit of benchmarking is to offer a new benchmark based on the material you learned. We are sure some case studies piqued your interest. If you could interest your boss in benchmarking a company that stands out in strategy, you can do the exercise without leaving your cubicle.

One of the most effective techniques for competitive strategy benchmarking is to draw an activity map[3] for your company and compare it, if possible, to the activity map of a competitor to see if there are *any* differences worth exploring. Primary activities are at the core of a company's competitive strategy. For Southwest Airlines, for example, one primary activity was to fly short haul between secondary airports. Another was to offer no reserved seating.

Comparing your map with a competitor's, you can see which map is more *coherent.* At times, we look at companies and wonder how did they decide to do X, Y, and Z when they do nothing that supports A, the pillar of their strategy.

Meanwhile, remember that whenever you wonder how you're doing relative to your classmates and colleagues, you are benchmarking! You will discover how easy it is to develop conspiracy theories. Relax. There's always someone doing better, there's always someone doing worse, there's always Meghan, Duchess of Sussex. She married a prince . . . and there is no "I" in Sussex.

---

[3] An activity map is a diagram of the main (primary) activities of your company vs. a competitor's, and the secondary activities that together support the primary activities. See Michael Porter's article "What is Strategy" in *Harvard Business Review*, November-December 1996, for two examples.

the consequences of sloppy, lazy thinking

"It is difficult to free fools from
the chains they revere."

—Voltaire

In the previous chapter, we derided Corporate's reflexive bench-marking whenever a consultant says, "Let's learn from the best." We also pointed out the folly of using success formulas. Formulaic thinking, though, is not limited to benchmarking processes. It goes to the heart of strategic decline.

"Something is rotten in the state of Denmark," wrote Shakespeare in *Hamlet*. Something is rotten in Corporate, wrote *The Economist* in a 2015 article about the benefits of hedge-fund activists, those billionaire investors who wage battles with underperforming management.

Hedge-fund activists attack companies that persistently show poor returns on equity. That's like locking the door after the thief has gotten away. It would be much more beneficial if companies had early-detection mechanisms to save wealth and jobs, *even the CEO's*. Companies need to spot sloppy thinking *before* it can cause trouble.

That's where you come in.

By nature, mavericks are mentally equipped to diagnose sloppy, rotten thinking—not thinking that's lousy, but thinking that's *rotting*—and fight it. You will find, however, that Corporate will pay a fortune for "used" ("pre-owned"?) perspectives and ignore your unorthodox thinking. But we are here, and we will provide advice on how you can push forward.

Diagnosing rot early is not nearly as difficult as some pundits claim. Corporate may look glitzy from the outside, but once you work on the inside, you see the cracks and rust and the inevitable decline, as the perfunctory rituals, formulaic thinking, and conformist attitudes of your colleagues are quite obvious. We've seen it in many of the leading companies and brands we've worked with. The issue is almost always a style of management that confuses process and thinking. The result—unintended but real nonetheless—is coasting, not competing.

In this chapter, we refute the ideas that formulaic thinking isn't all that bad, especially if you pay a lot for it, and that fresh thinking is not worth the price, even if it's free. With a few simple pointers, you'll find rot-diagnosis as easy as noticing a vegetarian in a steakhouse. First step: Look for the formula zombies.

YOU CAN'T AFFORD THE EXPENSIVE FREEMIUM FORMULA

Neglecting the skill of competing can hurt even the biggest brands. Think Barnes & Noble, Kmart, JC Penney, Nokia, Compaq, Kentucky Fried Chicken, Dr Pepper, Maxwell House Coffee, Snapple, Perrier, Pontiac, Blockbuster, House & Garden, Newsweek, MySpace, Corn Pops, and many more. Some bounce back with new management or new strategies (e.g., KFC). Some just die (e.g., Blockbuster).

It may take time, and it may show up first as small innocuous cracks, but if you are a maverick who hasn't drunk the Corporate Kool-Aid yet, you can spot the damage instantly behind the façade. Lucky for some coasting management teams, competitors' managements suffer from the same dysfunctions. Companies and competitors may coast for many years in happy harmony. And then an entrepreneurial disruptor comes in and wreaks havoc. Think Uber to the taxi industry, generics to pharma, Whole Foods to groceries, cable to traditional telecom, Facebook to advertising, and Google to door-to-door encyclopedia sales.

Is decline inevitable? Perhaps. Perhaps not.

After an exhaustive study surveying seven executives, consultants, academics, and employees (useable responses returned from five;

the other two's comments can't be printed here), we came to the following conclusion:

It's the freemium thinking.

The original idea behind freemium was ingenious. Offer basic features for free, but for *quality* features, you have to pay. The trick is, of course, to make the basics lousy enough to nudge people toward higher quality, but not so lousy they will be turned off completely.

In competitive strategy, *freemium thinking* is the act of repeating past strategy without putting a lot of effort and thought into how the future will be different. It is easy, and it costs little in cognitive effort. Just follow the formula that brought you success for so many years. But the most basic lesson from economics is that there really is no free lunch. You get what you pay for.

The problem is—say it with us—there is no free lunch. If you go for the freemium, expect the quality to be consistent with the price. And freemium thinking doesn't only make companies copy other companies. The basic axiom of "you get what you pay for" gets a *reverse* translation in Corporate: It pays a fortune for copying other companies via hiring "help." It pays a fortune for consulting that ends up making it look just like consultants' *other* clients. (See our discussion on benchmarking in Chapter 7.)

Next, Corporate's growing similarity to the other clients starts to erode the foundation of competitive advantage and strategic positioning that made the company great in the first place. The consultants are then hired away to the C-suite, since they are the only ones who understand who in the restructured organization reports to whom.

Finally, the consultants, now in the C-suite, proceed to hire *more* consultants in an attempt to slow the erosion. But that just accelerates the spread of the freemium thinking that gets more and more expensive. And now it's a race to turn the massive ship of industry. Will the inertia of coasting run the ship aground, or can the mavericks navigate skillfully enough?

Corporate also pays a fortune for advertising that can't prove its worth, agencies that advance the claims of "brand awareness" indexes, and lawyers who can prove anything you want. Corporate pays an army of vendors to work in every area of operations, then pays an army of bureaucrat-employees to coordinate those vendors. Like the consultants, many of the outside vendors sell their formulaic, off-the-shelf thinking to many clients. Corporate is happy to adopt the vendors' advice because freemium looks so *efficient*. After all, the vendors' list of *other* clients includes all the big names.

Original, rigorous thinking requires tremendous effort. It's premium thinking, and it is costly in terms of time and hard choices to be made. In war games where a company's outside consultants are allowed to participate, they almost invariably take over the thinking. After all, they are good at it. But no matter how articulate, what the company buys is freemium: Basic strategic thinking applied equally across the consultants' customer base.

We can imagine a meeting 200,000 years ago between an inventor and a Neanderthal clan's Chief Marketing Officer:

CMO: Gruuu . . . hmr . . . gawk . . . (What do you have here?)

Inventor: Grrrr . . . oooom . . . (I call it a wheel.)

CMO: What is it good for?

Inventor: Moving fast.

CMO: Who do we sell it to?

Inventor: Neanderthals who want to move fast.

CMO: Hmmm . . . No go. It is too out there. No one will pay to move faster. The consultants said we should focus on mammoth hair. All the other clans sell mammoth hair. It's a proven business model, even 200,000 years before we outsource to a lower-cost supplier. They said we should put it on a cloud (excited murmuring from the clan). Do you have a mammoth hair product?

It's easy for us to say that *competitive* strategy is about doing something your competitors aren't doing, but it is very hard work.

Did the Neanderthals go for a "proven business model"? Who knows. They disappeared, and so did the mammoths. If your company simply adapts a "proven business model" from the consultants, it may share their fate. The mammoths' fate, that is. The consultants still sell the "proven business model" successfully.

cost-cutting as sloppy freemium thinking

Following decades of formulaic thinking, market changes make cost-cutting to Corporate what a diet is to a monk: A natural adaptation to life in the barren mountains. In its endless quest to cut costs, however, Corporate ends up with low-quality, sloppy thinking, and not the premium ideas it needs. Yes, cost-cutting shouldn't be a knee-jerk mindless response to tough times. It should be strategic, unorthodox, and well-thought-out—not formulaic or reflexive like the overtightening you read about in Chapter 5.

So here is the irony of Corporate's cost-cutting folly: It saves a penny here or a penny there by cutting out real internal capabilities but then spends $50 million in investment bankers' fees for a billion-dollar acquisition that will recruit *talent,* which they cut out and that turns out to be almost as good as betting on the longevity of an opposition leader in Russia. Of course, the cost of the acquisition goes on the balance sheet, not the profit-and-loss statement, so investors don't mind.

Cost-cutting may seem the easiest, quickest, I'm-taking-action response to competitive pressures. It *is* easy, quick, and action-oriented, and Wall Street loves it unconditionally. But it's lazy thinking. Doing it *well*, rather than indiscriminately, is critical. If you want to lose weight, go on a diet; don't amputate a limb. You need to know where to cut without hurting the quality of management. Activist investors, for example, tend to cut

---

cost-cutting as sloppy freemium thinking, continued

costs while simultaneously increasing R&D, investing in capital equipment and infrastructure, and decreasing leverage. So if your company announces across-the-board cost-cutting, you are witnessing a Corporate dysfunction at work. Cuts across the board are freemium thinking: Easy, sloppy, orthodox, and low quality.

HOW TO DIAGNOSE FREEMIUM THINKING EARLY

How do you know your company is decaying at the foundation of its once-formidable competitive skill? Think of how pest specialists track termites.

Termites must be identified way before they settle in and eat your house. Specialists set "termite traps" around the house's perimeter. Traps include bait. If termites are in the area, they will show up in the traps. The pest-control company then comes in and sprays chemicals to clear the infestation before it does damage.

In Corporate, you can spot the "termites" by setting traps for conventional wisdom. Ask politely, "Why are we doing it this way?" See how many times the reply is basically "It worked before." When the accumulated weight of those replies exceeds a threshold in the traps, call the exterminator. OK, that last part is a joke. Call the activist? OK, that is probably illegal. Call Mom?

Some companies with impressive track records stick to their formula—why not, it works!—and keep executing it religiously until the house comes down or an activist comes in. P&G, Kodak, Anheuser-Busch InBev, Sears, Black & Decker, Sunbeam, Levi Strauss, Polaroid, Sharper Image, and Radio Shack are a few examples. Sticking to a formula is freemium. It's the cheapest way to select and execute a strategy without having to think too hard, develop foresight, anticipate change, go proactive, and all those tiring, resource-consuming mental activities.

Following the formula is also the least risky act in a successful company. Experiments demonstrate that people *seek* risk only to avoid the prospect of catastrophic loss and *avoid* risk if they face uncertain gains. This is known as *prospect theory*. Companies that don't believe they face catastrophic losses are, therefore, risk-averse: They will take the smaller, more-certain gains that come with repeating formulas over the big, hairy risks of a bold move. It is rational for a lower-level manager to be risk-averse in a risk-averse culture. But this rationality has its price: It is how Corporate sows the seeds of its own failure. It's easy to see in retrospect but hard to see in prospect.

Corporate coaches and consultants will tell you to go along with your peers and managers because team spirit and communication ability (their code for *shut up*) are high up in traditional advice. But freemium thinking is rampant because people with team spirit and an ability to shut up don't question it.

Formulaic thinking is easier, cheaper, and much less demanding than fresh, unorthodox ideas, but it is lazy. Mavericks in formulaic companies come under heavy pressure to accept the formula. Don't succumb! It would mean the death of your independent thinking.

advice to the maverick

Sloppy thinking lives on not just because people are lazy, but also because the burden of proof falls on those challenging the formula. Original thinking is an intense, energy-consuming mental activity; it is an *investment.* Busy people don't have the time or energy needed, and Corporate prefers to buy freemium from the consultants, deluding itself that it's receiving premium.

Daniel Kahneman won the Nobel prize in Economics despite never studying economics (he is a psychologist). In his 2011 book, *Thinking, Fast and Slow* (Farrar, Straus and Giroux), he describes slow, deliberative thinking (what we call premium) as System 2 thinking, and quick, seemingly instinctive thinking (what we call freemium) as System 1 thinking. System 1 is automatic and fast, intuitive, and effortless. System 2 is deliberate and slow, energy consuming, and tiring, and it is evoked only when System 1 determines *it doesn't know what to do.* Relying on a formula, whether the consultants' or the company's own, relieves the pain, embarrassment, and lowered status of saying, "I don't know what to do."

The alternative to "I don't know what to do" is typically a frenzy of activities aimed at reinforcing the formula that stopped working. It shouldn't be. Luckily, mavericks are there to offer fresh thinking . . . if only Corporate were interested.

We are not against using System 1 if you have the experience to marshal.[1] Intuition works when you can draw on *similar* situations or a pattern observed in many repeated situations in your past. System 1 is hardly ever appropriate, however, for strategic changes in the market if they are not repetitive or regular. Moreover, be wary of another trap, overconfidence: the "mother of all biases."

There is a safe and constructive path for the maverick. Although you may not question The Formula, you can question its assumptions. Be humble when your boss tells you, "This worked for a millennium, you sure you know better?" Just ask one minor, gentle, deferential question. The formula (!) for the question is this: Start with "what if," then change *just one* assumption underlying the strategy being perpetuated. For example, if you work for a consumer-product company where advertising is never questioned, and the

---

[1] Big Data doesn't count as experience, nor does habitually repeating an action.

marketing agency is entrenched, ask: What if millennials don't pay attention to ads the way older generations did?

"What ifs" are such powerful tools that Mark even named his website whati-fyourstrategy.com.[2] Use "what ifs" sparingly, cleverly, and politely. A formula can hurt the people in the room.

They may pour hot tar over you and cover you with feathers, but if they don't (where would you find feathers in the middle of the workday?), you may stand out as someone who asks good questions. This is better than someone who answers bad questions.

---

[2] Ben's website is called giladwargames.com, and it teaches how to create a "safe" environment for asking "what ifs."

how
corporate
communicates

the negative side of being positive

"Motivational products don't work. But our Demotivator® products don't work even better."

—Despair.com website

While formulaic ("freemium") thinking afflicts Corporate on many levels, no one is encouraged to say anything negative about it even if everyone knows the disastrous consequences of silence. Here is an example.

As reported in *Business Insider* in 2015, a very prestigious organization, the Corporate Executive Board, concluded, based on surveys, that 50 to 70 percent of executives fail within the first 18 months of promotion into an executive role. Among those 50 to 70 percent, 3 percent fail miserably and 50 percent struggle.

That's a horrible statistic and the end of the *Business Insider* story, but it's not the end of *our* story. Our story is about people's preferences for positive news.

Business Insider is a popular buzzfeed-type news site where stories pop up, compete, are ranked according to popularity, and disappear quickly if they fail to garner interest. The report on failing executives garnered about 1,400 reads on March 2, 2015, and was dropped before the end of the day. A story about Michael Jordan becoming a billionaire garnered 43,000 reads. The "40 Richest Hedge Funds in America" got 250,000 reads. The "Fabulous Life of Sir Jony Ive," about an Apple designer, got 300,000 reads.

Now this is by no means a scientific survey, but one doesn't need a scientific survey to see what's happening here: The masses love positive stories (success!) and hate negative stories (failure!). That doesn't bode well for our book, our attempt to create positive success through negative stories, but we don't fail to persist. Never!

In this chapter, we explore the negative consequences of the always-be-positive imperative. This imperative, enforced by Corporate culture, serves as an excuse to avoid facing reality. It leads to smoothing over real competitive issues, stifling debates, and hushing mavericks. And yet research suggests that the eternal optimists are not necessarily the best leaders.

Well, what do you expect? People dream. They love to read autobiographies of the rich and famous in the delusion that maybe one day *they* can be them.

So what's the downside? No damage done for individuals. The problem is when contagious, mandatory positivism—the dysfunction we call *Positivismitis*—infects Corporate. There, the damage is real, and it is the critical-thinking, "not-so-fast" mavericks who suffer.

Fortunately, we have the cure. No, it's not a counteracting dose of bad old Negativismitis. The cure is confronting reality; the cure is *honesty*.

~~NOTHING~~ ANYTHING BUT THE TRUTH

A few years after the second World War, America turned to positive thinking. The rationale behind it: America was the only economic superpower. Japan, China, and Korea, which would give American businesses and workers serious runs for their money later on, lay in ruins. So did most of Europe. Life was good in America. We could do anything we wanted! We knew we could *just do it!* because we *just did it!*

We are not going to say anything negative about the power of positive thinking or anything positive about the power of negative thinking. We are going to try hard to stay positive on positive thinking even if it hurts. It is precisely when it hurts that we have to turn the positivity down a notch. The opposite of positivity, you see, is not negativity. The opposite of both positivity and negativity is reality.

The willingness to acknowledge and face reality is a prerequisite for developing your skill at competing.

The essence of Positivismitis first appeared in COOC (to refresh your memory, that's Corporate Overconfident, Oblivious Culture) around the 1990s. Positivismitis is the obsessive need to smooth, silken, soften, and tone down anything that is not overtly positive, gushingly rewarding, loudly cheerful, or absolutely complimentary lest someone, somewhere, somehow be offended and start crying (not to mention complain to the ruthless HR department). The perpetual need to be positive manifests itself in every area of COOC from managers' performance reviews to company performance reviews to not commenting on the lukewarm and thin coffee (cost-cutting recipe: If you add water to coffee, you get more coffee) in the carafes brought to a meeting. Positivismitis has become so bad that when executives don't sugarcoat their views or see the silver lining in every tornado, the business world gasps in shock.

You might remember two 2015 incidents involving blatant honesty. In one, Fiat Chrysler publicly announced that some of its dealers defrauded customers by taking deposits for a hot car they would not be able to deliver. In another, Blackstone CEO Steven Schwarzman stated that his company, the largest private equity fund in the world, is working under the assumption that Europe will *never* grow.

The press reported that the Dodge division of Fiat Chrysler stated publicly that a number of dealers took more orders (and deposits) for the 2015 Dodge Challenger and Charger SRT Hellcat models than had been allocated to those dealers, which resulted in customers waiting months for their cars, if they got them at all. While Dodge didn't reveal the dealers' names (too much honesty?), the announcement was highly unusual for a car company.

In the case of Blackstone's CEO, in a 2015 interview for Bloomberg reported by *Business Insider*, the seasoned investor shocked the interviewer by declaring, "Our baked-in assumption is that Europe never grows." That is unusual, as heads of large funds never express such a pessimistic view in public. After all, it's bad for business.

A LIFE SPENT SPINNING

The idea that you must put a positive spin on every situation is deeply ingrained in Corporate. But positive spin, by definition, obscures reality, and without facing reality, jobs and wealth are doomed. Ironically, the ones who'll most likely be laid off are exactly those positive-thinking managers striving for harmony above all. Singing Kumbaya around the Corporate campfire is not confronting reality. It's not even a real campfire, as safety regulations prohibit the starting of fire in or near any office, trees, forests, parks, or houses that are not within five feet of a fire station.

Managers, theoretically, should be the ones *most* likely to promote truthful dialogue and debate because refusing to confront reality, especially when it is not pretty, can cost them their livelihoods. We have learned, though, that it is not so. Positivismitis, not to mention formulas and overtightening, get in the way. And, in our experience, that can even happen in a simulated environment, such as the ones we run for a living. Think about that for a second. If you can't be honest when you're *simulating* scenarios and risking *simulated* money, then why would you be honest in real life?

honesty wins the war game

Absolute honesty is a must in a business war game. We have run hundreds of them around the world, in giant companies, corporate workshops, and business schools.

War games simulate market "battles." They stress-test moves, countermoves, and counter-countermoves based on a realistic assessment of the host company vs. competitors' capabilities, constraints, commitments, histories, cultures, assumptions, and intentions. If you leave out the "realistic" part, war games are a waste of time and money. Yet that doesn't prevent nervous vice presidents, neurotic directors, and sensitive

honesty wins the war game, continued

managers from trying to steer their war games away from a bare-knuckle look at what a company and its competitors do well. Steering away turns a blind eye to real danger that can cost the company its future prosperity.

Interestingly, in smaller, entrepreneurial companies, war games are often brutally and decisively more honest, looking at practical strategic solutions rather than beautifying the ugly to prevent confronting reality (and top management). The simple explanation is that the smaller companies can't afford to paint everything happy while Corporate believes it can, (over)confident in the illusory refuge of its cash reserves.

However, size is not the critical factor in honesty. Culture and circumstance are.

The best war game Ben ran at a large company, a once-great manufacturer in decline, predicted its demise unless a drastic change in strategy and priorities took place. The company adopted this drastic change, and in three years moved from a losing business to what a trade magazine described as "leading a breakthrough in the industry." That was possible at that company, however, *only* because the war game was authorized by a new head of the division who had no emotional investment in the existing strategy and whose people thereby knew honesty was safe.

The best war game Ben ran outside large Fortune 500 companies was with a service provider where the CEO led the *competitor* team and portrayed her own company's strategy as a "hodgepodge of tactical initiatives with no clear direction."

honesty wins the war game, continued

Companies have different experiences with war games, but the mere fact that they run them shows some willingness to confront reality without the rose-colored glasses of Positivismitis. We've seen Fortune 50 companies change course 180 degrees after a two-day war game. We've seen some that realized one strategy is not ideal, but the other alternative would be disastrous. We've seen some realize that one strategy is not ideal but the alternative would be disastrous. We've heard people with 30-plus years of experience in their industries exclaim, "I didn't know our competitors could do *that*!"

Regardless of their final strategy choices, the common denominator for these companies was that they took war-game simulations as an antidote to Positivismitis. That is, except for a few. We've seen a handful of companies insist that a favored strategy would work even though it failed in the war game . . . and then the strategy real-life failed and people got real-life fired. Mark might have been undiplomatic in Chapter 1 when he said the president running the number-two company could not become the number-one company, but he—rather, the war game—was right.

A TEST FOR POSITIVISMITIS

As a maverick you will want to run war games every day, but that's a little too much medicine for those suffering from Positivismitis. But you can fight Positivismitis in your own way. Ask yourself questions like the ones below. The answers tell you whether your company is full or free of Positivismitis.

- Would your CEO have the guts—*yes, the guts*—to admit to "a hodgepodge of tactical initiatives" like that CEO? "Yes," means low Positivismitis. "No," doesn't.
- Does bad news arrive at your company from leading indicators? Example: Those newfangled cars are sure to drive down future demand for our buggy whips (low Positivismitis). Or does bad news arrive from lagging indicators? Example: Demand for our buggy whips has been down for several years (medium Positivismitis). Or does bad news not arrive at all? Example: Someone bought a buggy whip last month (terminal Positivismitis).
- Does the word *competitor* come up often during strategy, sales, marketing, or finance meetings? Does the phrase *our plan* come up? The higher the ratio of "competitor" to "our plan," the lower the Positivismitis.
- Does your company ask questions looking for disconfirmation that it's on track? Example: "What's interfering with reaching our targets?" signals the inoculation against Positivismitis has been effective. Or does it look for confirmation? Example: "How close are we to our targets?" signals risk of Positivismitis.

The more you scored your company positively on the questions above, the less susceptible it is to Positivismitis. That's a positive sign. See? We are not all about negativity.

SIDE EFFECTS OF POSITIVISMITIS

In psychotherapy, as in 12-step rehab programs, we are told that until we admit there is a problem, no progress can be made. Positive talk at any cost is a classic symptom of management who live in deep denial of a problem.

The most common side effect of Positivismitis is blindly going where one shouldn't and ending up looking for a new job. Denying honest dialogue causes the competing muscle to atrophy.

Honesty, however, doesn't mean being a Grinch. Let's talk, maverick.

Do I Have to be Nasty?

President Harry Truman said, "I never did give anybody hell. I just told the truth, and they thought it was hell."

In our war games, we tell people we are not there to be cheerleaders. First, we can't swing our legs above our heads even if you put a gun to our heads or our legs. Second, the market is not a field of flowers, and competitors are not running dreamily through it looking to hug you. While we don't think business is necessarily war (even though we run "war games," a misnomer for strategy stress-testing simulations), it is also not necessarily harmonious, reassuring, or supportive. Contested markets (an economic term for competition) are, well, contested.

So no, managers don't *have* to be nasty, but they have to be realistic. And sometimes reality itself is not very pleasant. Sugarcoating it doesn't lead to a "better work environment"; it leads to diabetes.

Oh Good! I Don't Like Being Nasty. I'm an Optimist. Can Leaders be Optimists?

Optimism is wonderful, until it is not. It is not when it gets in the way of reality.

It is impossible for an optimist to be pleasantly surprised. However, optimism is not always bad. It depends on the type of optimism. Here is a case in point.

In August 2013, a huge debate erupted in the business and tech sphere about who should succeed Steve Ballmer as Microsoft's CEO.

The tech community was torn between Microsoft friends and Microsoft foes (typically Linux fanatics). *TechCrunch* writer Alex Wilhelm saw Ballmer as a good CEO who was exiting at his peak. *ZDNet* writer Steven J. Vaughan-Nichols, a staunch Linux fanatic, regarded Ballmer as a flop. Both made their cases based on technology, personal preferences, and anecdotal evidence. Of course, none of those perspectives mattered.

The business perspective—Microsoft is a *business*, remember?—was expressed by savvier writers like *Time*'s Harry McCraken. Mr.

McCraken said any tech company's hegemony was bound to be relatively short-lived, and Microsoft's actually lasted quite a long time. He complimented Ballmer's skill at competing in such a rapidly changing world.

What do you think *PC Magazine*'s Samara Lynn said? You don't have to know anything about her. Just look at the title of her magazine. *PC?* Who uses a PC these days? It is soooo uncool. You don't see Jay-Z next to a desktop, do you? Well, it turns out all the companies that matter (sorry J-Z, sorry cool gamers) use PCs. Ms. Lynn rightly observed that Ballmer's tech "failures" (mobile, cloud, search) meant little at the time because he still led Microsoft to total dominance of the enterprise market. And indeed, later on, when Microsoft invested heavily in the cloud, its deep relationship with the business community made Azure, its cloud platform, a big success *despite* its late entry.[1] So Ballmer was a leader whose optimism was also checked by realizing some failures. He tried, he failed in some areas where Microsoft had to admit lackluster performance, but at the end he created a stronger base for the next CEO.

So who should have Microsoft selected as its next leader? We know who it did select (Satya Nadella), but before it did, who would you have recommended? Jay Ritter, a leading financial scholar and a professor at the University of Florida, had at the time this insight into competing reported in a 2013 piece by *USA Today*: "Microsoft's leadership must be open to new ideas but also must be sufficiently self-confident that the person is willing to acknowledge when there are no transformative opportunities."

In effect, Professor Ritter described a hybrid between an optimist and a pessimist, a balance of positive and negative thinking appropriate to the situation.

Sophia Chou, an organizational-psychology researcher from National Taiwan University, described a similar concept to Ritter's: The *realistic optimist*. Unlike optimists who see only the glass-half-full and limitless possibilities, and unlike pessimists who see only the glass-half-empty and no hope, the realistic optimists blend,

---

[1] Notice that "you have to be first to succeed" is a formulaic assumption.

uh, realism (which can have negative implications) and optimism. Quoted in Yahoo News at the time, she stated they choose "accuracy over self-enhancement."

According to the research findings, realist optimists have the positive outlook of the optimists with the reality checks of the pessimist. In the study, they had better grades than the other groups, as they realized they had to study to achieve academic success.

True, realistic optimists scored higher on tests of anxiety than "pure" optimists because they admit the possibility of failure. But, says Ms. Chou, they do not give up in the face of challenges. They come up with alternative plans. Alternative plans . . . that sounds like our maverick!

So with whom should Corporate replace its eternal optimists? We recommend realistic optimists. And if that doesn't work . . . well, we are positive we can come up with another plan.

advice to the maverick

Corporate consultants and HR coaches will tell you how important it is to create a "positive work environment." What they mean is don't be a party pooper! While no one objects to supportive management and loving teammates, they won't save your job when the Corporate axe falls because the rot has engulfed the positive work environment.

Companies put significant emphasis on teamwork. MBA programs in leading schools, therefore, subject their hapless students to endless team projects.

We, on the other hand, are much more skeptical about teamwork and positive outlook as a guiding principle to strategy work. In every team there is someone who comes up with strategic ideas, the inevitable free-riders, and the one taking the credit. *That's* a real-world team. And we're not pessimists! We are *realistic* optimists. If we were pessimists, there'd be no credit for someone to take.

advice to the maverick, continued

As a maverick, you'll be thrilled to be part of an exciting team and not averse to group hugs. Enjoy! Does it mean you should subscribe to the Positivismitis undoubtedly exhibited by the team leader? No. But you have to be smart about how you present your reality checks.

Never just come out and be negative. No one likes to work with negative people. Turn negativity into a question, as in: "This is a great plan, a great idea, a fantastic launch of our new and undoubtedly clinically superior drug! I truly don't mean to be a party pooper, but could we, *for just a second,* look at it from the perspective of competitor X? If I am competitor X and I see us communicating our launch message with key opinion leaders (KOLs), I may try to point out to *our* KOLs that our clinical trials are actually better because . . . Maybe we should just be ready with a response to that?" (This example is real, taken from a war game with a pharmaceutical firm about to launch a new drug with a multimillion-dollar marketing campaign and half a billion dollars invested in R&D.)

Of course, to do that you need to study a bit about Competitor X. Look at its history of responses, look at its culture, and read about it anywhere you can. Rest assured, *no one else* on your team actually does that.

And by this simple, humble, self-deprecating question, you just started to simulate competition using others' perspectives.

Alas, no one on your team will speak to you for a decade. You are a trouble-maker. You are a show-off. You actually want to compete.

No, we are messing with you. That was a pessimistic view. You'll be promoted overnight. See how easy and self-affirming it is to acquire Positivismitis?

what corporate obsesses and obsesses about

CHAPTER 10

"A man may dwell so long upon a thought that it may take him prisoner."

—George Savile

Positivismitis is a single, specific form of obsession. Corporate, however, doesn't restrict itself to obsessing about being positive all the time. For Corporate, being obsessive in itself is an obsession.

In this chapter, we obsess over Corporate obsessions, from reorganization, to growth, to the use of consultants. These obsessions pose special difficulty to mavericks as they may find themselves reporting to new bosses just as they may have been, perhaps, possibly, potentially, feasibly, conceivably able to make a difference with the old ones. (We worry about that all the time.) We advise mavericks that, rather than despairing and redespairing, they should think and rethink taking advantage of bad situations.

Obsessions are at times accompanied by rituals. When one of us was young, he was obsessed with a particular girl in his high school. He made sure to walk by her house on his way to school every morning for a year, though, he later realized her family had moved out months earlier. A ritual is a ritual, and there's no need to let it go due to little details.

To Corporate, rituals are not painful. *Lack* of rituals is what hurts.

Some COOC rituals are perfect examples of obsessions. We chose two: reorganizing and targeting.

REORGANIZING (A.K.A. "REORG" AMONG SURVIVORS)

Every two years or so, Corporate ritually reorganizes. If one is nitpicking, the second time around it should be called re-reorganization, since it reorganizes the original reorganization. But that's just *our* obsessive preoccupation with clear (semantic) logic. You can defend the relaxing of precise terminology after the fourth reorg, since it would become tedious and undignified to say re-re-re-reorg. On the other hand, it can simplify historical references. If we can have Henry the VIII, why not Reorg the VIII?

Reorganizing has an economic rationale. Markets are Darwinian instruments in the social realm, and to match changes in the market, companies should reorganize at times. It is an adaptive response.

Until it is not. The *ritual* reorg typically starts with slide 136 from the consultants. In that slide, a new organizational chart is presented as far better matching "the new competitive reality," which can be just about anything. "Disruption" is mentioned subtly 325 times. Management immediately buys into the idea since the job of management is to *do something,* and the excitement of "the new competitive reality" and the fear of "disruption" are effective action-triggers.

Management always buys into ideas that come from consultants. If the idea works, management can take credit for its quick action. If the idea bombs, explaining that the idea was proposed by one of the leading (always use "leading") consultancies in the world is a built-in CYA (cover-your-ass) shield. (In the UK, you can use "premiere" instead of "leading.") Any necessary explanation can also deflect both blame and attention by saying, "Anyway, the reorg achieved significant synergies and cost savings."

Reorganizing has its own peculiar logic that reverses itself every X years. ("X" is not a large number.) Scientists are still looking into the mechanism behind the regular about-face, but we already know some principles of the process. There are two main versions of reorganizing: Shuffling by sales and shuffling by business areas. We mean "shuffling" as in shuffling cards into a different order, not as in people who shuffle their feet as they walk.

The Reorg Cycle, Version 1: Sales

Here is a typical reorganization cycle based on the advice from whoever is the reigning consultant in the company at that time:

1. Based on a thorough study by the consultants, the company reorganizes itself by regions based on the rising sales in BRIC (Brazil, Russia, India, and China), the perennial decline of Europe, and the maturation of the North American region. Then BRIC becomes a brick around the company's neck as Russia implodes, China kicks it out after stealing its IP, India can't find the license it gave it, and Brazil loses another soccer match and commits suicide. The company then . . .

2. Follows the consultants' *new* chart reorganizing along strategic accounts, not sales regions. These are large customers who often require teams to work on their reluctant purchasing departments' employees until they capitulate and spend more than needed. (It's like coupons that make you buy 50 years' worth of dental floss.) Alas, a new company comes in with a "Blue Ocean" product,[1] and the strategic account runs to it with glee. The company then . . .

3. Hires a new consulting firm that recommends reorganizing by regions, a revolutionary new idea. Alas, the LATAM/MENA (Latin America, Middle East, and North Africa) region, combined due to the senior partner's inability to read the world map, collapses. The company then . . .

4. Goes back to step 2, but this is *completely* different and not a repetitive compulsive ritual because the organizational chart uses four colors for the accounts' profitability, not just three as in the former consultants' obsolete chart.

---

[1] A fashionable buzzword in the '90s, "blue ocean" refers to markets with no competition. It is based on a book called *Blue Ocean Strategy* (*Harvard Business Review Press*, 2005) by Renée Mauborgne and W. Chan Kim.

Where is the company at the end of the cycle? Trick question! There is no end; that's what makes it a cycle. The better question, the question only a maverick can (cautiously) ask, is *why do we keep oscillating between two points? If we're not satisfied with either of them, shouldn't we look for another?*

The Reorg Cycle, Version 2: Business Areas

Sometimes the reorganization is not by sales volume and emerging or lost continents but by product line or business areas. This goes as follows:

1. Based on a comprehensive study by The Keen and Old (TKaO) Consulting (one of the Big 2 consulting firms, or Giant 7, depending on its own reorg from last year), the company merges two business units with similar products and different markets into one, to "better serve the changing needs and the blurring lines between the consumer and business users" and to "increase the collaboration between the two business units, which brings complementary strengths to the customer."

2. The two merged units prove as siloed after as before, and customers do not take kindly to the two sets of salespeople showing up at their workplace within 15 minutes of each other and pitching competing messages. TKaO proposes tighter alignment with the global strategy by splitting the merged unit into business and consumer units so each can "better serve its market with its own unique qualities and specific expertise." Management hails the "Power of Two" and the better responsiveness that will be achieved in the market.

3. The company's CFO (who once used to be a partner at TKaO before being recruited by the company) retires. The new CFO hires (naturally) a new consulting outfit, Systematic Universal Consulting Karma Ecosystem Resources. SUCKER immediately recommends a reorg in which the business unit and the

consumer unit report to a new Enterprise and Small People Unit (ESP) for closer coordination. The company then recruits the partner to head its new ESP unit.

You think we are exaggerating for effect, right? It can't be that absurd, can it?

We wish. We actually are toning down the real havoc. According to a survey, reported by the (real) consulting firm The Clemmer Group, 50 to 70 percent of "reorgs" fail. Business school may have taught you that decisions at that level and with such expense are rational, carefully considered, and based on data. We are telling you how it is truly done. *Sorry.*

---

some reorg evidence

A 2015 article in Harvard Business Review, by Donald Sull, Rebecca Homkes, and Charles Sull, reports on a (real) survey of 8,000 executives and managers in 250 firms worldwide. "Why Strategy Execution Unravels—and What to Do about It" says, "fewer than one-third of managers believe that their organizations reallocate funds to the right places quickly enough to be effective. Only 20 percent of managers say their organizations do a good job of shifting people across units to support strategic priorities."

One third of the respondents report that their companies make shifts in ways that actually *disrupt other units.* We surmise that the other two thirds never received the survey since it was addressed to their old unit.

GROWTH TARGETS

Organizing and reorganizing and re-reorganizing and then back to organizing is one repetitive behavior typical of Corporate's dysfunction. Obsession with continuous growth represents another Corporate ritual.

Why do companies obsess about growth? There are several good reasons and one bad one.

Here are the good reasons why growth is good. Growth is motivating. It means more market power (maybe). It means higher bonuses to managers (definitely). It means Wall Street will welcome the CFO and CEO on conference calls and label them quick and agile. It means investors will buy the shares and push the stock price up. It means executives' stock options will be worth more. You can't fault Corporate for the constant-growth model because it underlies the entire semi-Ponzi scheme known as public companies.

In short: Companies obsess about growth because growth makes money.

Here is the bad reason. If you are a short-term investor in a public company, you buy shares not to hold but to sell. You want the share price to rise as quickly as possible so you can sell it before it falls to a sucker who thinks it will *keep* rising (or to a visionary who thinks you are the sucker). That is a legal and moral scheme of sorts at the heart of capitalism and which we completely (Ben) or gingerly (Mark) support but for one small issue on which we thoroughly agree: When markets change, sometimes the best strategy is to *lower* growth targets, not to raise them. That's the essence of defying Positivismitis and confronting reality. It is at the core of competing as a skill, which requires honesty and clarity. But what's good for the goose (the business) is not always good for some of the ganders (short-term shareholders).

In short: Companies obsess about growth because the sky falls when growth slows. And growth *always* slows, sooner or later.

In the Sull et al. study we cited above, "Eight in ten managers say their companies fail to exit declining businesses or to kill unsuccessful initiatives quickly enough."

Eight in ten! *80 percent (!)* believe their companies won't face reality. It seems their companies fear something more than they fear reality. Admitting limitations? Admitting failure?

private vs. public companies

The mentality of growth at all costs is obvious when you compare the world's largest private companies with the world's largest public companies. The public companies are so much bigger. Does it mean private companies are less efficient? Less profitable? Well, no one actually knows the profitability of private companies because they do not have to file quarterly reports about their earnings as public companies do. As Mark puts it, the dreaded quarterly report is the equivalent of "Will this be on the final exam?" for public companies.

What we do know is that the revenue growth of private companies significantly lags the revenue growth of public companies. One conclusion is that large private companies are not *obsessed* with growth, relative to public companies. They may care more about *longevity*.

The Pathology of Growth Targets

Growth is good. Obsessive growth targets are not. Why do executives keep pushing relentless, unrealistic, utterly delusional growth targets even if, at the end, it comes to bite them in a soft place?

Underlying growth targets is the belief—unexplained, deeply rooted, and unsupported by any evidence—that *if you stand still, you will die.*

If you work in a COOC (reminder: Corporate Overconfident, Oblivious Culture), you've probably heard this phrase at least ten times in the last ten video messages from the CEO. It's a Darwinian survival instinct dating back to the times our ancient ancestors ran away from charging saber-toothed tigers. Then, if you stood still, you indeed died.

Some sharks follow that model. They must keep moving even when they are asleep, or they'll die. The catch, however, is that when they do it, their brains are only half functional (literally: Only half the brain is working, the other half is asleep). Can that be the model emulated by Corporate? Are half the executives fully asleep, or are all the executives half asleep?

Tell it to Stihl, the world leader in chainsaws and other garden appliances, which has refused to sell at mass-market outlets, including Home Depot or Lowe's, for the past 50 years despite the temptation of huge growth if it relented. But then Stihl is German, and we saw in Chapter 7 on benchmarking that German companies must be talentless since they do not pay their CEOs enough to keep the talented ones. Or so goes the rationale of board of directors' executive-compensation committees in the U.S.

So ask yourself: Who says that growth is so necessary? What's wrong with stability? What's wrong with being satisfied with where you are and making sure you keep up that performance (which requires competing, not delusions)?

For Corporate, the answer apparently lies in the half of the brain that is asleep.

Growth Through a Different Prism

Corporate's obsessive growth targets reflect a real fear of the prospect of merely stable earning. Imagine how badly Corporate reacts to the possibility of *decline*.

Most pundits, industry observers, and Wall Street analysts drool over new hot markets. (China! Oh no, China is slowing down. Vietnam!) They drool over high-growth areas (tablets and mobile devices! healthy foods! e-cigarettes! digital readers! social media! artificial intelligence! Especially in China! Sorry, Vietnam!). They casually and quickly dismiss old industries threatened, or even merely overshadowed, by the new.

The same pundits predicted in the '90s that brick-and-mortar stores would disappear in a few years as Amazon and online shopping conquer the world. Yet in 2015, according to Ychart, online sales accounted for . . . 8 percent of retail sales in the U.S. That was double their share in 2011, and four times the 2004 level, but it is just *8 percent*. Moreover, the growth rate of ecommerce slowed from its annualized long-term rate of 16 percent. In 2017, it was just 14 percent.

Corporate's fear of decline is paradoxical. On the one hand, Corporate is slow to divest what needs to be divested, but on the other, it leaves a lot of money on the table by exiting or shunning industries it should be in with the right strategy. Remember Mark Twain's famous quip, "The reports of my death are greatly exaggerated"? The same is true of what the strategy literature describes as declining industries. Consider these examples:

1. According to Statista, the number of PC computers sold globally in 2015 was a puny 275 million, of which *113 million* were good old desktops. Yes, those dinosaurs that everyone under 25 assumes are extinct until they realize the box in their new cubicle is a computer. Wow. And it does not fit in your palm! OMG. And you can't bump it with another desktop and share music, or what they call music these days, but this is another topic altogether.

2. According to OTA, an organic food trade association, organic food sales in the U.S. in 2016 totaled $47 billion. Its growth rate far outpaced nonorganic food. Impressive, isn't it? Over the same period, however, U.S. fast-food chains sold $200 billion of nonhealthy, nonorganic, nonnutritional foods. McDonald's sales alone came close to $36 billion as reported by *Business Insider* in 2017.

3. Cigarettes, a dying industry in more ways than one, sold *258 million* units in the U.S. alone in 2016. That's a whole lot of dying. Some analysts quoted in an industry trade magazine in 2016 actually call our time the "golden age" of cigarette manufacturers. No, we are not advocating cigarettes. (Mark will not work in the tobacco industry. Ben will work for *any* private company catering to people's choices but not for governments.) The point is that money is being made with cigarettes.

The idea that the only winning strategy is to dive into high-growth markets is the bread and butter of Wall Street and its follow-the-money COOC-formula zealots. The more intriguing perspective is that opportunities exist in declining industries because acquisition prices are low, making it easier to make positive ROIs, and as long as companies learn to *position themselves correctly*, profit can be protected. Altria has 45 percent of the cigarette market in the U.S., and its margins would give smartphone makers heart attacks (as will its product). The health-food campaign is in full force in the mainstream media, telling us that fat is the enemy, sugar is the enemy, calories are the enemy, vegan is the future, and yeasts are the cure, yet fast-food and junk-food companies' profits are healthier than ever (and surely healthier than their customers). YCharts reports that McDonald's profit margin for September 2017 was an incredible 32 percent.

Knowing how to compete in Bloody Red Ocean markets (the opposite of those luscious "Blue Oceans") is a skill worth pursuing. MBA programs do not often teach about these dull industries that make money year after year, even without apps. How boring. Some 2,000 people—executives, students, consultants, professors—have entered Mark's Top Pricer Tournament™,[2] a strategy simulation involving only pricing decisions, that he uses in business school classes and corporate workshops on competitive strategy. As reported in his July 2015 article on HBR.org, 90 percent of the tournament's simulations in the Fast Growth industry produce profits lower than if everyone had done nothing at all, but that's true for only 40 to 50 percent of the simulations in the Ailing and Mature industries.

The latter point is perfectly demonstrated by the newspaper industry, which has been pronounced mortally wounded by most analysts, many writing for the same newspapers they were sure would die. The rise of the digital media led to many executives and staffers in the daily news media moving away from the mentality of "print

---

[2] The Tournament was inspired by, and expands upon, the MacArthur "genius" award-winning book *The Evolution of Cooperation* by political scientist Robert Axelrod of the University of Michigan.

first." That forced daily papers to increase analysis and perspectives, since those seeking the latest news now find it on the web. But to remain profitable and grow, the successful newspapers also adopted different market positioning. Gannett, a large publishing empire, focused on local news. *USA Today*, Gannett's national newspaper, includes a section covering local news in all 50 states with such important breakthrough items as a turtle seen crossing the road in Concord, New Hampshire. (Gannett's local dailies' disclosed even more—the turtle's name was Fluffy.) Thus, *The Des Moines Register* covers local politics (there is a reason Iowa holds the first primary), and the *Coloradoan* focuses on outdoor life. *The Washington Post* focuses on, well, Washington. *The New York Times* invests heavily in positioning itself as the leader in international coverage and has an international edition (formerly the *Herald Tribune*). *The Wall Street Journal*, a pioneer in many aspects of publishing, has always focused on business and investment analysis.

The fact that successful newspapers gravitated to focusing on different needs is a great example of the skill of competing in action. Instead of bleeding each other with price wars, rampant imitation, or casting the widest possible net (mass markets!), the smart players make money by segmenting the market. Competing in a declining industry is not just a tightening game as some analysts would have us believe. It's a positioning game.

But when we try to tell/sell it to Corporate, the response is swift: We are opening a new plant in China! If every Chinese person buys just one product from us, we'll be rich! It is in the spirit of the kid selling lemonade for $10,000 a glass—"I just have to sell one"—and it's not much better.

THE CONSULTANTS BEHIND THE CURTAIN

The obsessive, repetitive reliance on outside consultants (the "Bobs" for you *Office Space* fans) is like a Corporate eating disorder. A competitive-intelligence manager in a pharmaceutical giant told Ben she was instructed by her boss's boss to call a consultant and that "whatever the consultant says, that is our position." Some managers describe their companies as "infused with consultants at every level."

Mind you, we are not blaming the consultants one bit. We understand and agree that companies should "lease" specialists as needed. That makes sense. But when the consultants run the company, why do you need employees at all? Especially, why do you need *executives*? That's not so far-fetched. Companies have outsourced just about everything else.

The use of consultants, however, especially the giant ones, is much less common in China.

Just saying.

---

shirking responsibility

COOC's rituals are aimed at reducing anxiety. People may meditate or visit a hypnotherapist to allay their anxieties. Corporate hires consultants to reduce its anxiety. It becomes a reflex.

Consultants play an important role in Western economies. They spread best practices, diffuse innovations and technology, and help companies deal with areas where it would cost more to maintain the expertise in-house. As part of management doing what's best for the business (and its long-term stakeholders), hiring the best talent on a project basis (i.e., consultants) is smart. However, some companies abuse this practice and become chronic consumers of consulting services because they don't trust their own home-grown talent. Those companies are allowing their skill at competing to atrophy.

There are some roles and capabilities that Corporate should never ever *ever* outsource on a project basis. The number-one capability to keep in-house is strategy, the heart of competing.

---

shirking responsibility, continued

Executives are being paid handsomely to design, test, and carry out the company's strategy. If they farm it out to consultants, they (the executives) should be kicked out or—better—be forced to pay the consultants *out of pocket.* You'll be amazed at how fast multiyear contracts will shrink.

advice to the maverick

So what can you do about Corporate obsessions? Coaches will tell you to position yourself best for the reorganization (trivial), make sure your skills are up to date (trite), keep up with technology (What's that? Sorry, our Skype connection is spotty), and keep the line open to recruiters in case the reorg results in you being made "redundant." The recruiters' advice is always true, but do you need a coach to tell you to keep that line open?

We prefer to tell you the truth. Reorganization almost always hurts morale, confuses employees, and enriches the consultants. It might be appropriate if the market changes, but it is hardly correlating well with these changes, it is almost always late in the game after a crisis, and it covers up a lousy early-warning system at the top. If a reorganization follows a new strategy, it can make sense. If it follows the same strategy formula and is applied like fresh paint on a rusty car so management can appear agile and action-oriented, it's bad.

As a maverick, reorganization can threaten your job, your status, and your hard-earned reputation as the one who has unorthodox ideas. You may have to start over. This is demoralizing. It was hard enough to get your boss's boss to half-heartedly allow you to ask the tough questions, but now you have to train another boss's boss. But you can be prepared: Knowing it is a Corporate dysfunction, you can be proactive in a strategic way.

Being proactive doesn't mean learning R or C++ just because programming is a hot new skill. It does mean the following:

- Make friends across all the possible reorgs. If strategic accounts are the current theme, be sure to make friends in other strategic account teams. If regions are the theme, make friends in other regions. That's not only so you'll have lots of friends but also to learn other perspectives so you'll be especially valuable after the next spin in reorg roulette.

- To quote a rising star Ben worked with recently: Meet five new people a week. She said it was hard with a busy schedule, but it pays off in unexpected ways on many levels. One of them is that when the company reorganizes, she still knows where to find sources of expertise.

When it comes to growth targets, you can use the dysfunction in two ways:

- First, ask the tough questions we proposed in Chapter 9 on the Positivismitis dysfunction. Like this: "This is a great plan—a great idea! It should get us to the 10-percent growth target. I truly don't mean to make any trouble, and I don't have all the data, but could we, *for just a second*, look at it from the perspective of competitors X and Y? If we are to grow market share by 10 percent, are we taking it from X or Y? In which markets? What will they do to fight us?" If your growth target

advice to the maverick, continued

is for revenue, ask, "What are we going to do differently to get that growth?"

- Second, if competitor X announces its growth targets, ask yourself: "Is their plan going to reach this target? What if it doesn't? Are they desperate enough to risk hurting themselves, such as potentially triggering a price war, to reach it? Is their goal ambitious, or is it wishful thinking?"

- Finally, under no circumstances should you antagonize the consultants. They have deep roots in your management. Instead, impress them. They may use your ideas as their own, but then they may also mention your name at the right moment to the right people. Even if they don't, you may get a call from *their* recruiter, and you can have a chance to learn how it feels when the shoe is on the other foot.

Remember that we agree with the coaches on one thing: Keep an open line with recruiters at all times!

who said anything about chapter 11?

C hapter 11? What did you hear? Our cash flow is sound, and we are making progress in restructuring our operations.

does corporate mean what it says?

CHAPTER 12

"But if thought corrupts language, language can also corrupt thought."

—GEORGE ORWELL

Corporate-speak is a universal language heard in large staff meetings, videos from the CEO, interviews for the press, and annual report letters from the Chairman, not to mention spokespeople's responses to any revelation of Corporate wrongdoing and executive interviews on CNBC. It is a stream of words strung together to *appear* logical and meaningful while saying little and committing to nothing.

Corporate-speak is not to be confused with license agreements where language is used to hide or obscure meaning. You must click "agree" to the license agreement to use anything from a clothespin on up. You agree to abjure[1] all claims and give away all rights. You understand that every one of the 17,000 words in fine print shall be interpreted fully, legally, specifically, indubitably, irredeemably, and forever furthermore to favor Corporate.

But we are not here to prepare you for a career in law. We are here to help you survive, compete, and prosper by distinguishing Corporate-speak from real discourse. Of course, by continuing to read, you agree and abjure all claims.

In itself, what's the harm in spouting Corporate-speak like "we will remain vigilant about taking action" (a quotation from Fox Business News) if you are caught with your hand in the honey pot

---

[1] *Abjure* means to solemnly renounce, so be sure to turn that smile upside down when you click on "I agree."

like Wells Fargo? Well, after years of making statements that mean nothing, no one believes you even if you are sincere. It wouldn't matter anyway. "We will remain vigilant about taking action" *doesn't mean anything.*

Why does it matter that some companies can't seem to muster one sincere word in a year or even a decade? It's not as though companies are politicians, for whom our expectations are lower. After all, politicians by default are never sincere. If they mean what they say, they are ludicrous. If they say what they truly mean, no one will vote for them. So why should we have higher expectations for business? Because . . .

Sincerity pays. It pays not just because it is morally superior to lying but because it shows investors, analysts, and employees that you are capable of *facing reality.* Facing reality is a prerequisite to competing skillfully. It is hard to compete when you keep covering up with empty words. That's just slapping paint faster and faster on a crumbling building.

In business school, everyone faces reality when analyzing case studies. Your team project exposes with cold, incisive analysis that the company you dissected was full of undesirable crumbling. Facing that reality is easy because it's not your company and your analysis doesn't threaten your ego. But real life is not a case study. Even consultants find it hard to face reality even though the client is not their company. That's because they depend on the client. As Max Bazerman, a Harvard Business School professor, noted in an interview, that can lead to pleasing management, and management might have goals that conflict with the best interests of the company. In the book *Blind Spots* (Princeton University Press, 2011), Professors Bazerman and Ann Tenbrunsel said "motivated blindness" led Arthur Andersen auditors to vouch for Enron's "financial health during the time that Enron was concealing billions of dollars in debt from its shareholders." Andersen's $25 million in auditing fees and $27 million in consulting fees from Enron were strong motivation indeed.[2]

---

[2] Do not confuse this *Blind Spots* book with Ben's 1994 *Business Blindspots* book. Since Ben published his book, it seems there are blind spots as far as the eye can see.

We assume every company wants to be sincere once in a while. There is even a new company called Honest to highlight the problem with honesty in consumer products. Sure, *Time* magazine has reported that this company, created by actress Jessica Alba to sell nontoxic, eco-friendly products for parents, has been accused of deceptive labeling, but so it goes. It had been in talks (that eventually failed; we honestly don't know why) to be acquired by Unilever, which CNN reported bought Seventh Generation (apparently an honest Honest competitor) instead.

In this chapter, we expose for the first time in the history of the Western world the true meaning behind the words used by Corporate and its representatives. If our revelations shock you, you haven't been a maverick for very long. The older mavericks will say, "Don't worry, younger maverick, you'll get used to it," which is resigned-maverick-speak for "that part of your brain will shut down."

Part of *your* brain has probably shut down. Unless, that is, you (or your attorney) pay attention to the convenient asterisk.

FULL DISCLOSURE, OR THE CONVENIENT ASTERISK*

We ate healthful breakfasts in a hotel. Fresh fruit, plain Greek yogurt, and single-serving boxes of Raisin Bran cereal.

Each box practically promised immortality. "10%* daily value of 11 vitamins & minerals," it pledged. With each bite, we could feel ourselves bursting with fitness and glowing with health. Our biceps prepared to explode our shirtsleeves.

Then we noticed the asterisk. "*Based on a 53g serving. This box contains 33g." The box had 62 percent of the daily value of those 11 nutrients, and 38 percent baloney. Our shirts were safe.

Yes, the box disclosed the truth. Then again, it could have said "Lifetime* supply of 11 vitamins & minerals." The asterisk would then whisper, "*Based on a 1,547,600g serving. This box contains 33g." That would have been true, too.

The only reason for the 100 percent-plus-asterisk is that the company making the cereal decided they'd compete better with a grandiose claim^{and an asterisk} than with a straight-talking 62 percent. They didn't choose "100 percent*" because it was deceptive; they chose "100 percent*" because they thought it would create better results for the company.

To be fair, this company isn't the only one to use asterisks. As asterisks go, theirs was pretty tame. They didn't even ask the cereal-eater to abjure anything. And yet it's clear that no customer would prefer the slightly sneaky 100 percent claim over full disclosure or, better still, a claim of 100 percent combined with *delivery* of 100 percent.

By the way, the company is well-known. You have heard of it. You might like to know that its website lists its corporate values, of which the most prominent is "we do the right thing, all the time." No asterisk.

You might shrug and say, "So what?" After all, asterisks (and fine print and disclaimers) are everywhere. But the asterisks didn't write themselves and stick themselves on cereal boxes. People wrote them and stuck them, and they didn't do so because they love writing words they hope no one will read. They wrote them and stuck them because *they thought it was skillful competing.* And just as it's cheaper to put "do not overtighten" on assembly instructions than to make the product overtightening-proof, it's cheaper to put ink on the cereal box than it is to put more ingredients inside.

If you shrugged and said, "So what?" you have demonstrated the wholesale cheapening of customer expectations in the U.S. And *that,* maverick, is an opportunity because races to the bottom have left the field wide open in many industries to differentiate yourself with small-h honesty. If you want to compete, do something your competitors aren't doing.

FULL DISCLOSURE: MARKET LEADERSHIP

Corporate doesn't talk only to outsiders. It talks to itself, too.

---

the opposite of an asterisk

KIND, a small New York-based maker of healthy snacks, has this unusual statement on its website: "Daniel Lubetzky is on a mission to build bridges between people. He is the Founder & CEO of KIND, a not-*only*-for-profit that makes delicious and nutritious snack foods. Drawing on his experiences in the food industry, Lubetzky recently founded an independent organization called Feed the Truth, which seeks to improve public health by making truth and transparency the foremost values in today's food system." The company even registered a trademark, Nothing to hide®. In 2017, Mars bought a minority stake in this company that valued the company at $4 billion.

Honesty pays.

Corporate executives use the term "leadership" 1,008,976 times in every given year. It appears in every speech, to employees, shareholders, market analysts, and strangers on a plane alike. That's saying "leadership," give or take, every 31.3 seconds. Leaders "R" Us. How many companies have you come across that willingly describe themselves as risk-averse *followers*? (Hint: Pick a number very close to zero. *Very* close.)

Now, market leadership is a, shall we say, *flexible* concept. Leadership can be defined by quality, price, reliability, technology, customer service, prestige, or, well, anything. But leadership is most often defined as market share (or, almost equivalently, sales). That's still not entirely clear; market share in which market segment? When antitrust regulators march in, market leaders claim puny market share by defining the market in galactic terms. Naturally, if we assume there are at least a few more consuming societies in the Milky Way, how significant is 60 percent market share in the U.S.? Some investigators have been known to hold back their tears during meetings with these sad, hapless executives from global market-leader companies as they struggle to keep up with galactic forces.

Let's assume we *are* the market leader. What does it mean? We go first? We have the highest price? We have the lowest price? We have the biggest share? We have the most innovative products? We speak, and others obey? We are the oldest? We are the most respected? Says who, besides us?

"Market leader" implies more than size; it implies authority. What's a leader without followers? Curiously, though, we have only rarely heard managers describe their businesses (or themselves) as followers. (Perhaps only market leaders contact us.) And those who *do* call themselves "followers" add quickly that they are *fast* followers. They are *almost* leaders, without the risks of being first to leap.

If "market leadership" is so meaningless, why is it so important? Ego? A sense of accomplishment or security? Those would make "market leadership" *worse* than meaningless; they'd make the term dangerous because it is a *false* sense of security that lulls Corporate into overconfidence.

Leadership requires some distinction. If you look like the herd, how can you be the leader? Leaders walk up front. They lead by example. They make decisions that change industries. But if you look closely at some of the companies known as market leaders, you find little leadership. What you find is jockeying, where companies take turns nosing ahead of each other. This month, *we're* number one in sales growth for the coveted 18-to-35-year-old demographic! Of course, unfortunately, it means someone else has snatched the number-one title for 82-to-103-year-old marathon runners. We should address this oversight.

Competitive Convergence

In strategy, jockeying behavior is the result of "competitive convergence." Companies look alike, behave alike, make similar noises, and leave similar footprints. Some industries have completely competitively converged: pharmaceuticals, telecommunications, superhero movies.

Of course, if you ask pick-an-industry executives, they will vehemently deny convergence and, as proof, show you that the paper clips at their company are from a different supplier than the competitor across the street. *Completely* different supplier. And look, we've got 19.72 percent of the coveted 5-foot-9-inch-to-5-foot-10-inch, partially-balding male segment, a full 0.32 percent ahead of our competitors! We lead!

Competitive convergence is not a law of physics. Convergence is the result of how Corporate competes: Treat the market as "yours" by divine privilege and maximize our demand by selling everything to everyone at every price. If we abandon 54-to-55-year-old Norwegians in odd-numbered ZIP codes to focus on everyone else, our sales will *go down*.[3] Someone else will be the market leader!

case study: walmart and costco

Convergence is not inevitable, and "leadership" and "differentiation" are not just empty slogans or fantasy goals. For proof, look no further than retailing. We have Walmart, and we have Costco.

Walmart offers everything, more or less, to people looking for reasonable quality at relatively low prices (as opposed to poor quality at rock-bottom prices like some low-end retailers). It doesn't try to serve everyone, just the frugal shopper looking for reasonable quality. That's a big segment, but it is not everyone. It operates humongous stores because "everything"

---

[3] If you noted the logical fallacy, kudos to you! The fallacy is that sales must go down if we pull back from a segment. Sales *in that segment* will go down, but we will enhance our ability to customize our products for other segments, and that can cause sales in those segments to rise.

case study: walmart and costco, continued

is a lot. Offering everything to a lot of people in humongous stores requires armies of low-paid but happy-to-have-a-job "associates."

Anyone who tries to imitate Walmart at this point in time is irrational. Scale and bargaining power play a huge role when you want to keep prices down. So how come Costco succeeds, too? Costco doesn't try to imitate Walmart. Although it sells food and nonfood items just like Walmart, its business model is very different from Walmart's. Costco doesn't offer everything, and it doesn't sell to all frugal shoppers. It locates only in more affluent areas and sells to the affluent in bulk. Its prices are very good, but you have to buy in large quantity. It carries a limited number of high-quality brands, plus a high-quality private label. It employs relatively few people.

But most revealing about this retailer, which works diligently not to imitate other retailers, is its culture of openness and honesty. According to Exploringmarkets.com, Costco's cofounder James Sinegal was known to call reporters on Saturday and leave his cellphone number and has said publicly that he doesn't have lofty growth goals. Bloomberg reports that his successor, Craig Jelinek, has a faux-wood table in his boardroom, has no PR department, and preaches simplicity.

Walmart relies on bargain-hunting customers who come in and get out. Costco makes the store a "happening." It doesn't talk about leadership at all. Instead, it focuses on the best price for good quality and defines its competitive advantage not in vague leadership terms but as customer and employee loyalty.

case study: walmart and costco, continued

Quoted by Balance, a news site, Sinegal once said, "This is almost like show business. I mean, every day you're opening up and it's show time." Ben and Mark shop at Costco, at opposite ends of the country (Florida and Oregon), and they can attest to that. In both places, customers come to the store for social interaction with neighbors and workers who give free samples of featured foods as much as for purchases. In Florida, Costco employs senior citizens to operate food-sampling stations. The crowd loves freebies. *Loves* freebies, no matter what they are. The lines to get to the cheese-on-a-tiny-cracker are longer than the lines at the Department of Motor Vehicles.

In addition, Costco is "unreliable." It drops items without warning. You may buy a favorite brand for several months, and then, poof, it disappears. Why? Maybe the brand did not sell fast enough. Or maybe they just figured the buyer won't remember what they bought the week before. This unpredictability extends to shelf space. Every few months, Costco relocates some merchandise so customers have to search for their favorites. In that search, customers may serendipitously discover pickled herring. Impulse buying has been elevated to an art form at Costco. So has walking. To help the health of its shoppers, Costco never labels the aisles. Go search, Marty!

Costco and Walmart have not converged mostly because Costco's founders fought tooth and nail to keep its distinction without obsessing about "market leadership." Smartphone and laptop makers are converging: All of them can run all apps. (It wasn't always that way. BlackBerry and its "hard" keyboard used to lead the market. Now

---

case study: walmart and costco, continued

it specializes in high-security business communications.) AT&T and
Verizon converged. Domestic air travel in the U.S. has converged so
much that American Airlines, Delta Air Lines, and United Airlines are
almost adjacent on the Fortune 500 list. If you didn't know their distinctive colors, and if you couldn't hear the commotion of passengers being
dragged off flights, you wouldn't know whose aircraft you were on.

Convergence Is Not an Accident

Here's how convergence happens and where convergence leads.

As they develop their symptoms of Corporate, once-great
companies begin chasing each other's tails to keep being the "leader."
(We've seen that dynamic play out at warp speed in our business war
games.) One adds a new feature; the others say they must offer that
feature, too, or else they'll be at a competitive disadvantage. Sales
commissions incentivize salespeople to *demand* convergence because
they, rationally, don't want to lose the deal because they don't have
that feature. They abandon focus for fear of "leaving money on the
table" and no longer being hailed as the leader. As an ironic result,
buyers' price sensitivity increases since buyers see no differences in
the products or services themselves. Price is all that's left.

When price is all that's left, cost becomes all that matters.
Consequently, companies merge and acquire to attain economies of
scale to reduce costs even more. When every company has the same
goal—low costs to enable the best prices—they look more and more
alike. Buyers see even less difference between the companies than
before, and so on and so forth, until antitrust authorities do them
part . . . or until upstarts disrupt the convergence with an idea the
incumbents could have had if they'd spent less time jockeying and
more time strategizing.

You can't blame executives for pushing leadership. Investors love hearing that they've invested in market leaders. (So do the other investors who invested in the competing market leaders.) Employees cheer when they say it in large gatherings. From a classic *Harvard Business Review* article in 1999, "Why Good Companies Go Bad," Donald Sull charges that successful companies—market-leading companies—develop active inertia. The Corporate-speak overuse of "leading" becomes an obstacle to strategic change because when we believe we have achieved market-leader status, then we believe our competitive job is done.

CALLING INNOVATION WHAT IT IS

Nowhere is Corporate-speak more pronounced (hah!) than in the area of innovation. Being innovative is as much a Corporate mantra as being the market leader.

OK, folks, let's get real. Powered flight was an innovation. The internet was an innovation. Double-entry bookkeeping was an innovation designed to make business school students miserable for centuries (five, so far). Indoor plumbing, central heating, eyeglasses, paint, rulers, nails, algebra, antibiotics, pianos, money—they were innovations. Wall-to-wall carpeting, *American Idol*, and supersized fries are *not*. Detroit's resurrected old cars, or at least old car names— Camaro, Challenger, Charger, and Mustang—are also *not* innovations.

You already know how to get past Corporate-speak about innovations. All you have to do is *call things what they are*. A new flavor is a product-line extension, a new SKU, or just, well, a new flavor. It is not an innovation, and you are not innovative when you propose it.

How about competing without innovation? Now *there's* an innovative strategy! "New" isn't the only thing customers care about. Sometimes they just want a company to keep its promises, such as offering Raisin Bran cereal that delivers 100 percent and doesn't need an asterisk.

A corollary of "innovative" that has spread like wildfire in Corporate-speak is *disruptive*, a term made popular in the book

The Innovator's Dilemma (HarperBusiness, 2011) by Clayton Christensen. Christensen, a disruptive member of the Harvard Business School faculty, advocated that HBS go online with free courses. Christensen's most disruptive influence has been on strategic thinking. We remember days when competition was just that: competition. Now, in every war game we run, someone, sometime, will describe a competitor as a disruptor.

corporate-speak phrase book

To prepare you, dear maverick, for navigating the world of jargon and yes-people, you're going to need a translator. Consider this your quick guide to what Corporate is saying and what it really means.

Phrase: We will achieve our objectives by . . .
Translation: Let us pray . . .

P: We will leverage our substantial assets.
T: We'll figure it out later.

P: New and improved!
T: Warmed up and tweaked.

P: People are our most important asset.
T: Please think that we care about people.

P: People are our most important asset.
T: My HR person said I should say something nice about people.

P: People are our most important asset.
T: But I have more data about the number of staplers in the office.

P: People are our most important asset.
T: People are not our most important asset.

---

corporate-speak phrase book, continued

P: Rightsizing.

T: Making other people pay for my prior mistakes.

P: Core competency.

T: What I like to do.

P: Make it happen.

T: I haven't got a clue, so it's your problem.

P: Considering our alternatives to respond.

T: Full panic.

P: Big data.

T: 5,340,986,098,150,498,260,983,409,809,821,340,981.99

P: Strategic pricing.

T: Anything with .99 at the end.

P: Failure is not an option.

T: We're all going to die!

The real irony? Corporate probably wouldn't even realize we are poking fun at it. It takes a sense of humor to appreciate irony, but Corporate is a place where two senses, common and of-humor, may be scarce.

SCORE! CORPORATE-SPEAK SPORTS METAPHORS

Corporate *loves* sports metaphors. It is part of Corporate's infatuation with anything "motivational." Corporate relies on football during Super Bowl season. The rest of the year, it is typically business and baseball except for "slam dunk," which is always allowed.

What can business learn from football? Nothing. *Absolutely nothing.* But that won't stop companies from applying sports metaphors to business.

It takes less time than an instant replay to reveal that those metaphors just don't fit. Yes, football and business involve team play. So does kindergarten. Aside from that, football (or baseball, or synchronized swimming) has nothing to do with business.

The football season ends, while business is a bunch of going concerns.[4] A football season ends in victory or defeat, while it is far from clear what victory even looks like in business. Football deploys physical moves that have no parallel in business. What, "fake left and then go deep" is a lesson business should heed? Most important, football requires playing by rigidly enforced rules and regulations. There is nothing to innovate unless you consider avoiding concussions innovative.

There is one thing Corporate can learn from football. NFL teams take rivalry very seriously. They endlessly analyze the moves and countermoves of every team coming against them. They watch movies, send scouts, listen to the calls (no, that's the National Security Agency), and never take them for granted. They run simulations, war-game exercises, and more. Then they adjust their game plan (more beloved Corporate-sports-speak) to block the expected rival.

Compare that to the Corporate playbook: If we're trailing in the seventh inning, double down on what hasn't worked, but call it "game-changing strategy."

Game Changing, Corporate Style

Mavericks are all about changing the game (that's what disruption actually means), but if you call, say, an Oreo cookie with peanut-butter filling a "game changer," the term loses its meaning. But that is exactly what happened in this game-not-changing story.

---

[4] A "going concern" means the CEO keeps worrying.

Ben ran a war game for a large medical-device company. It was the market leader by volume. That was a new thing for the company. The former market leader—a consumer-marketing powerhouse—had fallen on hard times. The client, with a newer product portfolio and a smart strategy of marketing to doctors rather than to patients, moved to the number-one position.

Then, though, doctors became less important in making purchase decisions. Large corporate buyers, employing hundreds of doctors, took their place. Corporate buyers think differently from individual physicians: They want better terms, lower prices, and more flexibility, qualities that the client lacked. Worse, a competitor adapted to the corporate buyers' preferences, and rapidly gained market share in corporate clinics.

During the war-game simulation, a team proposed raising doctors' switching costs by training them on the company's medical device for a year after they graduated medical school. Moreover, during that year, the doctors could treat patients in facilities financed by the client. The trained doctors would then be matched with corporate buyers who won't have to invest in the doctors' training, and so will benefit from their practical experience. The newly minted doctors in their corporate jobs will more likely bring their device preferences with them.

The idea was risky, entrepreneurial, fraught with regulatory and other hurdles, far from being a sure thing. It was also utterly strategic. The idea's value was not that success was guaranteed, because it wasn't. Its value was the attempt to address directly the strategic risk of the rise of corporate buyers and the decline of independent practices.

In the months following that war game, the executive team decided instead to require doctors (mostly small practices) to buy a high percentage of their medical devices from the company if they wanted access to the more popular products. Not a bad strategy. Intel used it brilliantly with PC makers, for example. But PC makers had few alternatives, whereas doctors could switch easily to another supplier. Oh, well. The marketing VP then boldly proposed raising the trade incentives to these doctors from 10 percent to 12 percent.

The sticking point that made management uncomfortable was that the "train and imprint preferences" idea was "too much out there;" *too much* leadership. They didn't say it that way. They said it was too difficult to execute, but they were clearly uncomfortable with getting so far ahead of the pack. In effect, the executives reduced the skill of competing to repeating past behavior, only a bit more so. After all, they did propose to raise incentives by two whole percentage points!

We can understand, if not exactly admire, the executives' reluctance to adopt such a radical (in the sense of unprecedented) strategy. Unless the circumstances are dire, humans care more about avoiding losses than about achieving gains. Disappointments are not as bad, to the company or the career, as disasters. Boosting incentives might fall short, but "train and imprint preferences" might blow up. It is bad for the career, however, to admit risk aversion when Corporate culture pretends to encourage "bold leadership." When the executives harmonized that pretense with their risk aversion, they issued this Corporate-speak:

> *This war game successfully surfaced some long-term strategic challenges we must confront honestly and proactively. We thank the people participating in this excellent workshop for their hard work, innovative thinking, and great recommendations. After careful thought, management decided the best course of action is to continue our successful program of distribution with increased emphasis on distributors' incentives.*

The president of the division, by the way, was forced out about a year and a half later as the division's performance slipped. The entire division was spun off later.

advice to the maverick

Consultants and coaches will say there is nothing wrong in inspirational and motivational adjectives, such as *leading, game-changing, working diligently to solve the issues*, and so forth. They boost employees' morale, assuage the investing community, and calm the nervous nellies. But as a maverick, you should know better. Reread the quotation at the beginning of the chapter; it is powerful. Then, if you have to meet with a coach, ask them what they think about the quotation. If it makes them uncomfortable, walk away.

You may suspect we hate business because we mock insincere messages, sloppy language, and trite adjectives. So it's time to clarify: Corporate-speak is not the issue. What it *hides* is the issue.

It is also time to emphasize that Corporate is not enterprise in general. Enterprise is wonderful! It is responsible for our comfortable lives and the end of hardship for more and more of humanity. Without enterprise, we would still be serfs to kings toiling in small farms. Corporate with a capital "C," though, refers to companies exhibiting the symptoms of overconfident, oblivious cultures. The first survival rule for mavericks is to learn to distinguish between Kool-Aid and cool aid, between great-places-to-work corporations and Corporate, because no one in business school or job interviews says anything about Corporate-speak.

Corporate-speak permeates all the way down to your immediate boss. Team leaders, product managers, and sales managers will use Corporate-speak, perhaps subconsciously, perhaps to avoid the discomfort of straight talk. When we meet a straight talker, it is an unexpected pleasure. A straight talker is almost always a maverick.

advice to the maverick, continued

The risk to your career is that if you try to be a straight talker right away, seasoned managers, bosses, and peers are going to assume you are arrogant. If you challenge a statement on leading the market or a metaphor on slam-dunk initiatives, you are not a good team player. So as a maverick, go along. Nod, smile, cheer, and applaud. You can put in a humorous zinger once in a while, in response to another "touchdown," "home run," or "sweeping the series" metaphor, by suggesting (with a chuckle) that the similarity with your business is that both your company and the winning team know it's temporary. Next season, it all starts again.

what corporate does

corporate burns money as it gets big and "fat"

CHAPTER 13

"American consumers have
no problem with carcinogens,
but they will not purchase any
product, including floor wax,
that has fat in it."

—Dave Barry

If you learn to identify Corporate-speak, you are one step closer to being able to diagnose early signs of metabolic problems.

Some diseases have no early-warning signs, though. Like the flu, all of a sudden, they just flare up. Others start with very small indications. Unimportant and relatively harmless, these symptoms are typically ignored. Such is the case of skin cancer, for example, where a small mole may change its shape. And some diseases take years or decades to manifest, such as obesity.

People can be obese, and so, too, can companies. Obese companies tend to be bloated with money to burn, gathered over time until the Corporate scale breaks. In this chapter, we examine the various ways Corporate spends money on frivolous, uncompetitive activities. We equip you with diagnostic tools so you can recognize Corporate binging. We conclude with the biggest waste of all, acquisitions, which, as research suggests, are delicious to eat but hard to digest. The ultimate reason Corporate throws money down the drain: because it can.

To ensure that you read this chapter carefully, we designed a quick quiz of general knowledge (see Figure 13.1 on page 200). A prize for correct answers will be announced at the end of this chapter.

Q1: DRUGS
Which of the following is the name of an actual drug?

1. Mxyzptlk
2. Xeljanz
3. ArtiChoke Extra Strength
4. Margaret
5. Fubar

Q2: FAMOUS ADVICE
Famed business consultant and teacher Peter Drucker said:

1. Make sure you measure the right things.
2. If you can't measure it, you can't manage it.
3. If it's worth managing, you must measure it.
4. You can't measure what's really important, but it's OK.
5. True leaders lead. Only accountants and engineers measure.
6. Measure this! (obscene gesture)

Q3: PRUDENT USE OF MONEY
Unnecessary spending can be called:

1. Free cash flow
2. EBIDTA
3. Free fat flow
4. Executive prerogative
5. Investment
6. Taxes

FIGURE 13.1— **Test Your Pre-Existing Knowledge**

Q4: LIFE

The most dangerous stage in a company's lifecycle is:

1. Entrepreneurial start
2. Rapid growth
3. Consolidation
4. Convergence
5. Death
6. Right after it hired you

Q5: FAILURE

Famed strategist and Harvard Business School professor Michael Porter found that when corporations acquire a company in a different industry:

1. 12 percent of acquisitions fail
2. 33 percent of acquisitions fail
3. 50 percent of acquisitions fail
4. 74 percent of acquisitions fail
5. 90 percent of acquisitions fail
6. No acquisition ever fails

Q6: PILES OF CASH

The amount of cash held by American companies in 2017 was:

1. $1,900,000,000,000
2. $190,000,000,000
3. $19,000,000,000
4. $1,900,000,000
5. $190,000,000
6. $1.90

The answers are at the end of this chapter.

FIGURE 13.1— **Test Your Pre-Existing Knowledge,** continued

THE CORPORATE LIFECYCLE

The lifecycle theory of business, just like the lifecycle model of products, is about the progression of companies from beginning to end.

At the start, companies are lean, mean, motivated, and terrifically strategic. If they're not, they fail before we even know they've been there.

Then, as their terrific strategy bears fruit, the company becomes successful: bigger, happier, . . . and fatter. Its founders depart. The hired guns who take their places start to expand the portfolio of offerings. Inevitably, at this stage, the uniqueness of the strategy starts to fray at the edges as competitors enter the same space. The competitive race then moves away from the focused and distinct strategy of the founders and into an imitation game—the competitive convergence of the previous chapter—in which each company chases the others while providing the benchmarking consultants with a wonderful, richly rewarded lifecycle of their own.

The companies grow so big, the only way to grow more is to buy each other. They consolidate to gain economies of scale. Now we have a few very big, very happy, and very fat giants *that look alike*. They all offer everything to everybody in every market. They all use Big Data to tweak their products in ever-smaller ways. They all offer sales on the same holidays. If someone put you on an airplane with your eyes closed, could you tell which airline it is when you open them? Maybe only if you fly Emirates. When you open your eyes, you realize you are on a magic carpet.

And then, out of left field (remember the sports metaphors) comes a new company with a distinctive strategy and kills them all. The left field—it is always left field, never right field—can be doing completely different things or doing the same things differently, which turn out to be better for the customers. An alternative technology producing completely different products, like cellphones vs. corded phones, is an example of the former. Much more efficient operations that yield similar products at a cost that the incumbents just have no chance to match, like textiles made in Bangladesh or newspapers delivered over the internet, are examples of the latter.

Here's a hint: If surprises always come out of left field, perhaps you should watch what's going on in left field. Better still, *imagine* what *could* go on in left field, and do it yourself. And if the right field is the predictable one, your move to the left may surprise others. That's the "Circle of Life" (cue music from *The Lion King*, please).

In business-school case discussions, the teacher points at the incumbents' inability to adapt to change as the reason for their decline. But that explanation doesn't go far enough. *Why* can't the incumbents adapt? Because they have become too fat to move fast. They recognize the change; they are just stuck in the door frame.

Diagnosis: Corporate Obesity

What's obesity in business? As companies consolidate, grow, and prosper, they accumulate "fat" in several forms: Large cash reserves, surpluses in department budgets at the end of the year, or a bureaucratic maze of business units, product lines, partners, and subsidiaries. What started out as a lean and mean organization is now a fattened calf of a company. This phenomenon of huge, complex organizations accumulating additional businesses around the core at a rate faster than the accounting department can keep track is at times comical. How do they know who works for whom? How does HQ know which subsidiary is theirs or their competitor's?

No one talks about it as putting on weight, of course. It's Corporately incorrect and a negative word. Instead, executives use Corporate-speak to talk about "moving increasingly into . . . ," "securing our future with additional vital . . . ," "offering a wide range of solutions," "meeting new customers' needs," and the capstone, "ensuring our leadership position in a wide range of industries."

In human terms, we say, "This company has money to burn." It's like a rapper coming into a club with his entourage and buying a $15,000 bottle of champagne even though he can't even tell the difference between Dom Perignon and Pepsi.

There is no clear financial measure of Corporate fat that can be taught at a business school. Some small fat reserves become obvious toward the end of the annual budget cycle when departments and functions rush to spend what is left of their budget so they don't get their budget cut the next year. You know this spending is not essential because if it were, they would have already spent it. But this spending is just peanuts. Categorically corpulent Corporate spends billions on uncompetitive activities—a.k.a., free fat flow.

Free Fat Flow

We call silly, unnecessary, or outrageous spending or investments *free fat flow* (modeled after free cash flow, a financial concept). Free fat flow is clearly exhibited in investments and spending that defy competitive logic or economic principles but are publicly hailed by the CEOs and their Boards as essential to "positioning the company for the future." In some Corporate headquarters, teams of PR and Investor Relations people burn the midnight oil trying to recycle optimistic statements as the fat flows freer and faster than the available Corporate-speak.

Free fat flow is the classic warning sign that the company is approaching a heart attack. The classic home remedy following the crisis is to slim down considerably via laying off a third or more of the work force. So mavericks should be wary of free spending by top management even as they enjoy some of the perks. As a 2013 article in *Inc.* magazine proclaimed, big companies' perks grow old quickly, and nap pods, bike lanes, and video game rooms do not compensate for deaf top management. And when times turn bad (e.g., heart attacks), management takes away the perks and the loss feels worse than the happiness when it introduced them.

Today, Apple, Microsoft, Cisco, Alphabet (Google's parent), and other giants have enormous cash reserves tucked away in tax shelters outside the U.S. There is absolutely nothing illegal about it. But here is a prediction: When you have so much free fat, you'll be spending like the proverbial sailor on shore leave or like an unfortunate lottery winner.

A bulging cash stockpile is not necessarily evidence of free fat, though. It is not wasteful to use cash to make strategic acquisitions at a reasonable price, to experiment with ventures with good competitive strategies (not just wishful thinking), or even to pay dividends to stockholders. Holding profits as cash in low-tax countries to save on taxes may still serve the interests of stakeholders.

Also, the size of the stockpile is not necessarily an indicator of potential waste, depending on the size of the industry. Thus, pharmaceutical giants Amgen and Gilead Sciences have together about $60 billion stashed away as of June 2017, but as buying the rights to even one miracle drug can cost a fortune, this cash is not necessarily a sign of lax competitiveness.

So we conclude: Corporate fat would be a great predictor of decline . . . if only we could *measure* it.

Peter Drucker is *rumored* to have said, "If you can't measure it, you can't manage it." He didn't actually say it. What he said was make sure you measure the right things. So measuring the wrong things because they can be measured is one example of wasteful activity—and a little, clot-sized part of free fat flow. Bringing a famous basketball coach or a former president to an annual sales meeting for a motivational speech at $10,000 per motivated second is another. Bring in a less-famous person; *they're* motivated! Then there's good old CCH (Chapter 2). And spending $15 million on a commercial in the Super Bowl without a shred of evidence it raises sales in the long run (not just the Madison Avenue's hyped-up "awareness") is another.

We can't directly measure Corporate fat and its associated wasteful spending, but we can present a graph. Companies spend a lot of free fat flow on software that translates data into graphs even if the data is meaningless and (therefore) so is the graph. Executives love graphs. Hence, our graph of Corporate BMI (Body Mass Index) in Figure 13.2 on page 206.

At the entrepreneurial stage, companies have very little "fat." There's just enough to get coffee in the morning and rent a bicycle for the founders so they can travel from their garages to the nearest Kinko's office. Kinko's itself couldn't afford much fat since it served entrepreneurs with little free fat flow. FedEx bought Kinko's and renamed it FedEx Office. FedEx is relatively fat free because its

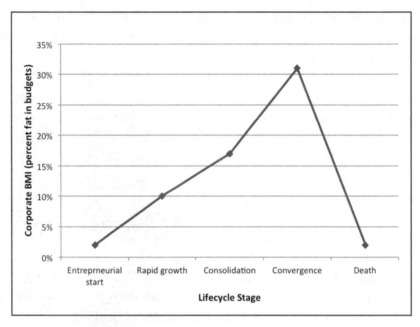

FIGURE 13.2—Gilad-Chussil Corporate BMI Index Measured Along
Various Lifecycle Stages

founder is still the boss. This is a great stage to work for a company as mavericks have real influence, see real action, and exercise real impact.

If the company grows rapidly, and especially if it expands globally, "fat" grows with it. Our carefully controlled double-blind studies ("double blind" as in neither of us can see where we put the files) suggest BMI at that stage is around 10 percent of the total budget, and mostly spent on more lavish executive travel (enough with the bicycle!) and dubious client entertainment. Some of that fat is diverted into free coffee or free snacks for all employees or even a chance to see an A-list movie star at a product launch party. But don't be fooled by the fun: That fat could be better spent on keeping the company competitive, funding your projects, or planning for the long run.

When the industry consolidates, our big player, one of the few remaining, has considerably more "fat"—around 17 percent on average (adjusted for industry's average profitability measured as risk-adjusted return on assets, or raROA, and if you believe this parenthetical note, you are already an OOP).

By the time convergence is complete, where the large incumbents look alike and chase each other's tails, Corporate fat is the highest, reaching a peak of around 31 percent. Naturally, some industries, like pharmaceuticals, are known to reach much higher nominal BMIs, but then pharma is a special case. You have no idea how expensive it is to invent, synthesize, and submit for clinical trials unpronounceable drug names starting with X or Z. The drug discovery process itself is a walk in the park by comparison.

But even the fortunes paid for unpronounceable drug names pale next to the fortunes paid for failed acquisitions. Failed acquisitions are the main Corporate route to metabolic disaster.

"ANOTHER SCOOP OF M&A, PLEASE"

Corporate gains weight through mergers and acquisitions (M&A). M&A are part and parcel of the business reality. They can serve to increase efficiencies, enter new markets, expand products, and acquire new technologies. If M&A activities follow competitive logic, they can be financially rewarding to *all* stakeholders.

Alas, they don't. On a grand scale. Instead, to Corporate leaders, acquisitions are just like playing Monopoly.

In 1987, Michael Porter, then a young academic at Harvard Business School, published a seminal research study called "From Competitive Advantage to Corporate Strategy" (*Harvard Business Review*, May-June 1987). In it, he explained that while business-unit strategy deals with achieving competitive advantage in a given industry (the hallmark of skill in competing), small-c corporate strategy deals with what industries/businesses the company should be in and how to manage the portfolio of businesses. These are two very different competing skills.

In that rather iconoclastic article, Porter made the claim that the "track record of corporate strategies has been dismal." He backed it up by showing that the diversification records of 33 large U.S. companies over the period of 36 years amounted to a colossal failure of previous acquisitions. On average, more than half the acquisitions in new industries and 60 percent in new fields were divested later. Almost *three quarters* of the acquisitions in unrelated industries failed. In other words, even companies that were bellwethers in their core businesses failed miserably when they wandered into adjacent territories through acquisitions.

Why is this "ancient" article important today? Because U.S. companies are awash in cash. Companies now have twice as much cash, as a percentage of total assets, as they did about 30 years ago. Their pockets are bulging with $1.9 *trillion* in cash. When companies are awash in cash, they, like any other consumer, want to spend it. No wonder companies are acquiring—and with that track record, most of the time they won't be happy.[1]

The reason companies hoard cash is that they are uncertain about the economic future. Just like individuals, they keep cash as a rainy-day buffer. But the pressure to use this cash is growing. You can shield yourself against torrential rain for many days with $1.9 trillion. And other than dividends or stock buybacks, what is the "safest," least controversial way to use cash, build legacies, and satisfy the need for instant growth? Acquisitions! Designing superior competitive strategies is hard. Buying *other* people's competitive successes is much easier.

So what does it all mean to you? Why should you care that your management is wasting billions or buying other peoples' success at inflated prices? Because, as we stated early, the reckoning day is getting closer. Mavericks everywhere want to see their companies stay competitive. If, instead, Corporate struggles to digest large acquisitions, you can bet that keeping it competitive will become

---

[1] When times are bad, such as the 2008 financial crisis, companies do the opposite: They clutch their cash and cut their costs. That's understandable, but it's also ironic. Ironic because prices go down in bad times, so buying is cheap. They wait instead for good times, and that's when prices go up. Buy high, sell low.

harder by the day. What can you do in your cubicle? Not much. M&A is the game reserved to the "big boys and girls." You can, however, advocate smarter spending in your corner of the world. Smarter spending now is better than cutting costs later. Always think about which activities are strategic and which spend money for no other reason than "this is how we always do things around here."

The attitude of "What do I care? It's not my money" is shortsighted. It is your money, eventually, because when free fat flow replaces strategic investments, you'll pay with your job. Just ask the managers at General Electric.

pricing pitfalls

We would expect companies to learn from Porter's breakthrough analysis. Well, you forget we're talking Corporate with a capital "C." While not every acquisition is bad and not every synergy is fictional, one prevalent problem is pricing an acquisition. A unique investment fund called the Merger Fund (symbol MERFX) takes advantage of the Corporate "winner's curse." The winner's curse stipulates that the winner of a bid (such as for a company's shares) doesn't just pay the highest price; it also tends to *over*pay.

One reasonable assumption is that if you are flush with cash—that is, if you are "fat"—you will find paying a high premium easy to digest (at least in comparison with other bidders who have to count every penny). The Merger Fund's first strategy is to buy the stock of target companies *after* a merger/acquisition deal is announced and to hold it *until* the deal is closed. *Barron's* explains that the theory behind that strategy is known as the takeover arbitrage spread: Prices of takeover companies are traded at a discount to the final deal price.

pricing pitfalls, continued

That strategy is not interesting in itself. It relies on simple risk-management reasoning: The uncertainty about whether the deal will close makes the target's stock price lag the deal price (that and the time value of money). But MERFX's second strategy is fascinating: It *shorts* the *acquiring* company's stock. It bets that the stock price of the *acquiring company* will *fall*.

Why would the price fall? Because of the winner's curse. History shows that it is likely that Corporate will *overpay for the acquisition*. (Or, equivalently, that Corporate will not produce the value from the acquisition that it expects.) Markets know that. Corporate has free-fat-flow money to burn, whether through excess cash or easy borrowing. While experts advise people who'd like to keep their BMI low to eat small portions and chew carefully, Corporate likes to gorge. Price is no object. "Supersize me," says Corporate.

Markets are typically (though not always) right. They represent the experience, beliefs, predictions, and analysis of thousands of experts and hundreds of M&A deals. Investing.com, a research site, reports that the Merger Fund posted positive returns for over ten years, supporting the hypothesis that acquirers pay too much. Acquirers overpay *even though they know acquirers typically overpay*.[2]

Isn't capitalism magnificent? Someone—not just Scott Adams and his Dilbert cartoons—found a way to make money off Corporate's dysfunction!

---

[2] If acquirers were getting better at not overpaying, we would expect MERFX's performance to turn zero to negative. But its recent performance is rising.

advice to the maverick

The quiz at the beginning of this chapter reminded you that we are not going to dispense trivial coaches' trivial advice. No conventional consultant would ask those questions.

Let's see how you did.

Question 1. We sympathize with pharmaceutical Corporate as they name their products. Just try to pronounce Xeljanz. We tried, but it hurt. If Xeljanz was your answer to Q1, *bingo!* We'd hoped it would be Mxyzptlk, an imp from old Superman comics, but the modern rule is that unpronounceable names must begin with X or Z.

Question 2. Since we can't really measure "fat"—cash is only a crude proxy—you may be tempted to ignore it. Peter Drucker had a famous line about measuring. Most of the answers were reasonable, but what he actually said was make sure you measure the right things. If that's what you said he said, *bingo!* Why didn't he say the others? They miss the point, and the point is that "fat" around the Corporate core makes it easy to spend money ineffectively whether one can measure it or not. Executives find it easy to spend when the times are good but take it all back when a crisis hits. Since when times are good the company is flush, who cares? You should. Competing skillfully means staying lean. Ask any athlete. (That's a sports metaphor; Corporate will understand.)

Question 3. What can you call unnecessary spending? Any of the answers is technically and/or arguably correct, but the term we've used over and over is free fat flow. *Bingo!* if you said so, too.

Question 4. Corporate tends to go on a binge of acquisitions when it is in its convergence stage in the lifecycle. If you answered convergence

advice to the maverick, continued

to Q4, *bingo!* That's where Corporate accumulates fat fast and where you will hear phrases like "economies of scale" as the key "success factor." From the Corporate perspective, it makes sense: Acquisitions create a behemoth that is harder to take over in a hostile bid, but it also makes the behemoth too big to save. As a maverick, think twice—no, three times—before you join a behemoth. If you are already in one, we hope it's in one of the business units that still allows for some competitive spirit.

Question 5. Corporate worships growth. The quickest, easiest way to grow is through acquisition. That's Corporate because buying more stuff doesn't always make your life better; sometimes it just adds clutter. Professor Porter did a study on the failure rate of mergers and acquisitions. If you answered 74 percent to Q5, *bingo!* As a maverick, you may want to keep this in mind: There are always alternatives to acquisitions. Startups are generally cheaper to launch and build. If you can make an argument to management about starting up rather than buying someone's else success (or failure), use examples from 3M, J&J, and United Technologies. Maybe the bosses will even let you lead the business plan project. Keep in mind, though, that you are competing with the senior partner of the famous investment company who has a personal relationship with the CEO and who benefits greatly from fees off the acquisition. Your only weapon is an astute business plan showing original thinking. Sometimes you will win. Often, you won't. When you don't, try to enjoy the free coffee and snacks.

Question 6. What makes M&A not only possible but attractive? Free fat flow, or in simple, crude terms: Lots of excess cash. How much cash? The answer is $1.9 trillion. Is that what you said? *Bingo!* This is not competitive because so much cash tempts Corporate into careless acquisitions and other wasteful spending. To Corporate, though, it's rational. "We can return the investment through synergies." If only. Fortunately, there's more cash where that came from . . . or went to. As a maverick, while you are working for a cash-rich Corporate on the hunt for buying anything that moves, think of becoming an entrepreneur and selling your company to them for an exorbitant sum.

The truth is, mavericks who come out against M&A wage an uphill battle. There are too many vested interests in M&A to fight: the CEO's desire for power and a legacy of "building;" the investment bankers' huge fees and free tickets to the playoffs; the law firms' enormous fees and free tickets to the other playoffs (whichever the bankers didn't offer). Be prepared to face Corporate resistance. Yes, it is easy, or at least dramatic, to acquire. Yes, some acquisitions work. What doesn't work is automatic, lazy-thinking anything.

Most managers are not involved in the acquisition game until they are vice presidents, but by then it is too late to become a maverick. Maverick VPs are rare. That's why we are intervening early. We encourage you to stay skeptical of grand promises of synergies and cost savings (beyond the immediate elimination of redundancies). We encourage you to ask yourself, in a quiet room where no one hears, "What is the competitive rationale behind the acquisition?" Beware that a fear trigger, such as, "what if our competitors got that company?" is often baseless. If that happens, it may be a good thing: After a hard-to-swallow M&A, your competitor is distracted for decades, trying in vain to "integrate."

advice to the maverick, continued

Question the knee-jerk response of buying someone else's success (and at top dollar since, by definition, no one else was willing to pay as much as you) rather than developing success in-house. The latter is much more difficult and time consuming, but it doesn't run into the high failure rate, cultural mismatch, and other acquisition maladies.

Closer to home: If you read that the company you wish to join is about to make a large acquisition, think twice. Digesting a large acquisition is a long, difficult process, and while it goes on, management will pay little attention to whatever part of the business is recruiting you. Benign neglect sounds good until it turns to just plain neglect. Then comes the restructuring.

By the way, if you answered all six questions correctly, bravo! Your prize is in the mail. It's a 1,906-page legal binder on the merger of AT&T and Time-Warner. Enjoy!

If you answered fewer than six questions correctly, re-read this book from the start. Please read carefully, as the questions have changed.

corporate
overpromises

"I went down the street to the
24-hour grocery. When I got
there, the guy was locking the
front door. I said, 'Hey, the sign
says you're open 24 hours.' He
said, 'Yes, but not in a row.'"

—STEVEN WRIGHT

Clear expectations inform and motivate. In competition, they do more: They signal. That's why people skilled at competing set expectations deliberately and strategically. Expectations declare boundaries to competitors: "This is my territory; stay away or we battle." Expectations announce capabilities to customers: "This is what we will do for you."

Expectations can be unconditional or conditional. An unconditional expectation is a promise. A conditional expectation depends on something else.

Conditional expectations are cautious and realistic. They spell out circumstances under which something may or may not happen. Given the no-place-to-hide ubiquity of Facebook and Twitter, they are also wise. But they are far from exciting. In the age of millions of MBAs in marketing, apparently that is a no-no. Unconditional expectations beat conditional expectations. We sacrifice the lesser good, wisdom, for the greater good, hype! (That's why we used an exclamation point instead of a period!)

In this chapter, we take a closer look at how Corporate sets expectations (and, ultimately, overpromises) in a way that resembles shooting itself in the foot. We strongly advise you not to do the same because the foot is never the same afterward.

SILLY PROMISES

A highly visible case of silly promises was brought home in 2013 when UPS and FedEx guaranteed next-day delivery throughout the holiday period. Even as they failed to deliver, their sites continued to make promises. Should the CEOs of UPS and FedEx have consulted a dictionary on the meaning of "guaranteed," or should we assume consumers would take "guaranteed" as implicitly conditional on good weather, low volume, and a merciful God? (Reminds us of the nutritious Raisin Bran asterisk from Chapter 12.)

In a conference call with analysts in April 2013, reported in *USA Today*, Apple CEO Tim Cook promised the company would introduce "amazing new hardware, software, and services" in the fall and through 2014. Turned out "amazing" meant an update to Apple's existing lines of iPhones and iPads. On the defensive, Cook "explained" his promise in a conference call on October 28: "What I said is that you'll see . . . some exciting new products . . . and I absolutely stand by that, and you've seen a lot of things over the last couple of months." Indeed, but none were amazing.[1]

In 2007 Tim Armstrong cofounded Patch Media, the hyperlocal news company, and subsequently bought it when he became CEO and chairman of AOL. He publicly pledged to bring Patch to profitability by the fourth quarter of 2013. After losing hundreds of millions of AOL's money in Patch, he failed to meet his promise. While Patch is not a major part of AOL, the failure is very personal and very public.

Everyone knows Tesla is exciting. What about Volvo, founded 1927 in Gothenburg, Sweden? Well, as quoted in *CNN Money*, Volvo has promised that "by 2020, no one will be killed or seriously injured in a new Volvo car or SUV." (Notice that Volvo shows its

---

[1] Perhaps there is a mathematical relationship between version numbers and amazing-ness. The first iPhone replaced no iPhone at all, and 1 divided by 0 is amazingly unknown. The second iPhone 2 replaced the first, and was $2 \div 1$, or twice, as amazing. The iPhone 8 was only 1.1429 times as amazing as the iPhone 7. Prepare to fall asleep around the iPhone 15 or so and not because of the arithmetic.

skill at competing: Their goal is compelling, distinctive, and a perfect fit with their brand.) We'll be watching . . . and hoping.[2]

We promise not to talk about politicians' promises.

WHY PROMISE?

So why promise? Promises seem dangerous. Why not a policy of "ask me no questions, I'll tell you no lies"?

One reason why Corporate leaders make promises they can't later meet comes from psychology, with studies by scholars like Ellen Jane Langer regarding the illusion of control. Powerful people actually believe they *can* meet their promises. After all, they became powerful people by achieving things.

As Professor Phil Rosenzweig observed in his book, *The Halo Effect* (Free Press, 2014), "any good strategy involves risk. If you think your strategy is foolproof, the fool may well be you."

The thing is, Corporate seeks and rewards bold promises, not bold actions. Timid is too timid; bold is visionary. A shot at glory excites Corporate.

If Columbus was Corporate, imagine his reaction to discovering the Bahamas rather than the route to India he sought. It might have gone something like this:

Sailor on the Pinta, seeing the Bahamas after months on the ocean: Land! Land!

Christopher Columbus: Hooray! At last we can return to Spain and tell the Queen we discovered a route to the riches of India! What do you see there, sailor?

---

[2] We also note that Volvo, more than 90 years old, has learned a thing or two about promises. Of course, Volvo does not extend the pledge to those who "really want to hurt themselves" or who are "just really, really stupid." And their goal seems achievable. According to the same *CNN Money* article, the Insurance Institute for Highway Safety said nine vehicle models—including the Volvo XC90—had zero deaths from 2009 to 2012, the latest data available at the time of the article. Still . . . Remember Numerology in Chapter 6? There is a self-selection bias here: People who buy Volvo may be careful people to begin with. We want to see Ferrari make the same claim!

Sailor: A few naked natives, one hotel, and a casino.

Columbus: Is that all? No jewels? No gold?

Sailor: No.

Columbus: Bummer. We promised the Queen more gold than in Fort Knox. Forget it, turn back, and let's not talk about this place again, eh?

Corporate promises often rely on short memories, a general societal attitude that forgives failure, or more cynically, the assumption that customers have few alternatives. If that is the case, a strategy of overpromising is a rational (if not ethical) tool in competing, until it isn't. The question is, does Corporate know when to stop?

VW made its reputation on promising and delivering engineering excellence. If you had a VW Beetle or Microbus, you know their reputation wasn't based on looks. The "creed," as it is called, can be stronger than the ugly, smelly truth: VW diesel technology was just not good enough to pass an emissions test in the U.S. or Europe. The overpromise of engineering (or marketing) led VW to design the cars' emission controls to kick in only when emissions were being measured. VW paid a hefty price in fines and lost trust, and VW executives paid with jail time.

---

customers are guilty, too

Customers have a role in promises, too. If you want honesty, reward honesty. First step: Lengthen your memories. Second step: Take the glitter out of your eyes.

Assuming customers value honesty, let's run a quick "back of the envelope" scenario using FedEx as an example. What would have happened if FedEx announced it would do its best to meet deadlines during the

---

customers are guilty, too, continued

holiday season but it wouldn't provide guarantees? Knowing the intense rivalry between FedEx and UPS, UPS sees an opportunity to pull ahead by retaining and touting its guarantee. Customers might even see UPS' boldness as a sign that it tries harder or has invented a secret delivery sauce. Many will then flock to UPS, exacerbating UPS' logistical problems and leading to rude surprises for its customers. A self-unfulfilling promise. Meanwhile, FedEx will deliver mostly on time, pleasantly surprising its customers and emerging as the honest one.

Reputation is everything in the game of express shipping. When companies compete as directly as UPS and FedEx, with few differentiators, FedEx might gain competitive advantage while UPS gets short-term sales at a longer-term cost.

Another option for FedEx and UPS would be to unbundle the delivery guarantees. FedEx and UPS charge by the day they'll deliver. They could charge by the strength of the guarantee rather than by the expected delivery date. Pay a premium, you get compensated by ten times your shipping cost if they don't deliver on time. Pay the regular price, accept the probability (whatever it is) that it will not be there on time but within two days. This is the management of expectations.

But that's just strategy. Let's return to the dysfunction you need to recognize as your boss promises you that a job making photocopies is fascinating and challenging and a step up the ladder to CEO: Overpromising leads to loss of trust. OK, maybe the example is not perfect. Who makes photocopies nowadays?

customers are guilty, too, continued

We contrast FedEx and UPS to regular U.S. Postal Service mail because they do not guarantee delivery at a specific time. At least there we know what to *expect,* and we can always be pleasantly surprised!

OVERPROMISING WORKS. FOR A WHILE. MAYBE.

Why is overpromising (as opposed to conditional, cautious promises) so seductive? The person who projects the most confidence, even if it's overconfidence, or the greatest competence, even if it's the illusion of control, is the one who gets the project, the capital, the votes, or according to *HuffPost*, even the hot babes and dudes on dating sites.

In Corporate, targets get missed all the time. CEO tenures get shorter and shorter as Wall Street's patience with missed targets gets shorter and shorter. Even the Ritalin doesn't help any longer. And promises not kept have given many a manager their first pushes down slippery slopes. Think Ponzi schemes and cooked books. May we remind you about Wells Fargo, where, according to CNN, pressure-cooked salespeople opened millions of unwanted accounts for unwitting customers? More fines, more trust squandered, another CEO gone . . . not to mention the people fired or burned out by the pressure-cooking.

Car emissions or bank accounts, Germany or the U.S.; on the surface, unkept promises can look different depending on the industry. But they all involve claims that benefit the claimant and shortfalls in delivery that the claimant hopes the customer will not notice. We can imagine the discussion between Moses and God on Mount Sinai:

Moses: I have to promise my tribe a happy ending, or they won't wander in this damn desert for 40 years!

God: Watch the language. There are kids around.

Moses: OK, darn desert. It's still (bleeping) dry.

God: OK, let's think of a promise. What do people like in the morning?

Moses: A little milk in their espresso and a little honey on their toast.

God: OK, promise them the Land of Milk and Honey.

Moses: But Canaan doesn't have cattle or bees. It's almost as dry as this (bleeping) desert.

God: Believe me, after 40 years of walking, anything looks like milk and honey.

If you know the biblical story, the land of milk and honey proved elusive. Scouts sent by Moses reported the difficulty of conquering the land (". . . and there are giants there . . ."). The Israelites rebelled against the idea. God became angry. The original Israelite tribes that escaped from Egypt then wandered in the desert for 40 more years until all of them died and only their children entered the land. One conclusion is that they could have used better GPS. Another is that overpromising sets up bad expectations.

advice to the maverick

Conventional wisdom and job-advice books say that eagerly accepting any assignment and promising to be up to any challenge will lead to great respect from peers and bosses. Our view is that the opposite is true: *Under-promising* allows for pleasantly surprising the client, the boss, or the really big boss with more than they expected.

Overpromising leads to loss of trust. Once trust is lost, it is doubly hard to regain it. Do you look forward to flying again on the airline that lost your bags? Do you frequent Chipotle as much as you did before its 2015 and

advice to the maverick, continued

2017 food scandals? Do you trust Facebook after its 2018 data privacy scandal?

By contrast, under-promising gives you the option to delight customers beyond their expectations. Delighting customers this way has been proven to work for companies such as Nuts.com, Relax the Back, and other niche retailers whose customer service is known for going *beyond* the call of duty.

So maverick, strive to delight. "Delight" is the operative word. There *is* an "I" in delight.

Politicians do, shall we say, the reverse. Draw your own conclusions about how well that works. But we advise that you *always* under-promise until you are made VP, whether of a company or a country. True, your road may be more difficult than that of the over-promising co-worker, but you may stay longer out of jail. Just ask Audi's CEO.[3]

Do that, and you could be the next Jeff Bezos. We promise.

---

[3] Arrested in 2018 for involvement with the diesel fraud scandal. See https://money.cnn.com/2018/06/18/investing/audi-ceo-arrested-volkswagen-rupert-stadler/index.html.

does corporate do strategic due diligence?

"If at first you don't succeed,
try, try again. Then quit.
There's no point in being a
damn fool about it."

—W.C. Fields

Overpromising runs the gamut from asterisks on cereal boxes to software that cheats on emissions tests. The good news is that the backlash (embarrassment, prison terms, etc.) can make the lessons stick, at least for a while. But it seems there's a kind of Corporate whose business model, in practice if not in theory, all but *demands* that it succumb to overpromises. That business is Corporate-like venture capital.

Are you familiar with the terms *schlimazel* and *schlemiel*? *Schlimazel* is the Yiddish word for a chronically unlucky person. *Schlemiel* is the Yiddish word for an inept, incompetent, clumsy person, a bungler. The difference between a schlemiel and a schlimazel is classically described like this: "The schlemiel spills his coffee on the schlimazel."

In business, luck plays a big role. Only overconfident or arrogant executives think every aspect of competition is under their control. Mark's current research and writing focus on how to know whether decision-makers were lucky or smart. (Or, of course, unlucky or not-smart.) When the results roll in, it's already too late to worry about luck or smarts.

In this chapter, we explore the difference between being unlucky (the schlimazel) and being strategically careless (the schlemiel). The first may be excused, but the latter may not. Luckily, you, the maverick, can play a constructive role: Your critical thinking and diplomatic interactions can produce *strategic due diligence.*

THE SCHLEMIEL AND SCHLIMAZEL IN CORPORATE

Preparation—using tools such as war games, computer-based simulation, scenarios, and other planning methods—reduces the *need* for luck but never ever eliminates it (unless one is working for Goldman Sachs[1]).

From a skill-at-competing perspective, one can't gripe about schlimazels (those with bad luck). Even the best-laid plans, the most brilliant products, and the cleverest approaches to the market can fail by bad luck.[2] Too early, too late, *force majeure*, spontaneous combustion; the reasons are immaterial here. The point is that luck, by definition, is no one's fault. Even when we understand risks and uncertainties, that doesn't mean we can know how they'll turn out. The market turns down (or up), the earth quakes (or rests), the court rules against you (or for you). You know the cards in the deck, but you don't know which you'll be dealt.

Corporate, frightened when it misses targets, rapidly deploys CYA and casts blame with "you should have known." But *should* have known implies *could* have known. That's a different case, as we will discuss later.

An OOP (remember, that's an Overconfident, Oblivious Person) is a kind of schlemiel, and OOPs do not foresee risks effectively even when they could in principle. They either discount risks (overconfidence), or they don't see risks (oblivious).

Operationally, schlemiel translates mostly to "careless." There are two risk factors that lead to carelessness in Corporate.

---

[1] If you are not familiar with how Goldman Sachs played both the government and its clients brilliantly prior to and during the 2008 financial crisis, read the piece by *The New York Times*, June 30, 2010; *Fortune*, March 16, 2017; or *Reuters*, March 17, 2009. If you are still not convinced, you are probably looking to be recruited by Goldman.

[2] Likewise about *good* luck: Even the dumbest plans, the lamest products, and the flakiest approaches to the market can succeed by good luck. The difference is people share their complaints about bad luck, but they cover their complaints about good luck with face-saving statements, such as "I *said* it would work!"

One is size. When you are rich and powerful, you can afford to be careless. Why worry? Your money and power make you less vulnerable.

The second is more insidious: success. Success in itself would seem a positive sign, a mark of competence. But beware: Instead of treating success as tenuous, Corporate declares "we found the golden rule.[3]" One example is the way venture capital, once the bastion of maverick thinking, has become Corporate in itself. Corporate-style VC (that is, VC with sloppy thinking) bases its decisions on faith—faith in the golden rule.

FAITH IN PEOPLE OVER STRATEGY

The "formula" for VC investments requires tolerating or even expecting failure in nine out of ten investments. As long as the VC hits it big one time in ten, it will prosper. For some VC funds, it pays off soon enough; for others it doesn't. Some VC funds prosper forever on Megabucks wins like Facebook or Google.

The VC industry as a whole is doing well. In 2017 alone, $71 billion in venture capital was invested in startups, a decline from 2015, but more capital was raised than in 2015. The question is, why they should accept such a high failure rate. Is it a *necessary* aspect of competing in the startup world?

In other words, *do startups obey different rules when it comes to competing?*

There is no doubt this is of major interest to new graduates of business schools. There isn't one MBA alive who doesn't dream of being recruited into a VC fund.[4]

Ben had a seat on the board of a VC fund in the 1990s and remembers the endless pitches by enthusiastic entrepreneurs. Few actually got to make these presentations to the board. The first step

---

[3] This "golden rule" is not in the sense of do-unto-others. Rather, it is in the sense that we know where the gold is.

[4] Well, maybe one, but he moved to Oregon.

in weeding out potential investments was to look at business plans. After reading hundreds, the conclusion he reached was quite simple:

> *Entrepreneurs assume competition doesn't exist. VC pretends it does.*

The few that do acknowledge competition are utterly confident they will overcome it with their incredibly ingenious product/service with a potential market size of $3.4 trillion by 2039. They back their fantasies with detailed cash flow and profit and loss (P&L) projections.

Smart and seasoned VC investors immediately discount these projections by 50 percent.

Let's accept that discounting 50 percent off startups' financial projections makes them more realistic. That's tantamount to accepting our children's promises they'll never get drunk in college, but we never got drunk, so we'll go along with it. Given the huge uncertainty surrounding the plans of startups, how do VC leaders actually decide where to invest?

Their golden rule is this: *Invest in people.* In other words, the most important element behind success is the management team, not the product/service offering.

This mantra is so deeply ingrained in the insular investor circles around the world that it has acquired the status of a law of thermodynamics. It is also very inspiring, playing right into everyone's belief in the entrepreneurial spirit (and perhaps thermodynamics). The problem is, it's a myth. People are *less* important than competitive strategy.

THE DELUSION OF SERIAL SUCCESS

According to a story in *The Verge* from November 2015, the first music-streaming service to arrive in America was Rdio. (Some will say Rhapsody, but we truly and utterly don't care to take sides in this important debate.) Its founders were Skype billionaires Janus Friis and Niklas Zennström, and the venture was backed by Atomico

---

the vc version of thermodynamics

For those not lucky enough to be intimately acquainted with the laws of thermodynamics, let us repeat them here. The four fundamental laws of thermodynamics[5] are:

1. Energy cannot be created or destroyed in an isolated system.

2. The entropy of any isolated system always increases.

3. The entropy of a system approaches a constant value as the temperature approaches absolute zero.

4. The management team is more important than understanding the nature of competition. (Also known in Jamaica as "no worries, *mon*.")

---

[5] We are not counting the zeroth law of thermodynamics. Seriously, the zeroth law. "If two bodies are each in thermal equilibrium with some third body, then they are also in equilibrium with each other." Go forth and amaze your friends with that fun fact. https://www.livescience.com/50833-zeroth-law-thermodynamics.html, retrieved 8/31/2018.

---

and Mangrove Capital Partners. In 2010, it was the first to offer a $5 web-only streaming plan and a BlackBerry app.

The product took two years to launch, as negotiations with record labels were tough. Record labels held all the cards (and made all the money). But Rdio was a slick product with many innovative features, such as the ability to show your friends in real time what you were streaming and a playlist that highlighted albums based on how many friends had listened to them.

There was only one problem: "Excellent product" is not synonymous with "excellent competitive strategy." While Rdio was enthusiastically adopted in San Francisco (where else?), people were already talking about the coming launch of the Swedish competitor, Spotify.

If the VCs hadn't been in love with the billionaire founders—a.k.a. the invest-in-people rule, a.k.a. lightning *likes* to strike twice in the same place—they might have war-gamed Rdio against the arrival of Spotify with the latter's free on-demand streaming supported by advertising. This is Competing 101. When Rdio eventually offered a free service, it was too late. Besides, imitating your competitor is hardly ever a winning strategy. Imitation prevents you from falling behind, but it does not help you leap ahead.

But it's not about strategy, is it? It's about the people. Skype founders are impressive!

Looking back, some former employees said Rdio invested heavily in technology and features no one wanted to pay for, such as a sophisticated method to collect music for later listening. Competitors also offered a queue, but it was simple. "At the end of the day, that was not a major differentiating factor," says Wilson Miner, a former design leader at Rdio. "If we hadn't had something like that, *nobody would have noticed, and it would have been fine*" [italics added].

Who Defines Value?

Rdio failed because *customers* define value as they compare your products/services to alternatives, and Rdio didn't fare well in their comparison.

Once Rdio decided to play defense (sports metaphor!), it implicitly accepted that it would carry two heavy burdens:

1. Suppliers, the record labels, have enormous bargaining power, so margins in streaming music are thin. When margins are thin and fixed costs are high, scale is essential. According to *Billboard*'s article from 2016, Spotify raised more than $1 billion to acquire subscribers to get that scale (and to counter suppliers' bargaining power). Amazon used a similar strategy. Competing without understanding economics is hazardous to your capital.
2. Imitation is not competitive strategy; it's operational strategy, and the deep pockets win. Competing well means offering

unique value for enough customers. If you ignore economics *and* competitors, "people" (the ones running the company as opposed to the ones buying the product) don't matter even if they had huge success in startups before . . . *when they competed well.* Tell them that next time you Skype with them.

Was Rdio's fate inevitable? Maybe. No one knows, and hindsight doesn't tell us what they should have done. But we do know that "first movers" can be done in by what might seem a strength: Their insular, internally focused culture. We sympathize: It's not easy to question, let alone abandon, what you believe caused your success. But as we said earlier in the book: If competitive threats come out of left field, watch left field. Anticipate left field. Go to left field yourself.

The flip side of this story is Spotify. They entered second or third or seventh (depending on how closely you pay attention to these statistics) against a first mover in an industry, striking deals with tough suppliers with high bargaining power. They needed a different business model. They had one. They also needed to survive on no profits for a long time. How did Spotify do it?

The only explanation we have is that one founder of Rdio was Swedish (the other was Danish), but *both* founders of Spotify were Swedish. There's no denying the data: Two Swedes are better than one.

FAITH IN STEREOTYPES

As reported in *Business Insider* in April 2014, mobile-payment app company Crinkle announced a $25 million round of seed financing from 12 leading VC firms and angel investors, among them Andreessen Horowitz and Accel Partners. It was the largest early investment raised in Silicon Valley history at the time. The company later raised $5 million more in the same year. Notable investors for that round included Stanford's StartX fund and Virgin CEO Sir Richard Branson.

Nine months later, Crinkle was crumbling.

Crinkle was the brainchild of Lucas Duplan, a 19-year-old first-time founder, a Stanford student, and the son of a software entrepreneur. When he took a class on entrepreneurship at Stanford with Professor Charles Eesley, he met VMware cofounder Diane Greene, who would later become an angel investor for the company. Greene also opened doors for Duplan to connect with Andreessen Horowitz and Accel Partners.

In the world of VC investing, there was nothing unusual about the way the deal got financed. It's a small community, friends bring friends, and no one is ever more than two degrees of separation away from $25 million. Greene sent a note to Marc Andreessen and Ben Horowitz urging them to meet with Duplan. They visited Crinkle's office and spent a *whole hour* with him. They came out very impressed. Duplan didn't have a formal presentation like other eager beggars. Instead, he showed them an animated demo of what the app might do, with a cute sound at the end.

That was all it took to get millions from the experienced dealmakers at Andreessen Horowitz.

What it took just wasn't enough.

When the app was launched in beta form in April 2014, what developers built bore little resemblance, in both appearance and function, to the demo.

Later in 2014, Crinkle laid off a third of its staff, brought in and quickly lost experienced executives from Netflix, Yahoo, and Twitter, and eventually went bust.

Being 19 and believing in luck is not surprising. But how did Marc Andreessen, Ben Horowitz, Branson, and other extremely smart and seasoned investors make such a careless, schlemiel-ish investment? As *Business Insider* explains, Duplan looked and sounded exactly like "the sort of Silicon Valley wunderkind who could build a billion-dollar business."

Entrepreneurs must believe in their ideas. As Mark observes, only optimists become entrepreneurs and investors. Being an optimist, however, is not synonymous with being a schlemiel. A schlemiel is *blindly* optimistic. In the immortal words of *Mad* magazine's Alfred E. Neuman: "What, me worry?" The schlemiel doesn't care about left field and might be unable to locate it.

To make due diligence diligently do the job it does, we must take it beyond the business equivalent of a spellcheck. We should not merely verify that the gold shimmering on the horizon isn't a mirage; we should also look out for cliffs on the way to the gold. We call it *strategic due diligence*. If you don't use strategic due diligence, you don't have skill at competing.

Looking at the flip side of your optimism does not make you a pessimist or a naysayer. It makes you the opposite of an OOP.[6] It makes you strategically diligent.

In the case of Crinkle, the OOP mentality appears not in the schlemiel saga but actually in what hasn't even come to the forefront. Let's assume the product could be built. Let's assume its majestic novelty of a cute sound when money is transferred would remain. How could this payment system compete with Apple Pay or Square? What bank or payment processor would take a risk on this product? "Your money is backed by the full faith and credit of a 19-year-old entrepreneur with a cute sound." We apologize for this, but the Crinkle episode is just barmy.[7]

FAITH IN TECHNOLOGY

The last bastion of some VC's sloppy thinking (and that of many other industries) is to have absolute faith in technology.

We don't know what word processing, spreadsheet, and presentation software you use at home, but we know that at work, you use Microsoft Office.

Why Microsoft Office? It's not because Microsoft was first. There's another reason.

WordStar, released in 1978, dominated word processing in the early to mid-1980s. It was overtaken by WordPerfect (released in

---

[6] The opposite of OOP is OOP—Open-minded, Observant Person. It might superficially look the same, but it is an utterly different animal.

[7] Our vocabulary word for the day! Thesaurus.com says it is British slang for "silly," and it sounds cute.

1980) around 1985. Microsoft Word made its debut in 1983 and didn't pull ahead of WordPerfect until the 1990s.

VisiCalc, the first interactive electronic spreadsheet and "the first killer app of the computer era"[8] came out in 1978. It was invented by the brilliant Dan Bricklin (a business school classmate of Mark) and Bob Frankston. It ran on the most popular computer at the time. Unfortunately for Bricklin and Frankston, the most popular computer at the time was the Apple II. Lotus introduced the 1-2-3 spreadsheet for the IBM PC in 1983.[9] Microsoft's Excel—not Microsoft's first spreadsheet, by the way—started to count in 1985.

Aldus Persuasion (later, Adobe Persuasion) came out about the same time as Microsoft PowerPoint.[10] Persuasion was shut down in 1997.

To say the least, there was vigorous competition in the three arenas at the start. There isn't any more. Don't byte us, we *know* Apple has Keynote, Numbers, and Pages, and Google has Docs, Sheets, and Slides. You might use them at home. But we said that *at work* you almost certainly use Office, even if it's under duress. Why?

Because at work almost *everyone* uses Office, and that means almost everyone can share files and tips. In short, everyone uses Office because everyone uses Office.

Go ahead, work on technology. Offer longer words, bigger numbers, and slicker slides. It won't matter. The switching costs, including your digital isolation, far outweigh the benefits.

---

[8] For those who want to know, VisiCalc was the world's first electronic spreadsheet. It preceded Lotus 1-2-3, which preceded Excel. In that citation, there's a photo of Bricklin and Frankston. Bricklin is the bearded guy on the right. Dan showed a prototype of VisiCalc in a class he and I were taking. I approached him immediately and asked to invest in his company. He said no. I made the right decision to ask. He made the right decision to say no. http://history-computer. com/ModernComputer/Software/Visicalc.html

[9] Lotus later acquired the rights to VisiCalc and shut it down.

[10] Microsoft acquired PowerPoint from its developers, at a company called Forethought Inc., for $14 million. It bought the software just three months after it first appeared.

Contrast word processing, spreadsheet, and presentation apps with internet browsers. There's robust competition among browsers.[11] That's because the cost of switching among browsers is about as close to zero as you can get without being zero. So sharpen your Edge *and* polish your Chrome. Go on Safari *and* be an Explorer. Sing your Opera *and* bada your Bing.

By the way, WordPerfect has kept itself in the game with its office suite. Among the features it touts: "Extensive compatibility, including Microsoft Office." Technology can be cool, but it doesn't make money without strategy.

LESSONS FROM THE SCHLEMIELS, AND *FOR* THE SCHLEMIELS

Neither a stellar management team, nor a performance pedigree, nor a radical technology can compensate for the lack of competitive strategy. That lesson is so basic we are afraid you are going to miss it as you worship the famous VCs and other Corporate stalwarts who get it right one time in ten. Here is a checklist to help you remember:

- It's *always* strategy first.
- Competitive strategy requires that you always, always pay attention to what others are doing.
- Good people can't save bad strategy but . . .
- . . . even the dullest of people can thrive with a good strategy. Who made money during the Gold Rush in the 19th century? Manufacturers of pickaxes, shovels, and gold pans.
- Strategy uses technology. Technology is not strategy. Repeat: Technology is not strategy. Ask Alexa: Are you strategy?
- If you don't have a good (i.e., competitive) strategy, your only route to success is relying on good luck. That, in itself, is a bad strategy.

---

[11] It's odd to call it "competition" since the browsers are all free. But the customer isn't you, the person doing the browsing. The customer is the advertiser. You are the product.

Whether you're entering the Corporate world, well-established in it, or thinking of going out on your own, you need to read this statement from an entrepreneur cited in Inc.com's article, "Why Silicon Valley Loves Failures": "Starting companies these days is akin to *doing research* in the past."

Therein lies the catch. Investing Monopoly money on a whim is not akin to research. Backing half-baked ideas with no strategy other than "we'll be first" is not akin to research. Falling under the spell of a charming entrepreneur-salesperson with no careful assessment of the economics is not akin to research. Having faith in people, stereotypes, and technology is not akin to research. Those activities *are* akin to something else: gambling.

Strategic due diligence is akin to research.

advice to the maverick

When an individual takes risks without due diligence, we call him or her careless. When a community—a business or a group of investors—takes such risks as its *modus operandi*, we call it a dysfunction.

Faith is common among humans. We approach it gingerly. There is nothing touchier than challenging core ideas based on faith. So it is with the delicacy of a bull charging into a china shop that we suggest you reconsider your Corporate faith (whether it's Corporate VC or Corporate Corporate). "Trust, but verify" in business means trust the people, the stereotypes, and the technology, but verify the strategy. Ask questions, such as if someone less wealthy or photogenic brought you the same business plan, would you believe it? Financial due diligence often concentrates on why numbers *will* work. Strategic due diligence means paying attention to why business models *won't* work. (Note also that financial due diligence looks at a different set of numbers from strategic due diligence.)

advice to the maverick, continued

We *could* say, in a serious voice, "Always think, 'What's our (my) strategy?'" and only after that is carefully laid out, think about people and technology.

We *could* recommend that you first address why the business will work, and only after that address why people will want to work there.

We *could* tell you to ask in meetings, as you listen to people discuss *your company's* strategy, "What are *others* doing? What are others not seeing that we could exploit? What are the switching costs for customers to adopt our technology? What are the potential improvements to the old technology that may derail our new technology?"

But that is just wishful thinking on our part. If a VC fund offers you a job as an analyst, or a researcher, or even a bike messenger, are you going to listen to *us*?

Still, trust us on this. Watch out for schlemiels carrying coffee.

performance addiction: or, corporate wants results *today*

CHAPTER 16

"After all, tomorrow
is another day."

—Scarlett O'Hara,

Gone with the Wind

You've been studying this book all along, right? Because you know there's going to be a quiz. Here it is:

Imagine that you can design your dream job. At which company do you want to enjoy that dream job?

1. Cisco
2. Sysco
3. Is this a trick question? They sound the same.

We'd bet you'd choose Cisco. Cisco is high tech (it makes networking gear). Its headquarters are in San Francisco. Age-wise, it's in its 30s. Therefore, it is cool.

We'd bet you haven't heard of Sysco even though you've almost certainly eaten the products it distributes throughout your life. Sysco is the top wholesale food distributor in the U.S. Its headquarters are in Houston. It was founded in 1969. Food is not cool unless it is inside one of Sysco's refrigerated trucks.

Cisco and Sysco are almost adjacent on the 2018 Fortune 500 list of the largest companies in the U.S. Cisco Systems is #62, with 2017 sales of $48 billion. Its profits and revenue were down that year, but it was still highly profitable. Sysco is #54, with sales of $55 billion. It's profitable, though much less so than Cisco. Sysco's profits and revenue rose in 2017.

Googling "Cisco" on June 21, 2018, yielded "about 145,000,000 results." Googling "Sysco" a minute later produced "about 4,310,000 results." That makes Cisco exactly 33.64269 times cooler than Sysco.

Why do we emulate and venerate the cool, sexy, volatile companies rather than the larger ones who've managed to survive for decades, even *centuries*, more?

Because we love shiny objects.

Cisco is shiny. Still, there's an object even shinier than Cisco. A company whose name is synonymous with an activity. A company bigger than Cisco and even Sysco. A company we've already mentioned twice in this chapter, but you haven't noticed. That company is Google. (Well, it's Alphabet now, but we don't mind.)

Google—sorry, Alphabet—is Fortune #22 in 2018. Its sales, $111 billion, exceed Cisco's and Sysco's combined. And when we Googled "Google," we got *9,960,000,000* results.[1] It's 69 times cooler than Cisco and 2,311 times cooler than Sysco. Wouldn't you like to work there?

"God" got 2.7 billion results.

"Money" got 2.8 billion results.

"Sex" got 3 billion results.

"Google"—10 billion results—is cooler than God, money, and sex *combined*. Strangest of all (and maybe not so strange), that doesn't even seem surprising. We love shiny objects. You love shiny objects. And Corporate loves shiny objects.

In this chapter, we examine Corporate and investors' addictions to stellar performance. The source of this addiction is evolutionary and dates back to the days people spoke Latin. Anything less than stellar, or (god forbid) less than adequate, or (argh!) a *decline* in performance, triggers a panic response. But don't panic; we are here to help. If not today, tomorrow.

---

[1] Oddly, when we *Binged* Google we got only 65 million results. Hmmm . . .

GROSS GALACTIC PRODUCT

Ten years ago, an eternity in cool-time, Google (not yet Alphabet) was on track to earn profits of about $5 billion on revenue over $20 billion. At the time, that amounted to 26 percent growth in earnings and 31 percent growth in revenue. Alphabet's data on the 2017 *Fortune 500* list said profits of $12.7 billion on revenue of $110.8 billion.

Alphabet's sales growth, starting from an already huge-by-any-standards $20 billion, has compounded annually at 18.7 percent.

Let's put those numbers in perspective. At that rate of growth, Alphabet would equal the rest of the entire American economy in 2055 or so. A few more years, it would equal the non-Alphabet gross *world* product. A few more years (depending on whether there is monetary life on planets other than our own), the gross *galactic* product.

Facebook will get there even sooner. It's smaller than Alphabet now, but it's growing faster.

Obviously, these numbers are not accurate even though they are based on real data and calculated to n decimal points.

With the possible exception of the universe itself (even that is debatable among physicists), nothing sustains a positive rate of growth forever because nothing grows forever. However, the expectation, the demand, the requirement that each year be bigger and better than the previous leads Corporate to deceive itself and its investors, overreach, cut corners, build houses of cards, and do "whatever it takes" to "make the numbers."

We all know growth eventually slows. No one expects Alphabet to dominate the world. But even though we all know growth eventually slows, we don't expect it to slow *today*.

This is the lesson to ask Alexa to remember for all of us: No executive, and no investor who buys a stock, expects a decline *today*.

It will happen, sure, one day, but NOT TODAY.

Some management gurus call this short-termism. But that's not it. No CEO in his or her right mind will admit to being a short-termist.

In interviews, they all talk about the long term. The long term, by the way, starts tomorrow. Not today.

The disease is not short-termism, it's just Not Today.

SICUT NON HODIE

Practice saying *sicut non hodie* ("SNH" in a TLA[2]). *Sicut non hodie* means "just not today" in Latin. Why Latin? Because it sounds better. It sounds scientific. And it might be on a quiz in a later chapter.

We can now talk about anaphylactic SNH, a severe allergic reaction to a possible slowing or (shudder) reversal of growth. In other words: *Decline* (sound of gasping executives lunging for the EpiPen).

Suffering from anaphylactic SNH, management reasonably wants to maintain or enhance performance. That's not inherently bad; it's how capitalism is supposed to work. But management has little clear guidance on knowing when their efforts go from:

building up, to
propping up, to
puffing up.

When did airlines' cost-cutting go from sensible to requiring that passengers exhale before they can fit in their seats? They know someday a backlash will disrupt the model of sardines-in-a-can. But . . .

Not Today. (They are probably right on that.)

When did VW's engineering pride go from superior technology solutions to software that cheats? They knew one day they'd have to admit diesel is just not that clean an alternative to regular fuel, but . . .

Not Today.

When did pharma's infatuation with blockbuster drugs go from delightful jackpot to essential lifeline? Every pharma executive we've

---

[2] We're not sure how to pronounce it. Ask the nearest ancient Roman, or Siri. TLA means three-letter acronym. Corporate loves TLAs.

worked with—and we've worked with hundreds over the years—laments the overreliance on a few blockbusters and the culture that pushes lesser drugs off the development track. They know it will have to change because pipelines of the Next Big Thing are running dry, but . . .

Not Today.

The problem is not that feverish growth won't last forever. The problem is not that stock prices rise and eventually fall. The problem is that, judging by results, Corporate has no idea what to do when growth stalls. Yes: Today.

Not Today (chant: *Sicut non hodie, sicut non hodie*) means that when Today happens, the inevitable is greeted as if the sky is falling. It's a complete and utter shock. Who would ever have predicted?

Today happens. And it happens in what looks like a sudden and unexpected decline even as signs might have been accumulating under Corporate noses for *years*.

Today is always sudden. COOCs never recognize Today until it is Yesterday.

When Corporate pushes too hard to keep the growth going, it creates a bubble that ends up like the financial crisis of 2008. It blows up in its face.

When Corporate squeezes too hard to keep costs down, it starves the investment it needs to run the business in the future. When Corporate polishes its numbers to make them shine, it creates new expectations that are even harder to satisfy. According to a story in *The New York Times* on January 16, 2018, shareholders of GE, the once-venerable industrial giant, are suing a former CEO, Jeffrey Immelt, for polishing GE's numbers as GE was deteriorating fast. His successor, John Flannery, is facing reality.

Underlying the decline of executives' and managers' skill at competing is the inability to accept bad news. But the fault isn't all theirs. It comes, too, from the investors and the boards of directors who say, "If you can't get the job done, I'll get someone who can TODAY."

RESILIENCE AS A BUSINESS MODEL

How do you get past the performance addiction once you're embedded in Corporate? As part of learning and practicing your skill at competing, you need to develop resilience.

The best way we know to develop some resilience for bad news is to live through a bad situation.

One of us (Mark) was fortunate (his word) to be on a flight when an engine exploded in midair. He was fortunate both in that he lived to tell the tale (no one was injured) and in that he was lucky to have had the experience. While he does not recommend that we blow up lots of engines at 5,000 feet so all of us can enjoy growth experiences, he sees it as an utterly cheap way to learn an important lesson. (Cheap for him, not the airline.) No pain, no side effects, over in 20 minutes; that's about as cheap as it gets.

That's the key: *A quick and cheap way to learn an important lesson.* The military does it with war games. Lawyers do it by arguing in front of mock juries. One of these days, virtual reality devices will make this a common tool for other professions and occasions. Not today, but soon.

Interestingly, the exploding-engine incident was a learning experience for Mark but not for the pilots of his aircraft. They'd already had their learning experiences in flight simulators!

Which is exactly the point.[3]

In business, the quick and cheap way to learn important lessons and develop resilience is through business war games and strategy simulations, especially because they make it possible to turn the clock back and what-if a different move by you or your competitors.

Facing strategy challenges rarely requires calculating more decimal points. It almost always requires thinking differently. Thinking differently doesn't happen automatically or overnight.

---

[3] Notice that it's "interestingly," not "luckily." "Luckily" would imply that it happened by chance that the pilots were well-prepared. That they were well-prepared was most assuredly *not* by chance.

We know because each of us has spent a lifetime—*invested* a lifetime—discovering and implementing our approaches. But thinking differently is possible. And you're learning it now because those who learn can pass the lesson on to others.

Perhaps the most insightful, useful, and important part of thinking differently is asking what can go wrong and developing robust strategies to enable resilience.

One way of looking at resilience is to test strategies against various scenarios.[4] "What happens if" questions are not negative but positive because they help companies modify their strategies to survive various states of the world. If you happen to work in the automobile industry, for example, you might ask, "What happens to my brand if the acceptance of electric vehicles reaches a critical number?" That question is more than legitimate; it's *necessary* as part of your company's strategic due diligence (see Chapter 15). The answer might be to develop hybrid models because they are more acceptable to many consumers than pure electric cars. In other words, the strategy of hybrid is *robust* in several scenarios.

You can apply this thinking to your own proposals and recommendations. Resilience and robustness mean making choices that don't depend on everything going just right. They can intrigue even a Not-Today executive overconfidently committed to heroic performance objectives.

Big bets require a sense of looming change. It is legitimate to make big bets as long as the decision-maker accepts the possibility of failure. Given its Not-Today mentality, though, Corporate doesn't believe in big bets. For Corporate, improving thinking is the fastest, cheapest, surest, and highest-leverage way to improve the quality of decisions if they can only take their eyes of the shiny objects for one day. Start today.

---

[4] "Various" can be a large number, though it doesn't have to be. Mark's simulations test hundreds, millions, or even billions of scenarios to see which strategies are most robust. Ben's Blindspots' war games typically focus on a few strategically damaging (blindsiding) ones.

advice to the maverick

If you're not lucky enough to be prospering at Alphabet, what should you do amid the slowing of the global economy, or the maturing of the North American market, or the deflationary pressures in Europe, or the rise of China, or whatever other excuse Corporate dreams up for the inevitable slowing of its galactic expansion? Whatever it is, it increases the pressure to perform even as it makes the goal harder to reach.

You are a maverick. You sense the pressure, and you see the frenzy. You can offer unconventional strategies, but you'll face Corporate's preferred solution: Deny, then panic.

Here are two of the generic things that generic others might urge you to do: Get back to basics, or hunker down to wait it out.

And here's what you *should* do: Outthink your competitors. Growing in a no-growth market means a zero-sum game because *they* have to lose for *you* to win. They won't volunteer to lose, so you have to find ways to help them lose. Simulate ways in which their decline accelerates your growth. Start by reverse-engineering a scenario in which competitor X has lost market share. How did that happen? Then select the most promising tactic that can bring about or "encourage" that share loss for that competitor. Naturally, for you to outsmart a competitor, you need to look at the world from its perspective, to dive deep into its thinking and tactics.[5]

---

[5] It's a little different if you focus on profits rather than market share. Market share is a zero-sum game because there is always, always exactly 100 percent market share in a market, and the only way you can raise yours is to take it from someone else. Profit is not necessarily a zero-sum game; it is possible for everyone's profits to rise or everyone's to fall. Not forever, of course; when profits get too high (collusion?), new competitors have an incentive to enter the market, and when profits get too low (price wars?), competitors go bankrupt.

advice to the maverick, continued

If your competitor is Corporate through and through, count yourself lucky. Corporate never considers others' perspectives. It's too proud and overconfident its plans will work out if only they are executed perfectly. Be warned, though, that when your Corporate competitor misses its goals, it might flail around in a panic. Factor it into your predictions and strategy.

Then bring up your idea at the first meeting. Ask: Why don't we do this or that to increase our competitors' discomfort? What must we do to avoid imitating their mistakes in our desire to *do something*? How can we turn their decline into our opportunity?

Your idea may not get buy-in at first since you are a maverick and Corporate's instinct is to go for the formula (and call it "getting back to basics"). Don't get discouraged. Your name will be mentioned somewhere, sometime, as someone who has interesting ideas. "Interesting" is the golden ticket. It's better than "hard worker" or "doing a good job."

"Interesting" is the first step to being recognized as a "fresh thinker." Fresh thinking is in desperately short supply precisely when management needs it most: during times of slow growth or decline. As it panics, management actually narrows its focus rather than broadening it. It thinks short-term: Make the pain stop! It thinks tactically: Put everything on sale! It thinks historically: What did we do last time to get out of this pickle?

Be aware that management is in a state of altered consciousness. Be gentle, be considerate, and above all, make sure your unconventional ideas offer solutions and relief. Being blinded by stellar performance means that for a while management can't see too well. It will ignore your unorthodox, proactive strategies as fixing something that isn't broken. When *Today* hits,

advice to the maverick, continued

management is blinded by grief. It can't believe Not Today has become Today. Tell them what T. S. Eliot said: "If you aren't in over your head, how do you know how tall you are?"

circling the wagons is not a strategy

CHAPTER 17

"Reality is the leading cause
of stress among those
in touch with it."

—LILY TOMLIN

Some readers may question whether we exaggerate in this book. Even though each of us has worked with Corporate for several decades, some readers may dare to question our objectivity in ascribing sloppy thinking to esteemed and powerful leaders worshipped by millions.

How dare you question us? We are the world's *leading* consultants.

People's desire to see their business idols remain the heroes is fully understandable. They often ascribe magical powers to individual executives, seeing them as the embodiment of progress. If the heroes and heroines just put their minds to it, they can rekindle complacent companies, rejuvenate aging innovators, recapture market dominance, and cure baldness.

Sometimes they can. Often, they can't. No matter how hard Paul Otellini tried, he could not break through Intel's PC-centric mentality. Carly Fiorina did not rescue HP from decline. Eddie Lampert did not keep Sears from bankruptcy. We like to believe in heroes and heroines. Disney has this effect on us. But even Disney couldn't save ABC TV from its decline in the face of cable, streaming services, and boycotts. In reality, executives often work within environments, internal and external, that determine outcomes more than the "heroes" and "heroines" themselves.

In this chapter, we explore the internal Corporate environment for factors that hinder leaders from accomplishing their visions. We answer the question: Is it the CEO, or is it the culture? We leave no stone unturned in looking for reasons why Corporate actually digs itself deeper when it could have avoided the quicksand. OK, sometimes the sand is not that quick, but the principle holds.

COVER UP THE CRACKS AT ALL TIMES

It is hard to know Corporate from the outside. Occasionally, however, we get a glimpse, and it is scary.

Consider General Motors. Its current CEO is Mary Barra. When Barra took over GM, press releases described her as a competent executive with a long and successful track record as GM's product chief. Her predecessor as product chief was the *legendary* Robert (Bob) Lutz.

Bob Lutz had been a legend in Detroit. When Barra replaced him in 2011, a press release said, "Bob Lutz, the longtime auto industry executive who led nearly a complete overhaul of General Motors' lineup, will retire May 1. 'My work here is done,' the 78-year-old executive said in an e-mail to The Associated Press." In the same press release, one analyst, who was quoted by the *Huffington Post,* went even further: "Bob had an uncanny ability to champion an idea or a concept through the organization," said Michael Robinet, a former automotive analyst with CSM Worldwide in Michigan. "While at GM, he was able to globalize the company and make it think like one GM. He was the ultimate car guy."

Sounds good, doesn't it? The ultimate car guy.

Yet when Barra was appointed CEO, *USA Today* on January 12, 2014 quoted Dan Akerson (then GM's CEO) saying ". . . when she took the global product chief's job, she stepped into a confused nightmare and put it right better and faster than expected." Praise and accolades to a new appointment are what one expects from a well-oiled PR machine. But this was more than stock PR. That was a moment of honesty like no other. "Confused nightmare?" Who was responsible for the confused nightmare Barra put right? Could it be the legendary Bob Lutz, *the ultimate car guy?*

Analysts, historians, Harvard Business School case writers, and every auto columnist on the planet have analyzed GM's decline since the 1960s. The list of external events (determined foreign competitors, rising gasoline prices) and internal constraints (union work rules) undoubtedly count for a hefty portion of the decline but not all. Just for perspective, in the 1960s, GM alone had 50 percent of the U.S. market. In 2014, when Barra stepped in, GM had 17.9 percent. If one believes this decline is purely the result of external factors and labor costs, fine. We don't. Airbus has been a determined and sophisticated competitor to Boeing, but Boeing did not flounder. Samsung has been a determined competitor to Apple, but if Apple is in trouble, then we'd like to have trouble like that.

When competition intensifies, one expects to lose some market share. For GM, however, the issue was not mere "competitive pressure." It was a massacre. Its rivals stayed superior to GM for decades.

Have you ever wondered why GM did not receive *Consumer Reports* "buy" recommendations for its products *even once* for decades? Why couldn't GM design cars that people would love to buy more than imports? How difficult is it to look around, see where you stand, and try to make your position *distinct*? Even Audi succeeded in that, and they are Germans, and Germans abhor marketing concepts such as "distinct."

A potential explanation glimpsed from Akerson's refreshing honesty—by no means is this the whole story—is a culture of *mirror, mirror, on the wall*. Corporate loves mirrors. Every morning for 50 years, GM executives have looked in the mirror (their subordinates) and asked, "Who are the fairest car guys of them all?" And the subordinates sang in unison, "We are, you are, oh ultimate car guys." Customers, though, went with reliable, high-fuel-mileage Snow White.

Think about that: *50 years*. It was not a single CEO who led GM from world dominance to bankruptcy. It was not a single management team. It was not a single event or a single decision. It was *half a century* of decisions, *generations* of smart, motivated, educated, experienced managers and executives who *wanted to succeed* but trapped themselves.

And if you *really* want to be scared sober in your job, think about this: Those managers and executives started off just like you. "I would never advance such sloppy thinking," you tell your mirror. They had the same conversations with their mirrors.

DON'T FALL FOR PR

Corporate is not an intellectual construct. It is a real, breathing, uncompetitive culture of human beings who forgot how to compete. Mavericks should think twice before falling for Corporate's PR. Read between the lines. Put the press release in context of industry developments and try to discern fluffery from reality. Ask yourself a *disconfirming* question: What *negative* events or results would make this company want to release a statement full of artificial sweeteners? Who's the real audience: Customers, employees, competitors, or investors?

Think twice and remember Positivismitis. "We used to have 50 percent of the U.S. car market. There's no reason why we can't have it again." It's nice that you had it before, but do you have sufficiently unique value to warrant 50 percent again? When you see your share plummeting for, oh, a decade or so, it's not wise to assume it's an aberration.

Think twice, and watch out for overtightening. You want to maintain profits to keep the share price up, but you don't head off a serious competitive threat by going on a diet. You need muscle and energy. You need fresh perspectives. You need to stay in front, not try to catch up from behind and run out of breath. Car guys? How about car gals? How about car juniors?

Think twice and call things what they are. When you have to stuff dealerships full of cars the dealers can't sell, when you have to bribe customers with cheap financing (cheap for them, expensive for you), when you have to unload inventory through fleet sales, call it what it is: an existential threat.

It's a tall task, but it will help you survive in business. Looking inside, surrounding yourself with sycophants who describe you as the ultimate [your industry] guys/gals, and gushing about the "great team" will make you feel proud to stick your finger in a leaking dike, but the problem is not to find a spare finger. The problem is to make the dike *stop leaking*.

HOW TO MAKE DECLINE WORSE

According to *The Economist's* article, "The Age of the Torporation," published on October 24, 2015, the good times for Corporate may be over.

Over the past 15 years, Fortune 500 executives could make up for declining fortunes in mature markets with fresh growth in emerging markets. Alas, that golden age is at or near its end.

Half the big companies saw falling profits in recent years. For the first time in a decade, even Nestlé, the largest food conglomerate in the world, has missed its sales target for three years resulting in the scrapping of the target in 2017 by its (not coincidentally) new CEO. Knowing how Nestlé is run by Swiss bankers, this must be a serious shock. Bellwether companies, such as IBM, Walmart, GE, Kraft, and InBev (the beer giant), saw growth slow, stall, or outright reverse. Even the tech industry's profits, *The Economist* says, have been overall flat.

While annual profits fluctuate, *The Economist* predicts large companies may face a *long-term* decline because they have lost three of their most important profit-boosters: Emerging markets, financial leverage, and low relative wages. While some financial leverage may be temporarily restored with lower corporate tax rates in the U.S., rising interest rates are inevitable. This may not be just a short-term blip. Emerging markets (e.g., China and even Brazil) are on an inevitable trend of creating their own powerhouses. They may yet turn Corporate as well (which will help the Western Corporate), but it may take decades. Until then, they are fearsome competitors. The golden age of Western corporations may be ending.

Successful executives have a lot to lose. It is natural, then, for them to avoid risk and attempt to guard existing profits. They have more to lose than gain from being bold. However, when growth stalls, risk-averse executives unwilling to think creatively and competitively lose out to those who have *less to lose* . . . and those who see *opportunity* when risk-averse companies overtighten both thinking and investment in fresh ideas.

Corporate's knee-jerk response to decline—circle the wagons, cover up, maintain the façade, praise the "team"—only speeds and deepens the decline. In the end, it is the next generation that will face the music. But if you think rap is music, maybe you deserve facing it. Sorry—we are just old-fashioned rockers and folkies.

IS YOUR COMPANY STUCK, OR IS IT THE WHOLE INDUSTRY?

One classic example of a stagnating company was Yahoo! In 2017, *Business Insider* reported that the company sold at a fraction— about 4 percent—of its old value to Verizon to disappear into its belly like plankton into a whale's. In comparing Yahoo! with AOL, *The Economist* notes that the difference between Marissa Mayer (Yahoo!'s former CEO) and Tim Armstrong (AOL's former CEO) is in how boldly they acted.

It is easy in retrospect to call one strategy bold and another not-bold. "Bold" is vague enough to accommodate a lot of variations. What is clear, though, was that Armstrong's strategy of turning AOL into Aol.—a tech platform for high-growth areas such as programmatic advertising and video advertising—worked, while Mayer's strategy of adding scale, but not much technology, didn't. AOL and Yahoo! remind us of Kodak and Fuji. Both recognized the decline in film, but while Kodak's strategy of staying with digital photography failed (margins were too low), Fuji took its technical expertise and applied it to growth areas such as healthcare, pharmaceuticals, and LCD screens. It is not enough to do things right; we must do the *right* things right. That's the hallmark of strategy. *Recognizing* the right things often requires bold, anti-Corporate thinking . . . and that's why Corporate needs mavericks.

The end for Yahoo! was sad. What can you learn from it?

Sometimes, you can look at an industry and see it stagnating under conservative, formulaic Corporate management. Take transportation and banking, for example. In transportation, rail (in Europe) and taxis (in the U.S.) are threatened by substitutes. In Europe, the opening of the transportation market resembles the opening of the skies: Dozens of bus companies are growing at neck-breaking speed. Even the age-old hitchhiking substitute to paid transport is being pumped up with technology (via the sharing app, BlaBlaCar.) In the banking industry, deregulation of data allows aggregation and analysis of consumers' financial portfolios (by firms like Mint and Bankin') so nonbanks can target consumers with specific products at a lower cost/lower price than banks (including a P2P lending app). And we didn't even mention cryptocurrencies because our Bitcoin just went from $18,000 to $3. We are a bit dizzy.

If the whole industry is mired in formulaic, traditional, bureaucratic thinking, and it closes itself to disruptive technologies, adopting Corporate-speak about "agility" will not solve anything. Stagnating industries need bold moves the way fluttering hearts need shocks.

MOST MANAGERS THINK THEIR EXECUTIVES ARE TIMID

The fact that technology can disrupt existing business models is neither surprising nor new. Undoubtedly, the invention of the sharpened stick disrupted the trade in big stones used for hunting and killing mammoths.

A lot has been written lately on the virtue of being agile. Agile is the new black. Agility, however, comprises mostly quick adjustments to existing strategy on a local (tactical) level. Applying bandages faster is not enough to lift a company out of stagnation or allow it to fight disruption, real or imaginary.

the NEW employee manual

We imagine a conversation between a Homo Habilis trader and a Homo Erectus buyer. Homo Habilis disappeared when the more advanced Homo Erectus showed up (we came later still). We believe it was because Homo Habilis was all about agility. Don't believe us? Ask them:

H. Erectus chief: Hi, Habilis. What do you have for us today?

H. Habilis trader: Chief, the latest in sharp stones.

H. Erectus chief: Sorry, pre-man. We now go with the new disruptor, the spear. You see, we attach the sharp edge to this long branch, and we get an aerodynamic . . .

H. Habilis trader: Aerodynamic, shmerodynamic. Chief, don't go with this cockamamie new gadget. It is dangerous. Look what happened to Jamie—he stabbed his own foot!

Jamie (at a distance): Argh, argh, arghhhhhh!

H. Erectus chief: Yeah, but we can throw it at a really large mammoth from 200 feet!

H. Habilis trader: Of course, Chief, but we just came out with Stone version 2.0, and you can actually see the improvements. It comes with sharper edges than before! See for yourself. I am throwing it now at the mammoth over there.

Jamie (yelling at a distance): Arghhhhhh!!!!!! (Thud.)

H. Erectus chief: I think you killed Jamie instead.

Many in Corporate assume, erroneously, that improving operations will let them fend off disruptive technologies. At times, one can hold off a disruptive alternative by coexisting with it, making improvements to existing products or services (example: cloud computing vs. local storage). As the fictional Homo Habilis trader shows, however, one has to make sure this is not a delusion. Fixing stagnation requires the *opposite* of risk aversion, which means bold thinking. Moves to end stagnation may appear risky, but the real risk—the risk they *should* be averting—is *not* to move. The problem is that the same executives who reigned during the *good* times might be unsuitable for reviving companies. They might be brilliant, powerful, visionary people, but they have become prisoners of their own success, singers of their own legends, guardians of their track records (not the galaxy). The more they focus on their past and their legacies, the more they worry it is risky to change and the more they

larry the lion

Not everyone is complacent. Larry Ellison, the fearsome founder and chairman of Oracle, has been leading the company's strategy for over 40 years. When most of his peers fell into hesitant, risk-avoiding "man-agership," Ellison remained as focused as always on competing. When cloud computing made an appearance on the enterprise IT horizon, many predicted Oracle, with its huge legacy business of on-premises databases, would be replaced by pure-cloud vendors. Instead, Ellison focused on *clients'* risk aversion. When it comes to managing their data, the vast majority of companies prefer the hybrid model: Keeping some data on-premises while placing other data in the cloud. Moreover, Ellison never forgot his famous focus on competitors, including the ones that still rely on Oracle. His example? Amazon. A competitor with its own database and cloud products uses an Oracle database to run its own business.

Covering up the cracks by throwing buzzwords like "we must become more agile" (translation: "How come I didn't even know about com-petitor X's move?") is not the same as boldly going where no one has gone before and where no one is going now. But going somewhere new requires perspectives not easily found in Corporate.

feel they lose by admitting their strategy doesn't work any longer. Meanwhile, their senior positions and their histories of success mean others won't challenge them in time. A not-very-funny comedy of errors.

Many managers think their big bosses are slow to act, but more significantly, when they *do* act, it is with incremental, hesitant, small tactical moves insufficient to turn the ocean liner away from the iceberg. It is often just the "same old same old," trying to prop up leading positions with existing strategies. However, as Gary Stibel, a famous consultant, observes in a stinging LinkedIn post, even savvy, brand-driven companies that depend on creative thinking for their success can fall into a mediocre marketing strategy.

HYPERBOLIC FORECASTS

Corporate responses to dwindling fortunes follow a predictable script: Keep a brave front, make optimistic forecasts, claim the strategy is *about* to work, and express confidence in the future. *Mirror, mirror on the wall.* One recent victim of wishful thinking, reported in a 2015 *USA Today* story, was UnitedHealth, which demonstrated the hyperbole with optimistic projections about the Affordable Care Act, also known as Obamacare. The frantic waves of consolidation in so many industries—pharma, consumer products, food, and IT, to mention a few—reflect another desperate move to prop up sagging growth curves.

The decision to go bold requires that the top must grant impunity to those proposing solutions. (Impunity from *top management itself.*) A timid top makes it dangerous for middle management (and mavericks like you) even to propose bold moves. Risk-averse middle management has its assistants fetch stale coffee, not brew fresh ideas.

When "judgment" day comes, though, it's the young managers who will pay, not senior executives. Last in, first out. But the problem goes beyond who gets the not-so-golden, just-a-little-porous parachutes. Those remaining at the company will face rising challenges, such as China and AI, that were left unattended, delayed, or ignored because their older bosses chose to circle the wagons rather than compete.

WHICH IS MORE IMPORTANT: STRATEGY OR EXECUTION?

Bold moves are never easy. We don't claim they're cheap and safe. But one reason leaders discard mavericks' thinking is because they pay three seconds' attention to strategy and immediately proceed to execution challenges.

Which is more important strategy or execution?[1] That's a perennial debate among strategists, and it proves strategists know how to have a good time. Three strategists walk into a bar, and everyone else leaves.

Those who don't like to take sides say "both." This is the vanilla answer from people who also follow (and like!) the popular posts on LinkedIn that claim the secrets to getting hired, promoted, living long, and/or being wealthy are to be kind, work hard, and avoid hitting bosses in the face.

You need to make a choice. Do you know why? Because strategy is all about choices. Leadership is about motivating. Management is about organizing and controlling. Strategy is about one thing and one thing only: Making choices.

Making choices is the hardest thing in the world for successful companies with well-compensated executives. It's hard because it means *not* doing something, and that sounds red-flag-waving, emergency-siren-blaring risky. The biggest risk for well-compensated executives in successful companies is that they will make a mistake and cause that compensation and success to come crashing to an end. Refusing to choose—"covering all the bases" in Corporate-sports-speak—seems so much safer.

---

[1] In case they didn't clarify in business school, "executing a strategy" does *not* mean killing it, though at times this is exactly what happens.

why is strategy so hard?

We suggest three reasons:

1. *When you make a choice, you have to sacrifice something.* Old product lines, big markets that are getting commoditized, customers who demand more than you should give. But you don't "lose" something; you *gain* distinction. Giving up revenue in the short term for better positioning in the long term is soul-tearing. Saying "goodbye" to something that worked so well for a decade or longer and may still be working is torture. It's like the sun's rays on a vampire's skin. Just remember: Strategy is for the future, not the past.

2. *Strategy is not marketing.* Strategy has to be logically consistent across R&D, manufacturing, logistics, purchasing, human resources (talent management), and other value-chain activities that *together* produce unique value. Unique value is what makes strategy *competitive* strategy.

3. *But the most important factor of all: Strategy is hard because competitors will do what is necessary to foil it,*[2] *and other high-impact third parties will determine its final outcome.* That simple fact means that you can execute a strategy perfectly and still fail miserably because competitors' strategies were superior to yours or you just didn't understand fully the influence of other parties. The skill of competing doesn't guarantee success; it just helps you not to shoot yourself in the foot using other parties' weapons.

---

[2] If they don't, then you got lucky.

People who think strategy and execution are equally important don't tell you that they really think strategy is overrated and execution is extremely hard. That's why they spend three seconds on strategy and fret endlessly about "New Package! Same Great Taste!"

They might be right, but that's only when the strategy is a mere continuation of the current strategy with a tactical tweak here or there. And that's what often passes at Corporate for strategy.

The vast majority of employees—99.99937 percent to be exact and scientific (we checked)—are dedicated to execution. That is, by definition, the role of employees and managers but not leaders. In a typical Corporate unit, that translates into thousands, tens of thousands, *hundreds* of thousands, of people who toil day and night and often on the weekends and during vacations in Spain to implement their company's strategy. If 100,000 employees putting checkmarks on tasks accomplished, meetings attended, quotas met, emails sent, and vendors contracted can't execute, who can? The North Korean military? The Argentinian finance minister?

So why do managers think execution is hard and strategy is easy? Probably because no one gathers them to take a break from the relentless execution for one day and think strategically. When someone does, as we do in simulations, managers are often shocked at how hard strategy is.

The crux of the issue is not actually what's harder. Who cares? The crux is the underlying belief that if execution were just a bit better (or actually, perfect), the company will prosper, competition will shrivel, and peace will dawn on Earth. That underlying belief fits well with the knee-jerk response to stagnation (or god forbid) decline: Circle the wagons and execute the wrong strategy harder!

GOOD STRATEGY TRIUMPHS

Excellent execution cannot save bad strategy any more than fine china can save bad food.

Strategy stumbling on execution *might be* saved with honest communication from leaders who prefer confronting reality to listening to the "mirror, mirror on the wall" chorus. U.S. airlines' strategy of constant price wars was replaced by quiet "territorial division" where the U.S. was neatly carved up by dominating hubs (Delta in Atlanta, American in Dallas, and United in Newark, among others). Prices could then be raised given the fewer options available to passengers, and, coupled with reducing capacity and charging for *everything* extra (baggage, meals, seat selection; next: bathrooms?), proved a breakthrough to an industry that was once a perennial loser. No one in their right mind would call airline service outstanding, and dragging passengers bleeding from their seats because of overbooking has done little to gain admiration. But the profits keep soaring. And when the strategy of overbooking became a huge PR problem, airlines showed (tactical) agility by quickly replacing the practice of offering a cheese sandwich and a recycled water bottle as compensation for those volunteering to give up their seats with thousands of dollars in incentives.

The strategy of dominating hubs was the result of consolidation. It created barriers to entry. Loyalty programs—a truly innovative marketing strategy—put smaller regional airlines at a crushing disadvantage and further promoted consolidation into big ones. It may have been less than cherished by consumer advocates, but the alternative, when every second day a new airline popped up with two old airplanes and tickets costing one chicken, was bankruptcy.

Imagine if consolidation hadn't occurred and there were 10,000 airlines cruising the skies.

"Hello, this is your captain speaking. Unfortunately, our airline has just declared bankruptcy. Our credit cards are maxed out, and we didn't have enough money to fuel the plane all the way to our destination. The company also reneged on its maintenance contract, so our GPS system gives directions only to Vladivostok, and we think no one on board wants to go there." (Sound of papers rustling.) "Right, no one for Vladivostok. We will land in what we believe is the island of Samoa."

Then the flight attendant comes on the intercom. "If Samoa is your final destination, we wish you a good day. If not, we expect another airline to start serving this route within the next year or so.

In the meantime, we would like to offer you a variety of nuts, but we have only peanuts. This is flight 539 to Akron, Ohio."

But interestingly enough, Southwest Airlines, which (among other features) has proudly kept the strategy of being *the only* domestic airline that doesn't charge for the first two checked bags, is also the *only* airline that has been profitable for 44 years. Now that's a competitive strategy that doesn't even need to correct for bad execution.

Why can't Corporate do the same? Giora Keinan, of Tel Aviv University, and several other researchers studied the effect of stress on perception. His 1999 study, reported in the journal *Anxiety, Stress & Coping*, revealed that especially during periods of stress, our human tendency is to narrow our focus: "Let's just do what the others are doing, only execute it *better*. We have a 6.5-inch entertainment screen while *they* only have 5.8 inches."

Strategy is hard—but it's worth the effort. Execution is hard, but if the strategy is wrong, at best it is not worth the effort.

advice to the maverick

Search for "coach" on LinkedIn. There is Coach the company and 1.9 million people with titles that include "coach" in them, from team coach, success coach, results coach, professional coach, business coach, and executive coach to agile coach (!) and a million other titles. We are certain these people add value and dispense useful advice or the field of coaching would have disappeared by now. Many are former executives. Some are organizational psychologists. Some probably came from declining companies that laid them off. Have they learned the lessons of those companies?

We are none of the above. We are entrepreneurs and students of strategy. We have worked with most major firms in the U.S. and many in Europe and elsewhere. Our advice is based on being there in the strategy trenches where

advice to the maverick, continued

the skill of competing should take center stage. When we say mavericks are the most valuable asset for companies in distress, this is not just empty, inspirational pandering to the mavericks reading our book. Mavericks can offer fresh thinking years *before* the axe comes down. Mavericks could have saved GM from bankruptcy if its culture weren't so devoted.

It's hard to offer advice to a maverick working in a culture that values conformity, whose mentality is "circle the wagons," whose strategy is dispensed with three slides, and where execution takes center stage. The irony is that during stagnation and decline, Corporate needs mavericks the most but uses them the least.

Is being inexperienced a real obstacle to bold ideas? No, it's not, but experienced Corporate lifers like to hold on to that feeling of, "I've seen it all and it won't work, so go back to stapling this presentation's handouts, OK?"

We don't blame them. They often feel overwhelmed with the competitive landscape erupting. But waiting patiently for the layers above you to recognize your fresh strategic mindset is also not a viable solution. Instead, we propose this: Strategize in your own little Corporate corner.

Everything you do, every task you carry out in your cubicle, involves strategy. How you *choose* to come across is a strategy question. If your strategy is to blend in, do as you are told, and hope for the best, you are imitating what millions of small-c corporate managers and professionals do around the globe. Those who will rise, however, are those who take chances and try a bold move. It may involve not playing the mirror-mirror-on-the-wall game when a big boss asks, "What do you guys think?" This opportunity may appear unexpectedly, and you should be prepared. Make your move. Yes, it is risky, as bosses do not often listen to mavericks, and it requires crafty execution so as not to turn the boss into an enemy. But it beats murmuring, "You are the fairest of them all."

Our suggestion, based on years of never playing the mirror game even if that meant the client would never ask us back, is to say: "If I may, I'd like to suggest that we take a different direction. I believe this new direction will be hard for our competitors to follow quickly for the following reasons. I further believe we can test it in a war game to see how it fares against all high-impact players."

Make sure you suggest, not complain. Research by Charles Okuonzi of Uganda Technology and Management University shows suggestions (so-called "promotive messages" in psychological jargon) have better chance of affecting leaders. In general, it is always better to suggest an opportunity than to report a risk.

Stay very respectful. A confident but *respectful* voice is, according to a 2017 post on HBR.org, one of the best ways to get the right attention. Try not to show your nervousness. Be concise. Do not under any circumstances start crying. Control the shaking in your hands. Wait for the response.

May we *suggest* this is your *opportunity* to shine?

corporate
believes
in
magic
formulas

"The problem with being a
leader is that you're never sure
if you're being followed
or chased."

—Claire A. Murray

When archeologists dig into the ground near the Mediterranean, they find artifacts from ancient cities. When 2,000 years from now, archeologists dig into the ground of a modern city, they'll find artifacts, too: Presentations with 2x2 matrices.

There is no Corporate artifact more ubiquitous, sacred, and worshipped than the 2x2 matrix as seen in Figure 18.1.

That is especially true if you can label one of the four quadrants a Magic Quadrant. The magic multiplies if you call the *entire* 2x2

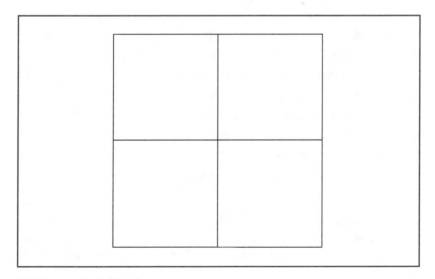

FIGURE 18.1—**2x2 Matrix**

matrix the Magic Quadrant even though there are four quadrants in a matrix. That's Gartner's Magic Quadrant matrix.

Gartner Inc. presents an entire market analysis in a 2x2 matrix. One axis is "completeness of vision" and the other is "ability to execute." The report is called the Magic Quadrant. We are not making that up. We are also not making up that they call the entire matrix (containing four quadrants) the Magic Quadrant, rather than, well, calling one quadrant magic. Who are we to argue with Dumbledore?

Gartner calls the upper right quadrant the leader, meaning companies high on execution and vision. If any quadrant is magical, that's probably the one since Gartner says on its own website, "keep in mind that focusing on the leaders' quadrant isn't always the best course of action," which implies that it *usually* is, but Gartner wants some magic wiggle room.

Do you know how kids in the pre-K class get excited when they are told they are the day's best listener or the day's neatest kid who collected all the toys?

That's how Corporate in the IT space reacts to Gartner's analysis—one that determines which companies go into the leader quadrant and which are magically condemned to mediocrity in the non-leader quadrants.

And do you know how the politically correct culture today demands that everyone's a winner for just showing up?[1]

That's Gartner's markets. If you are big and powerful and famous, and full of free fat flow, and not a leader in one category, Gartner will define a market in which you are. At last call, Gartner had defined 65 categories (markets).

Gartner's 2x2 is so influential, so powerful, so *magical*, that when you search for it on the internet, there are thousands of hits,

---

[1] Not just today's culture. Mark entered a homemade movie contest and got a fancy, embossed, suitable-for-framing "Certificate of Entry" 47 years ago. The company that issued it, Kodak, is gone, but the Certificate is ready for its archaeologist.

either of Gartner itself or of companies shouting: Look everybody, Gartner placed us in the leader quadrant!

There is little doubt Gartner takes its ranking seriously. The companies and technologies it covers are all well researched. Despite persistent rumors of "pay-to-play," no one has ever proved Gartner is anything but independent. Of course, until 2008 and the financial collapse, no one had ever proved rating agencies in the financial space, like Moody's and Standard & Poor's, were producing questionable ratings.

In a now-famous lawsuit in 2009, a company claimed Gartner defamed it. Networkworld.com reports the suit was dismissed for lack of specifics, but the intriguing point was Gartner's defense: It claimed First Amendment protection because its ratings were "pure opinion." In other words, legally speaking, the ratings didn't have anything to do with facts. As we said . . . Magic.

You'd think that would put a crimp in IT legends' use of the Magic Quadrant for marketing purposes.

Not by a mile.

Such 2x2s are pure magic, and don't expect the Magic Quadrant to change regardless of evidence it is "pure opinion." Even if a study shows that companies Gartner pronounced leaders have gone to the dogs one by one over a short period of time, people will still pay millions to get the 2x2.

In this chapter, we journey down Alice in Wonderland's rabbit hole: We examine Corporate's fascination with any formula by any author or vendor that promises an easy route to the Promised Land of greatness. From Gartner to Jim Collins, there's a magic formula out there for every COOC. We're going to examine these further and end up with a serious look at your future.

FROM GREAT TO . . . ?

In 2014, Professor Phil Rosenzweig of the famed IMD business school in Switzerland eviscerated Jim Collins's *Good to Great* (HarperBusiness, 2001) book and many other popular "success formula" management books. Rosenzweig used a simple and elegant argument to show that the methodology behind those lists suffers a fatal flaw, called the halo effect.

The halo effect (also the name of Rosenzweig's book) is the psychological tendency to confuse dependent and independent variables in explaining success. In other words, explaining the dependent variable (success) with variables that are actually influenced by that dependent variable, and thus are not *independent,* muddies and can even nullify the analysis. A company's performance creates a "halo" that influences the way the firm is *perceived.* When the company is performing well, people conclude it has visionary leaders, a superb strategy, and a culture that brings out the best in employees. When performance goes down, the *same* attributes and behaviors that haven't changed one iota are suddenly judged as "bad."

Rosenzweig writes, "In fact, many things we commonly claim drive company performance are simply attributes based on prior performance."

Publishers Weekly summed up Rosenzweig's argument against following "success formulas" as follows:

"Following these delusions might provide managers with a comforting story that helps them frame their actions, but it also leads them to gross simplification and to ignore the constant demands of changing technologies, markets, customers and situations."

You'd think Rosenzweig's meticulously documented case against *Good to Great* would cause the business crowd to stop buying that book, right?

Ha. Don't make us laugh; it hurts.

Collins's *Good to Great* is still number one in the Kindle store for books on "strategic management." Gartner would call it a Magic Quadrant leader. We call it a fairy tale.

But people love magic.

do *you* believe in magic?

A baseball game is about to begin. The coach of Team A goes over to Team B's dugout.

Coach (addressing Team B's shortstop and second baseman): Tinker and Evers, you guys show incredible hustle out there. You're legendary for your double plays. Can you tone it down a bit, though? It's dangerous when our guys slide into second base.

Tinker (looking sheepish): Sorry, Coach. I guess we got carried away. (Evers nods in vigorous agreement.)

Chance (the opposing team's first baseman): And I won't try to block first so much.

Coach (to Team B's pitcher): Harold, I want you to lay off all those curveballs. Too many the last time we played. Put a few more right over the center of the plate.

Harold: Sure thing, Coach! Sorry if I was rude last time.

Some people in Corporate seem to believe in that kind of magic, the belief that your competitors are on your side. Odds are about 40 percent that *you* believe in it. We are not making up that number.

Remember Mark's Top Pricer Tournament, that about 2,000 people have entered? (See page 164.) The Tournament's entry form is clear that competition is involved. The instructions include statements as blunt as "The only way to outperform your competitors is to out-strategize them."

do *you* believe in magic?, continued

Participants can take as much time as they want—it's handled as a kind of homework assignment—to develop their strategies.

There are plenty of pricing options to choose from: 14,739 possible combinations of pricing decisions and moves, to be exact.[2] The strategies play out over a simulated three-year time horizon.

Mark asks his audiences a simple question when he debriefs and discusses their Tournament results: What did you assume your competitors would do? That question is generally met with silence. People spend their time focusing on their businesses, not competitors'. That's not entirely surprising, given that business education and tools (forecasts, targets, spreadsheets, operations, etc.) are about what *we* are going to do. Corporate goals are all about *us*. If you can't get the job done, I'll get someone who can! Implicit: The job can be done. (Use magic if necessary.) The same thing happens often in the business war games we both facilitate. Corporate is all about what *it* will do, not what competitors could or would.

But back to the 40 percent odds that *you* believe in helpful-competitor magic. Why 40 percent?

The Tournament entry form does not ask "did you ignore the competition when you designed your pricing strategy?" It's a useless question. No one would answer yes.

---

[2] That is not a joke. And neither is this: In each of its three simulated industries with three simulated competitors, there are 3,201,872,665,419 possible scenarios.

do *you* believe in magic?, continued

However, 40 percent of entrants think so little (or so ineffectively) about competitors that their Tournament strategies perform worse than a strategy that says, "Stay on course and wake me up in three years." Perhaps they think competitors will not attack. Or they think their attack on competitors is certain to succeed. Or they think their attack on competitors will not provoke a counter-attack. Or they think competitors will follow them ("we are the leader") and will take a nap, too. They are the equivalent of the coach who believes the *other* team will play by his playbook. They find a strategy *they* like, and they implicitly assume competitors will help it come true.

It's not surprising that they manage rather than compete because Corporate is organized around managing rather than competing. The MBA degree is a Master's in Business Administration, not a Master's in Business Competing. "If you can't get the job done, I'll get someone who can" means we believe it's within your power to get the job done, so if I'm disappointed, then it's your fault.

Mark notes that the most common (by far) question from Tournament participants is: "How did I do?" What he says they *should* ask (and a few do) is: "How does it work?" Those who do are mavericks. They're not looking for confirmation or platitudes about themselves; they're looking for insight about others.

What Corporate needs—and how *you* boost your personal competitive advantage, maverick—to learn the skill of competing is "how does it work" thinking. If you understand how markets work and how competitors work, you are learning to compete.

Not Magic? Not Interested.

Here, again from the *Publishers Weekly* review of *The Halo Effect*: "[Rosenzweig's] . . . argument about the complexity of sustained achievement may end up limiting the market for this smart and spicy critique."

If success doesn't follow a simple formula, so-called savvy managers just don't read it. The herd prefers the "How Buffett Made His First $10 Billion" story over a success-has-no-formula book. On the other hand, we notice you're still reading our book. You are a maverick.

Alas, belief in magic comes at a price. As we contended in the previous chapter, circling the wagons around a "formula" that (seems to have) worked before, and making hesitant tactical tweaks (in the name of "agility"), is relying more on luck than on strategic thinking. Down the road, those who are young managers today will have to deal with huge challenges left to them by Corporate's management-by-magic tomorrow.

Back to the Magic and Matrices

All 2x2 matrices are easy, comforting tools. It doesn't really matter what the 2x2 is about. Just imagine a 2x2 matrix (see Figure 18.1 on page 275 for assistance). If you can imagine one right away, you are probably a consultant. If not, a consultant can imagine one for you.

A 2x2 framework divides something into categories so as to:

1. Make the speaker sound smart and insightful and . . .
2. Simultaneously frame a problem or solution in a desired direction.

Here's a story, vaguely connected to 2x2. It is a true story; Mark was there. A guy he worked with had an elaborate theory about the economy, which he drew on a graph as a series of squiggles going from the lower left to the upper left, then from the upper left to the upper right, then from the upper right to the lower right. He spent a few minutes explaining it to the audience. He was full of words that seemed to mean something. Then someone in the audience pointed out that he'd rotated the graph by 90 degrees, so his explanation didn't hold. The consultant didn't skip a beat. He rotated the graph (this was in the days of transparencies) and re-explained it with a different message.

As the world's *leading* consultants, we have been exposed to so many 2x2 matrices we've had to have them surgically removed. But now, freed from cows and dogs and stars—labels for three quadrants in another famous matrix[3]—we are getting better every day.

advice to the maverick

Coaches and consultants will not hand you *The Halo Effect* when they meet you. More likely, they will ask if you've read *Good to Great* so they can bond with you over their enthusiasm. They will even be able to quote whole passages from it.

Rosenzweig's book became a runaway bestseller, but among more-discerning readers who valued his insight regarding the huge impact of factors outside their control on business success, however defined. As a maverick, his book should be in your library. (Finish ours first, please.)

One of the toughest issues you'll face is how to compete against magic. That requires master's-level mavericking. Magic doesn't *have* a great strategy; magic *is* a great strategy. It's differentiated and low-cost, and it has nothing but enthusiastic customer reviews on its website. Don't try to beat magic at its game. Instead, remember what we said about imitation (bad) and unique value (good). Make magic play *your* game. Your game is clarity and reality. If that doesn't work, you can even put up a magical 2x2 matrix of your own.

---

[3] We refer to the famous BCG Growth-Share Matrix. See www.netmba.com/strategy/matrix/bcg/.

advice to the maverick, continued

Mavericks face many more *internal* challenges outside their control. Yet mavericks must focus on outsmarting the competition even as they are bogged down with "busy work" of little value. That's what a choice of a business career is all about.

On a more personal level, how about drawing your own personal 2x2 (see Figure 18.2) of which jobs you'd like to go for (or stay in) and in which companies? According to a recent post on LinkedIn, there is evidence that the labor market is favoring sellers in some fields. In other words, if you are a professional, you may get to choose to which company you will sell your services including not selling them to any company at all (that is, becoming an entrepreneur). Of course, the question is, what do you put on the axes?

Potential for meaningful impact	This food truck is *mine!*	Ah, the startup life! No glamor, l-o-n-g hours, but enormous pride.	Safe and secure. Your family owns the company.
	I am a cog in the machine	Corporate *without* the benefits. Why are you here??	Corporate *with* benefits. Do not confuse with friends with benefits.
		Parents' basement until 45	Full health insurance
		Level of security	

FIGURE 18.2—**To Be or Not to Be Matrix**

Our experience with small-c corporate managers is that when they are young, what they crave the most is for someone to affirm the importance of their work. When they are older, that drops to seventh place behind providing for their kids' college tuition, saving for retirement, not moving again,

advice to the maverick, continued

having sex with their partner at least once a year, and remembering how to count to seven.[4] Choose wisely, maverick, before the kids come in.

---

[4] Did you notice we listed only *five* items, so importance-of-work drops to *sixth* place, not seventh? If you did, kudos. You pay attention. See the Executive Summary.

corporate
filters
inconvenient
information

"The funny thing is, I look at these magazines that make me so insecure and neurotic, but I'm in them!"

—Heather Graham

W e've introduced you to a long list (but wait, there's more!) of dysfunctions that can afflict Corporate. All of them could be reduced, mended, and even banished if Corporate allowed its people to discuss them freely. You can't address a problem if you don't first acknowledge it, said Freud, who immediately proceeded to deny his.

Smart and hard-working top executives should be especially motivated to listen to mavericks' voices in their own companies. That is true in theory, and it is true in many enterprises. But part of what makes Corporate Corporate is that its top executives *hear nothing.* The reason is: Corporate is neurotic.

The dictionary defines neurotic behavior as "overanxious." Woody Allen made this behavior popular in his movies—almost loveable.

We all know neurotic people. Sometimes even *we* are neurotic, just a charming little bit.

We think companies can be neurotic, too—especially when it comes to filtering inconvenient information. We would not bother to document this statement if it did not relate to the skill of competing and mavericks' career prospects. In this chapter, we'll cover that and offer a new tool called the Neurotic Index, or NIX. Use it to assess how your organization's neurotic behavior affects its skill at competing. Don't get neurotic about it, though.

GET TO KNOW THE NIX

We were inspired to create the NIX by a personal experience with a Fortune 500 company. We've dealt with Fortune 500 companies our entire professional lives, so we're used to a certain level of neurosis. Mid-level managers are often subject to unpredictable demands from the top level, which turns the mid-level managers mid-level neurotic from time to time. But this was different.

This company, an icon in the chemical industry that shall remain nameless to protect the innocent (including us), asked Ben to participate in a half-day executive retreat. The role was to make a presentation to the CEO and her or his top echelon on the topic of *external focus*. This is a core expertise for Ben, to which he has devoted a considerable part of his professional life. He even wrote a book or two about it.

What followed was a series of calls and emails in which at least two VPs (or SVPs, we are not sure) told him what to tell the CEO and his or her lieutenants, how to tell it, and most important, what *not* to dare tell her or him. He turned this "opportunity" down, naturally, but it got him thinking.

We all assume that top executives, especially of the biggest and most powerful companies, are enlightened masters of their own fates. They are knowledgeable, smart, and well-informed.

Well, they may be knowledgeable and smart, but in some companies they are definitely not well-informed. In such companies— the one Ben dealt with is an extreme example but not an isolated case— the information reaching the top of the top is totally and absolutely controlled, filtered, massaged, and directed by the subordinates. To what end? Here's the answer:

> (*Censor's note: Sorry, it's on a need-to-know basis, and you don't need to know.*)

The CEO and others at the top of the information chain live in the dark as to what is really happening out there (or in there).

As a maverick, you probably know your great insight may never make it to the top *even if it could save your product/service/company/planet.* On the flip side, executives can't exercise their skill at competing without strategic intelligence. If middle management isn't allowed to deliver intelligence to the top, executives will do the equivalent of running on mountain trails at night while wearing a blindfold. You can run, you can even win a race, but at great and unnecessary risk.

CEOs are smart. They know there is a lot of "window dressing" and filtering going on around them. Jamie Dimon of JPMorgan Chase famously said in a 2006 interview with *Fortune,* "In a big company, it's easy for people to BS you. A lot of them have been practicing for decades." But they delude *themselves* if they think they can overcome it by getting a close, trusted circle to "tell them the truth." Indeed, some are becoming puppets, and *they don't even know it.* They haven't gotten the memo, *literally.*

Which brings us back to the topic of competing as a skill. The ability of a company to compete depends on a relatively unfiltered flow of strategic intelligence reaching the decision-makers who can act on it. Decision-makers, from product managers to the board of directors, don't need to know *everything,* but they do need to know *something.* They need at least a trickle of truth and insight. Some amount of filtering is to be expected. The internal competition among executives for the attention of the leader—and by implication the power and resources that come with this attention—is part of the skill of competing among individuals. But the *ratio* of competing internally to competing externally should be kept within reasonable limits.

That ratio is what we call the Neurotic Index (NIX).

While scientists and statisticians haven't yet found a rigorous way to measure this ratio (if they have, they are too neurotic to tell us), we can think of ways to assess it.

Most managers recognize the state of neurosis in their companies. Let's assume that the NIX measures the focus on competing externally *vis-à-vis* competing internally. We can operationalize—a favorite Corporate term—the NIX as follows:

$$NIX = \frac{\text{Effort and energy devoted to acting on intelligence reaching the top}}{\text{Effort and energy devoted to filtering information \textit{from} reaching the top}}$$

If we further assume, arbitrarily, that in the typical Fortune 500's company the NIX is 100, how would you rate your company?

Here's a way you can quickly assess the answer. Would you pass this book up the ladder at your company? If you would, you and your company pass the test of the *denial tree* below.

The CEO of that iconic company, the one who was protected from reality by a "trusted circle" of handlers, stepped down in a surprising move a year after our experience with the presentation at the retreat that we declined. It might have surprised Wall Street, but it didn't surprise us. Executives can no more make good decisions without intelligence flowing freely upstairs than they can without oxygen flowing freely "upstairs." CEOs who want their companies to compete effectively should heed this lesson. But we are not talking to them, as they can hardly hear us through the thick protective layer of filters. We are talking to you.

Are you listening to us? Hello?

THE DENIAL TREE

An insidious form of neurosis in filtering information that replaces the skill of competing with wishful and sloppy thinking is the common, unconscious use of denial trees.

In an episode of CBS' enormously successful legal drama *The Good Wife*, a client of the law firm at the center of the show faces a tough business decision. He is the CEO of a fictional "power drink" company, and a 16-year-old girl has died after guzzling several of his company's beverages. The family sues. The law firm representing the company offers to settle for $800,000. The family's lawyer demands $14 million.

is your company neurotic?

Here, making its world debut, is a way to assess whether your company is a Corporate neurotic:

Step 1. "Ambush" a senior executive in the elevator. While trapped there with you for a whole minute, ask politely if they received the memo you sent about the rising quality of competing products by Chinese companies. Chances are they don't know who you are and, of course, never received your memo because you didn't send one. Then tell them you didn't send one, but you wanted them to know there is a whole lot of filtering going on and maybe they would like to conduct an experiment with you. They'll be either curious or furious. The latter means you need to look for a new job.[1] The former is a breakthrough for you.

Step 2. If they are curious, propose an experiment. You will send a provocative email about an unpleasant fact through company channels and see how much of the original remains intact as it crosses their doorstep. Example: "Millennials are increasingly reluctant to pay for our products," or "Our bureaucracy is bloated, our R&D is wasteful, and our high-growth projects lag behind smaller firms." You may have played this game as a child, and you all laughed at what came out at the other end. Naturally, your elevator executive must cooperate in this experiment, and they must have a doorstep. They usually do, as "open-space office" is for "our most valuable assets" (see Positivismitis in Chapter 9) but not for top executives. At any rate, chances are the email will be killed

---

[1] It might be safer to try the elevator ambush when you're interviewing, not after you've taken the job and moved your family. Also, make sure the elevator can't stop between floors.

---

is your company neurotic?, continued

by your immediate boss, so if you like them, bring them in on the experiment. If you don't, well . . . If Steps 1 and 2, fail, simply ask your next-wall cubicle dwellers, "Is this company neurotic?" Assure absolute confidentiality to the trembling few who reply. Information may not get all the way to the top, but it can still get around.

The law firm's senior partners recommend going to court. If the senior partners spoke "decision trees" instead of words, this is what they would say (see Figure 19.1).

Fearing an unpredictable and emotional jury—and, the show tells us, six more wrongful-death claims wait offstage—the CEO tells the senior partners he wants "certainty." What kind of certainty? "A war game."

(As Shakespeare could have said, a mock trial by any other name would be a war game.)

The client allocates $100,000 for the exercise. The senior partners role-play the Blue Team, the law firm representing the client. They assign their two brightest associates to the Red Team

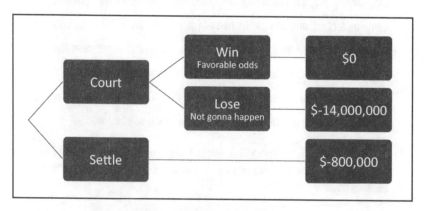

FIGURE 19.1—The Senior Partners' Decision Tree

with orders to "give it your all" as they role-play the family's legal team. They recruit a mock jury. An equity partner, a retired judge, will preside. They stuff a mock courtroom with cameras to tailgate jurors' reactions. They give the Red Team $10,000 to hire an expert witness to testify. The teams hiss "see you in court."

The Red Team role-plays aggressively. They show photos of the (previously) vibrant 16-year-old. They trace an IP address and confront a company executive who touted the weight-loss virtues of energy drinks on pro-anorexia websites. They hire an actress to cry hysterically on the stand as the girl's grandmother. It's hard to remember that the Red Team's lawyers are actually actors role-playing a Red Team's lawyers who hired actors who are role-playing actors who are role-playing . . . we can't keep it straight. So sue us.

Midway through the mock trial, a poll of the jury shows unanimous victory for the Red Team, awarding the family $45 million. Break for commercial.

The furious senior partner leading the Blue Team screams at the associate leading the Red Team. She stands firm: After all, there's no point to a war game if you pull your punches.

At the end—spoiler alert—the Red Team wins. The mock jury recommends $50 million in compensation to the family.

The CEO orders the senior partners to settle with an offer of $12 million.

That episode should be a required part of every MBA curriculum. It shows the difference between a decision tree and a denial tree. Denial trees are decision trees from which inconvenient truths have been pruned, and they are dangerously popular in real-life business decisions. The CEO wanted a decision tree. The senior partners provided a denial tree. Figure 19.1 (page 294) was a denial tree presented as a decision tree.

The war game lets us draw a much more realistic decision tree (see Figure 19.2 on page 296). Based on it, we can calculate X, the probability of winning at which the CEO should offer to settle. In this case, the CEO should settle if X, the probability of winning in

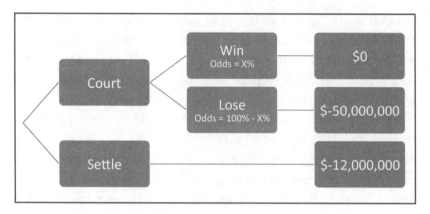

FIGURE 19.2—The Actual Decision Tree

court, is less than 76 percent. This is the mathematical solution to the X in the diagram above; it is the point at which the decision-maker would be indifferent, mathematically, to going to court or settling out of court. Any probability of winning that's less than 76 percent tilts the balance in favor of settling.

A key point about the drama: *The senior partners didn't know they were providing a denial tree.* They thought they were giving their client good advice. That's what's so insidious about denial trees and the overconfidence that fertilizes them.

We have each run hundreds of business war games around the world, and we've seen the same decision-making benefit portrayed on that TV show. We've learned that war games don't only tell you what you don't know; they tell you what you don't expect and even what you don't want to know. An inconvenient insight is still better than fake certainty. Denial can destroy wealth and careers.

Were we in denial that a TV drama could teach valuable lessons about strategy decisions? Not anymore.

But the real issue raised by the example above is not just the billions of dollars companies waste recklessly by not running war games to weed out denial trees and fight neurotic behaviors. The most pressing issue is actually much more profound: Should Alicia Florrick have gone back to Peter Florrick, her cheating governor-of-

Illinois husband in *The Good Wife?* If you think billions of dollars is more important, well, you're entitled to your opinion. Or to Gartner's.

OVERCOMING DENIAL AND NEUROSIS

One effective method to overcome Corporate's tendency to filter inconvenient information is to create a community of practice (COP). COPs are groups of like-minded managers and experts sharing perspectives on issues without filters.

Ericsson uses an extensive informal network called Strategy Perspectives. Royal Dutch Shell created an extensive network of technical experts. We note that both companies are rooted in relatively egalitarian cultures (Swedish and Dutch).

Informal flows of information do not compete with or replace formal channels, so they do not threaten the existing power structure. Instead, they empower middle management and, if used well, provide top management (CEO, business unit presidents, general managers, and so on) with sensible, useful *context* to competitive developments.

COPs thrive only if allowed to discuss issues freely without "supervision" and censorship. They need a positive, unorthodox-idea airing, left-field-watching attitude. Those who run COPs must gently, patiently, and invariably guide them away from griping and complaining. They can even grow into communities of collaboration, which take the discussions to the higher level of actual projects.

To the maverick, the COP is not just strategically sound; it's also psychologically sound. Being a maverick can be lonely in a conformist culture. COPs help mavericks form networks that help the company and help each other. If nothing else, you get a sense that you are neither weird nor alone.[2]

For executives, tapping into an informal group lower in the organization is sound advice as well. By the time the activist's fund

---

[2] One of us had a similar validating experience simply by reading Susan Cain's wonderful book *Quiet: The Power of Introverts in a World That Can't Stop Talking* and realizing that introversion is not a flaw to be cured.

swoops in, problems have been festering, fat has been accumulating, and waste has been piling up for years. While executives blame activists for "short-termism," they forget to notice the long-term sloppy thinking that brought the activists to the table. Mavericks can be the COPs who help keep the company, including the executives, from getting into trouble.

advice to the maverick

Corporate coaches will advise you to be a good team player, respect others, and listen actively. Then you land in Corporate and discover no one does that. (You go back to the coaches and tell them, but they don't listen.) Listening actively makes you better informed, and perhaps even smarter, but Corporate doesn't give out quarterly prizes for the nicest silent sponge. Being better informed and perhaps even smarter does not, in itself, make a difference. We advise you to take the next step. Take an active role in remedying the filtering.

The time pressure on executives is beyond human. The dysfunction of filtering information and sending only what executives want to hear—or only what middle-management thinks executives want to hear—is as old as management itself. Executives are just too busy to listen to 30,000 employees. The problem can be so severe and deadly that in government the intelligence community designed a parallel system to the formal communication channels with the president. That process, known as the President's Daily Brief, designates a structure within the structure and bypasses the formal hierarchy. The briefers move freely between various agencies and cabinet members and serve the top decision-maker (the president).

Companies don't yet have the CEO's Daily Brief, at least not formally. What can a maverick do? Suggest to your boss to suggest to her boss, to suggest to his boss, to suggest to her boss, and we lost the train of thought . . . oh, yes, to become a briefer to the Big Boss (say a unit president or an SVP) based on a strategic early warning system (SEWS).[3]

If your boss latches onto the idea, assemble a small, informal network of mavericks like you who are interested in informally (and perhaps heretically) discussing external events as they relate to the company's strategy. Funnel their insights (in summary form) to your boss. Over time, hopefully, this small effort pays off with your boss telling you what the Big Boss found intriguing. If you provide ample credit to those providing the interesting perspectives and they know the Big Boss is noticing their names, you'll become popular. If you also provide "cover" for negative perspectives by keeping them anonymous or spinning their views in "promotive" wording (opportunities opened rather than just risks looming), you'll be allowed to eat lunch with the bosses in the cafeteria. From there, the route to glory is short, if uncertain. (If we said "certain," we would be selling you hype. We stay true to ourselves by adding an honest qualifier and not a slippery asterisk.)

In the case of the company we mentioned at the beginning of the chapter, whose CEO was filtered like a mug of high-quality coffee, the turnaround replacement went on a ruthless cost-cutting drive, cut 40 percent of the company's overhead, spun off and merged businesses, called R&D projects white elephants, brought in the consultants, and reorganized the original reorganization to appease the activists. One wonders how much of this herculean effort and mayhem could have been avoided if the previous CEOs were better informed of mavericks' perspectives.

---

[3] If you want to build an SEWS, consult Benjamin Gilad's, *Early Warning* (Amacom, 2003).

we are with you, maverick

can corporate heal itself?

"Get your facts first, then
you can distort them
as you please."

—MARK TWAIN

Mavericks always face a dilemma: Should you go for the security, resources, scope, and health benefits of a large corporation, or should you open a kiosk for stuffed animals in the nearby mall? We don't envy you for having to make this decision.

In Chapter 18, we offered a 2x2 magic matrix (all rights reserved) to help you make this decision. You may decide more on timing and opportunities than on careful deliberation, but if you read this book, your decision will be more realistic. There are few things as bad as entering what looks like a promising career and finding out you are actually stuck in an anthill.

By now you may have realized the dysfunctions we outline in this book are real. We may have wrapped them in humor because we like to lampoon, but the reality is not so funny. Why do generations of managers, directors, and VPs take off their competing caps at the height of their careers? Why do they settle for formulas instead of continually sharpening their skill at competing? Why do they deny and filter when they should adapt to, or even *cause*, Big Hairy Change in the market?

A factor analysis of our pseudo-survey responses combined with logistic regression analysis on the main factors (statistical significance level of 1 percent or less under the right lighting conditions) confirmed our presurvey suspicion: Corporate regards investment in training for the skill of competing as unnecessary. It believes it already has competing down pat. When hedge-fund activists start to reform a company, here's what they find: Complacent, reactive, self-congratulatory, insulated management following a 30-year-old formula perplexed in the face of change. In short, everything we captured in this book as (Corporate) dysfunctions.

Competing is not well defined as a skill. Is it an innate talent propelling strategic geniuses like Patton, Washington, and Jobs to lead armies, nations, and companies? Perhaps. Is it a skill relying on patient and incisive observations and *ego-free, humble* analysis of what works, what doesn't, and why? We believe it is. It is a muscle that needs practice, encouragement, testing, and retesting to stay fit and ready.

Learning the skill of competing requires you to *internalize* three essential ideas: Success is ephemeral, luck is always a factor, and many things are outside one's control but not necessarily outside one's planning. That's how the late Andy Grove of Intel approached competition with his management team. Intel's luck ran out a few decades later when it missed the boat on smartphones, or maybe luck just followed Andy Grove while he was there.

"Internalize" isn't mere recall, like knowing the capital of Tennessee is Memphis.[1] "Internalize" isn't just a checklist or a best practice, like making sure your car has gas as you pass the sign that says, "next gas station, 300 miles." "Internalize" is not a formula or a tool, as in running for the hammer whenever you see a nail. "Internalize" is a mental habit, a cognitive schema: This is how you view the world.

When you don't invest in the skill of competing, you're left hoping for luck. Do you feel lucky? Chrysler, Countrywide Mortgage Bank, Alta Vista, Jawbone, Aeropostale, Payless, Theranos, Nine West, and many others felt lucky . . . until they weren't.

In this chapter, we point the finger at Corporate's lack of interest in training you to compete, which is consistent with its lack of interest in letting your unorthodox thinking percolate upstairs,

---

[1] Especially because it's Nashville.

affect strategy, and impact future initiatives. So what can you do if Corporate doesn't invest in your training? Train yourself. (You've already begun.) We offer a few principles to guide you in that. They are simple but not easy.

COMPETING: MISSING FROM THE CORPORATE COURSE CATALOG

What do we mean when we say Corporate doesn't invest in the skill of competing? After all, Corporate spends millions on training its managers. It erects corporate universities, sends managers to "rising-star" camps, and pays for horrendously expensive Executive MBA programs. Corporate buys the latest online courses and MOOC courses, TED talks, and any other learning technology on the market. If there was a MOOC teaching how to MOOC, Corporate would buy it.

Yet the skill of competing is the most neglected of all skills in Corporate. A study by Forrester Consulting on behalf of IBM and reported on IBM's website extols the benefits of design thinking in improving performance and urges companies to train all teams in design thinking (by IBM, of course). Interestingly, not one word in the entire design-thinking process or the study is dedicated to competition. It's as though we expect our competitors will curl into whimpering, helpless fetal balls when our employees, freshly trained in design thinking, produce invincibly superior results. The problem is that as common-sensible as it is to streamline design processes by centering them on the users, competing is not just solving users' problems but solving them in ways that competitors can't or won't. IBM demonstrated this point as competitors successfully challenged its position.

We imagine that somewhere in the enormous Corporate sphere, organizational training and development may include courses in "ergonomic fretting," "knitting during meetings," "360° gossip," "how to cram more data onto a slide," "contracts: Try 'em without legal!" and "leading with the aid of a deck of tarot cards." The only skill they don't train continually? Competing. And without training and practice, there is no skill.

COMPETING IS NOT MANAGING

Maybe Corporate thinks investing in the same subjects one learns in an MBA program creates competitive managers, though that confuses competing with financial-ratio analysis, or linear programming to optimize operations, or proficiency in Excel. Business schools teach the skill of solving problems but not the skill of competing.

As we said in Chapter 1: Competition is not a problem to be solved. Competition is a condition of being in business.

Maybe Corporate thinks competing is the same as catch-all "leadership" training. Send managers to a wooded resort to be screamed at by tough guys as they build rafts, cross rivers, and learn the value of teamwork. Teamwork is essential to crossing a river, but when it comes to thinking strategically on how to position your company more distinctively than competitors for the next ten years, or how to compete with China where your products have been stymied by unfair play for a decade, we suspect other skills are as pertinent. We should really find out if Dr. Oh-Hyun Kwon, the CEO of Samsung, was in one of those forest survival skills camps. The way he transformed his once laggard, imitator company into the market leader in many segments seems nothing short of crossing the ocean alone in a kayak against hurricane-force winds, but the skill he actually applied had nothing to do with paddling.

When we understand that competing involves the *integration* of a maverick mentality and strategic thinking, we gain the insight that practicing competing via simulations is the most effective tool that companies should employ routinely, just like they employ budgeting, planning, office cleaning, and replacing coffee filters (or Keurig pods).

Leaving the continuous practicing of the skill of competing to HR's formula of managerial "development" is like entrusting the combat training of the Marines to the USO. HR is just not the right conduit.

So who should be responsible for turning competing skill into a *fundamental* requirement like speaking English and wearing shirts? We suggest Thomas Jefferson. Yes, the forefather.

We can imagine a meeting with President Thomas Jefferson in the early days of the Republic. Jefferson was an early proponent of breaking with Great Britain:

Jefferson: Gentlemen, we need to free our citizens to pursue opportunities in our vast country! We need to compete with the vast British Empire, and we need to win!

HR: Hmm. Sorry, sir, which course would you like to add to our training program?

Jefferson: Discovering entrepreneurial skills! Understanding market realities! Predicting competitors' moves before they happen!

HR: No problem, sir. We have a course in Dining Etiquette of the Royal British Court. Would that do?

Jefferson: No! We need original thinking! We need strategies! We need visionaries! We need mavericks who take the initiative and take risks and think like owners!

HR: Oh! No problem! We have a famous professor from the great University of Hamburg who developed an intriguing theory about motivating the serfs to increase the production of cotton in the Southern Alps area.

Jefferson: How much does he ask for teaching it?

HR: We could get it for nothing. It's freemium.

Jefferson: You are all noodleheads. Bring me Andy Grove.

Without strong commitment from the top to cultivate competing as a skill throughout the company, and to use it as a promotion criterion and a mandatory ingredient in leadership development, don't expect Corporate to compete like Andy Grove.

THE BATTLE FOR YOUR DREAM COMPANY

Free-market competition alone may not cure Corporate. If it were, they'd be small-c corporate and not capital-C Corporate. However, it seems a new force on the horizon is taking shots at Corporate and scoring some hits.

The Economist's 2015 article "Capitalism's Unlikely Heroes" suggests the rise of activist hedge-fund investors is a true revolution. It might even cure complacent Corporate of its dysfunctions.

These brash and vocal billionaires take small positions in huge public companies and act to fix mismanagement by trying to convince *other* shareholders to support cutting fat, consider spin-offs, and return cash to shareholders instead of wasting it on bloated acquisitions.

Unlike buyout private equity, the activist hedge funds buy only a few shares. They neither burden the target with loads of debt nor strip companies of their assets (that's *so* 1980s and Michael Douglas[2]). Unlike Wall Street (the street, not the movie) investors, activists get actively involved in management decisions with the goal of making it more competitive. Naturally, companies' chiefs abhor them. Critics call them vultures. Boards try to "poison-pill" them.

Why is there such an increase in activists' funds? Have companies gotten worse and caused an immune response?

Well, *yes.* We've been trying to warn you from page one. You may dream of a dream job with the dream company, but your dream company may have turned Corporate while you were sleeping.

And also, hmmm, you know . . . *China.*

So before you say *yes!* to the recruiter, check out if the company is embattled. The results, in the longer run, may be good for competing, but in the short run, the company is like an ADHD kid in a video game arcade who forgot to take their Adderall. The anti-activist frenzy is gruesome to watch.

---

[2] See the movie *Wall Street*, with Michael Douglas playing "greed is good" Gordon Gekko.

cozy, insular, fat, and temporarily happy

Activists' funds are a significant development in the race to make public companies more competitive. The fundamental advantage these activists bring is an external perspective. If management's perspective was so great, activists would have no way to increase long-term profit or convince shareholders to place their nominees on the board. If executives know how to compete effectively—that's how they got to be executives, isn't it?—then why don't they act like the activists themselves? Putting egos and track records on the back burner, looking at themselves from the outside via war games, or just deliberately seeking different perspectives can take them a long way towards seeing what activists see. At the same time, if they just made sure internal mavericks with unorthodox thinking get a voice, that may be a better move than this:

Activist: "Good morning, Mr. CEO, this is Bill from KickInThePants Hedge fund. I would like to discuss with you a few ways to compete better. "

CEO (imitates static noise): "tssssssss . . . I am driving into a tunnel right now . . . No reception . . . tssssss . . ."

If you are an executive, perhaps getting your activist investor to head a competitor team in a war-game simulation may be more profitable than calling him a scumbag, as Sotheby's ousted chairman and CEO, William Ruprecht, did (and Reuters reported).

CEO turnover at companies targeted by activists has averaged 23 percent since 2013. For non-targets, the annualized CEO turnover rate, reports Forbes, was only 12 percent over the same period. Conclusion? Maybe listening to your own mavericks will save your job from outside mavericks. The latter are far meaner.

JOIN THE 13 PERCENT

Peer pressure, conforming to authority, respect for traditions, and belief in autobiographies of the rich and famous. Those are just some of the obstacles in the way of mavericks, young or old, who are determined not to slack off once they gain employment with the dream company that turns out to be not-so-dreamy Corporate. Busy work that fries their brains, endless routine tasks full of challenges such as "Where did I leave my stapler?" meetings that can make a chicken forget why it crossed the road, and relentless pressure to follow "the formula," that get in the way too. Mavericks who want their ambitions to stand out, who want to stick their heads up, who want to think differently, and who want to exercise their skill of competing, are squashed early on.

If you don't want to become an uncompetitive, coasting, oblivious manager, you can either find a company still infused with the entrepreneurial spirit and making high-quality, informed decisions, *or become an entrepreneur yourself.*

About 13 percent of Americans start their own business, according to *Business Insider*. That leaves 87 percent as employees of other people's small, medium, and large companies. Since lack of skill at competing is easier to hide in a large, fat, market-leading company, we can safely rule out the employees and managers of solvent small- and medium-size firms as *habitual* coasters. Since privately owned companies are less tolerant of sloppy thinking, we can eliminate them as well.

It is impossible to know how many managers work for the public companies on the Fortune 1000 list. The companies may not know, either ("People are our number-one asset; we regret so many have to leave us now"). Census data shows that 40 to 50 percent of employment is provided by large companies.

That means there may be millions of repressed cogs in Corporate's machines. The cogs' survival strategy is not making waves, marking time, doing what is expected, and trying not to stick out. These managers are not bad people; they are just not the ones making a company competitive.

As a maverick, taking initiative, standing out and questioning authority means taking risks. "The nail that sticks up gets hammered down" is a common saying of people who lost their skill at competing.[3] Corporate calls the latter good team players who fit in.

We call them clones. Corporate loves clones. Send in the clones!

Put differently: Genius.com quotes Steven Jobs, in a 1982 speech to the Academy of Achievement, saying, "If you're going to make connections which are innovative . . . you have to not have the same bag of experiences as everyone else does."

Now there we go, joining the clones quoting Jobs. So sorry. Will not happen again. Let's quote Groucho Marx instead: "Why, a four-year-old child could understand this report. Run out and find me a four-year-old child. I can't make head or tail of it."

THE HARD WAY OUT

Safety and security are important for most people. Millions toil for Corporate. Entrepreneurs buck the trend, swim against the tide, and venture out on their own. The herd finds safety in numbers. Entrepreneurs find anxiety there. The herd finds anxiety in separation. Entrepreneurs find fulfillment.

Believe us, we know. We are both entrepreneurs.

To strike out on one's own, one has to see an opportunity for oneself. Seeing opportunities where others don't is the same quality as being a small-c corporate strategic intelligence analyst, with one difference. Analysts see opportunities for their employers. Entrepreneurs take the next step and see opportunities for themselves. Entrepreneurship is always about an opportunity for oneself. It doesn't have to be an innovation or a breakthrough, web-based startup. It can be a location across from your home where you noticed a store for lease and decided it is an opportunity to at last open your soaps-looking-like-small-furry-animals store.

---

[3] Contrast with "the squeaky wheel gets the grease." Nails, hammers, wheels, grease . . . a malfunctioning machine is not safe for cogs.

Mind you, we do not condemn or disrespect those who join large companies. There is a lot of satisfaction with making a *big* difference. With the resources of a big company, their impact can go beyond furry-animal-looking soaps. It can go as far as sweetened, flavored, carbonated water. Sometimes even *farther*.

We are saying that working for yourself means you just can't be an OOP for long. Or, more accurately, as an OOP, you'd last about two seconds (unless you find an OOP VC to keep funding you). Free markets have this wonderful mechanism that eliminates incompetence quickly. In Corporate, with the mass and momentum of a gigantic cruise ship at top speed, it takes longer—unless an iceberg gets in the way.

It's your choice. You can conform, adjust, accept Corporate norms, never speak the truth about anything substantial, always use platitudes and clichés, cover up, kiss up, steal credit from those underneath you, and when the time comes, retire comfortably, and have fun complaining about the younger generation being unrealistic dreamers.

Or you can rebel, chafe at the Corporate shackles and rituals, speak honestly, question sloppy thinking, point out blindspots, be passed over for promotion, get tarred as not a good match for the "culture," get laid off the first time an OOP screws up, and never be able to afford retirement. But do not despair: You can always end up selling pot in your small kiosk in Denver while smiling broadly all day long. If you ask us, that's a better fate than dying slowly in a mindless job. Alas, only one of us lives in a state where it's legal to smile broadly all day long in a small kiosk. The other one lives in a state where people smile all day long whether it's legal or not.

There are probably some sensible readers who think, "There must be other choices.[4] Not all companies are bad."

---

[4] Excellent maverick thinking! When confronted with options the maverick doesn't like, the maverick doesn't choose the lesser of the evils. The maverick looks for more options.

Of course. But if you are young and ambitious and eagerly looking forward to joining a famous company, let this book be your guide and your warning: Not every green pasture is safe for your slick, shiny city shoes. If you are a maverick already working in Corporate and feeling frustrated, let this book affirm and validate that mavericks make a difference, while sloppy thinkers destroy wealth and jobs. This book is your shield against mediocrity. *Protego!*[5]

advice to the maverick

As a maverick, it's important that you keep honing your skill at competing. If you find yourself in an oppressive Corporate, use the elevator's repair room, where no one can see you or hear you, to tell yourself daily:

- Never let go of the strategic mindset. Always, always, always place developments in the context of the big picture. Always consider other market players' perspectives. Once you get good at it, you are *guaranteed* to outperform your peers and identify opportunities and risks others—including your bosses—*can't yet see.*

- If you get your big break and you are entrusted with a small team, remember that leadership is not just reading books on or by Warren Buffet. Leadership is the ability to show the internal logic of your perspective to others so they are *persuaded* to follow, not ordered to do so. This is much more difficult, and much more valuable, than you think.

- Your ability to manage—planning and executing your superior strategy for your small job in the remote cubicle on floor D—will always depend on being alert to other players' moves that can chip away at your

---

[5] For those of you, like one of us, who don't get their vocabulary from Harry Potter movies: *Protego* creates an invisible shield to protect the person casting the spell. Harry Potter was a real maverick, especially for a fictional character.

strategy's core. When you are a maverick without the protection of exalted rank or a magical shield, your strategy must reckon with insiders' reactions (your boss, peers, big boss, HR, etc.). As you climb your company's ladder, you must go beyond the advice on "interpersonal skills." They won't help you if you ignore the perspectives and intended moves of other players in the market who may not be charmed by your interpersonal skills.

- Simulate market dynamics as often as feasible for decisions under your control or in which you take part. Running a war game can be as simple as you role-playing against two of your friends or three of the experts you engage. It can be done by email, group chat, or, preferably, face to face. It can also be a bigger effort with 20 or 30 participants, if called for, computer-based simulation, and an executive sponsor who finds the idea intriguing and is open-minded enough to listen to *conflicting* perspectives. The more war gaming you do, the more you make it second nature to consider other players' reaction in your plans. That's how skillful strategists are made.

It's a bit different if you're a budding entrepreneur:

Mom: So Johnny, who are you going to work for?

Johnny: I am going to start my own company, Mom.

Mom: Doing what?

Johnny: I will sell a career advice books to students on campuses.

Mom: Oh, Johnny, why can't you be a lawyer? Your cousin Henry is a lawyer.

Johnny: Cousin Henry is just a cog in a machine, Mom."

advice to the maverick, continued

Mom: Ok, big shot, but how many books do you need to sell to make money?

Johnny: About 25,000.

Mom: I'll clear the basement then. You can live here as long as you want.

Ben and Mark: Thanks, Johnny! Thanks, Mom!

executive
summary

"If I only had a little humility,
I would be perfect."

—TED TURNER

E xecutive summaries are meant for executives who have no intention whatsoever to do what the executive summaries urge them to do but want to be fully informed *at all times*. They are also the bread and butter of business students who were forced to read 800 case studies and are hoping this executive summary will save them the need to read this book.

We fully intend to honor them. We summarize the main points made by this book and what our years of experience of building companies' skill of competing have taught us. Mind you, business schools do not teach *any* of these lessons.

Unproductive, uncompetitive, and sometimes simply bizarre rituals stand between a company and lasting success. It would seem we could help with clear consciences. But in writing this book, we faced a serious moral dilemma. On the one hand, we know managers *love* formulas for success not lessons about how companies undo their own success with sloppy thinking. On the other hand, we have our integrity. We know formulas *don't* work, and we have these exemplars of great authorities, such as Porter and Rosenzweig, who told it as it is and found enough intelligent people to read their nonformulaic books.

So what to do? Should we write a negative book? (Do not be fooled. We are not negative simply because we wrote about dysfunctions. No, no, no. We are just dysfunctional.)

Think about our maverick publisher. They are taking a chance on this dynamic dysfunctional duo.[1] We do not fit the formula for success because we are not (yet) Big Names, and we do not lead companies with hundreds of thousands of employees who we can "encourage" to buy our book. If our publisher hadn't been so brilliant, insightful, innovative, gracious, holy (are we going too far?), etc., etc. and had instead followed the formula for success, this is what would have happened:

Editors: Please sit down, Mr.?

JD: Salinger.

Editors: Thank you for coming in. We have finished reading your manuscript—*Catcher in the Rye*, is it?—and we are quite impressed. The only item left to discuss is how to market it. How many speaking opportunities do you have for the coming year?

Salinger: Hmmm . . . look, I don't have any. I don't like public appearances.

Editors: Get out of here.

Salinger: No, really, I am just not comfortable with . . .

Editors: No, we mean, GET OUT OF HERE! Next!

Moses: Hi, I am so excited to be here.

Editors: Yeah, yeah. So how many copies can you sell of this, what do you call it? Old . . .

Moses: Testament. I think 600.

Editors: What?? 600 thousand?

Moses: No, 600. My tribe is leaving Egypt, and it's about 600 people, including babies.

---

[1] Thank you, maverick publisher!

Editors: Hold on, Mr. Moses. We understood from your proposal that you have links to the royal pharaohs in Egypt.

Moses: Well, yes, but . . .

Editors: Well, can you sell 50,000 to the Egyptian military?

Moses: We are not on good terms.

Editors: Next!

We followed our own entrepreneurial advice to get this book to you. We rose early, worked hard, and struck publisher. Thank you, publisher.

THE ANTI-FORMULA FORMULA FOR THE MAVERICK
Lesson 1: When Examining a Potential Employer, Look Beyond Its Website or Job Description.

Throughout this book, we reported on and advocated the use of simulations in testing a move, a strategy, or a vision. That is because your move is only one piece in a puzzle where many other high-impact players will affect your success.

When you think of joining a company, the first simulation will be inside your head. (You do have Intel inside, right?) Look at the company's positioning in its market. Try to see that company from the perspective of its customers, current employees, and competitors. Do you like what you see? Does it have a distinctive strategy? Do you understand the core activities forming this strategy? You can get some of this information by reading comments about the company on the web and on social networks. Reading the company's own website is a waste of time. It's PR. PR stands for Positively Ridiculous.

Try this trick: Go on the company's website and search for how many times it mentions the words "leader" or "leading." Leading companies are less likely to listen to mavericks. "Our formula works," they figure, "so why change it? Mavericks need to listen to *us*."

Lesson 2: Once You Are on the Job, Collect Perspectives.

Scientific American reports that there is now a substantial body of research that shows the value of incorporating alternative perspectives. A 2013 *Harvard Business Review* article says, "Leaders who give diverse voices equal airtime are nearly twice as likely as others to unleash value-driving insights." The mere presentation of alternative perspectives for consideration improves decision making, according to the management textbook *Strategic Management: Concepts: Competitiveness and Globalization* by Michael Hitt, R. Duane Ireland, and Robert Hoskisson (Cengage Learning, 2014).

Uncovering and airing diverse perspectives is the essential power of simulation. Simulations come in many forms, and even though we have our own favorite methodologies—Ben favors intelligence-based role-playing, while Mark favors human + computer simulations—both consider *explicitly* and to the best of their ability what *others* intend to do, how others intend to respond, and what alternatives you face. Answering a "what if" question can save your career and many millions of dollars.[2] You can start with your own little world in your cubicle. Just keep looking at your actions from the perspective of others. You don't come to work naked because you can predict what others (including the police) will say, but when it comes to strategy, only *your* moves matter?

As a maverick, make it a habit to talk to as many people as you can. Not for the "relationship" as the trite coaching advice goes but for absorbing *perspectives*. Ask each and every one of them a simple question: "What is your take on . . . ?" People love being considered an "expert" who is consulted even if it is just by a lowly co-worker, a newbie, or an errand boy. We know. We get emails from people we don't know from all over the world, and despite the clear waste of

---

[2] See the chapter "Putting the Lesson before the Test," by David J. Reibstein and Mark J. Chussil, in *Wharton on Dynamic Competitive Strategy* (John Wiley & Sons, 1997). The chapter starts (on page 396) with the story of Shell Oil, which saved $133 million in the 1990s by stress-testing a strategy decision through simulation.

our time, we reply as long as the email starts with: "I found out you are the foremost world expert on this. Would you be kind enough to tell us what you think about XYZ?" We know we shouldn't fall for this, but we do, every time. So would people in your company.

Lesson 3: Be Realistically Optimistic.

The nature of simulation is to put pressure on strategy ideas from the perspective of other parties. An unbridled enthusiasm, required in some cultures whenever an SVP or higher-ranked officer dreams up a move, is not conducive to stress-testing anything. If you are a realistic optimist who can face facts and find solutions to every situation, stress-testing is a dream come true. If you are an unrealistic optimist, you are a nightmare to work for and with. Please stay out of the market. People may depend on your dysfunctional judgment.

Being negative doesn't mean being cranky or belligerent. It means being a realist who can discern risks and opportunities that are actually there. And if you are a maverick, it is exactly that relatively unbiased perspective that should be cherished by your employer. Alas, it won't be. At times, you'll have to pretend to agree and support initiatives about which you are personally quite skeptical. Write down your thoughts about why you think the initiative may fail. Date the entry. Journals are a fantastic aid to improving your skill of competing. Then when reality unfolds, check your reasoning against outcomes. What did the team leader miss? What did *you* miss? Was there a way to see that earlier, or was it unexpected? Can't blame anyone for not expecting the unexpected. Well, you *can*, but it's oxymoronic.

Once you have a good enough relationship with your team leader and some trust (very important), carefully share your journal entry with him or her. Be very humble and respectful. Say things like, "I think *we* missed the piece whereby they hired an executive from the government agency and used him to open doors for their atypical solution. I wish I picked up on that earlier." Of course, *you* didn't miss anything, but never ever point a finger at your boss and say he or she missed it. Take the blame. Then offer for the next project to do some preliminary competitive surveillance to see if you can pick up some clues. We bet she or he will say that's a grand idea.

Lesson 4: Do Not Judge Solely on Outcomes.

Outcomes are as dependent on others' moves as much or more than on your decisions and foresight. Barring the availability of a crystal ball, you can't ever have total control of outcomes, at least not legally. You are not a Too-Big-to-Fail financial institution that is guaranteed never to fail. The fact that your strategy is currently working, the bottom line is strong, and growth is in the air does not guarantee a happy future. This is the most important point we make in this book, and we know, like Don Quixote, we are fighting a lost cause. Executives will forever fall back on "but *it's working*" reasoning until it stops working (not today; maybe tomorrow), and then they'll panic.

The best you can do is to ensure *your* decisions are made well. With luck, the outcomes will be a resounding success. *High-quality decisions—that is, ones based on competitive intelligence, early-warning signals, appropriate decision analysis, and stress-test simulations of strategic moves (including what-if scenarios)—simply raise the probability of good results.* But fortunes and careers are made and lost on those probabilities.

A BIT OF HUMILITY

This section is capital-S Serious. It's person-to-person, not consultant-to-manager or oldie-to-newbie. You are welcome to skip the next 632 words if you like.

No one pokes fun at knowledge. The laws of physics and thermodynamics aren't particularly funny and, for practical matters, aren't in dispute. But ideas, unlike knowledge, said J. Robert Oppenheimer in his 1954 book *Science and the Common Understanding* (Simon & Schuster), are provisional and worth challenging. Ideas are poke-worthy, and we have poked fun at many in this book. We hope we've shown that what some businesspeople consider knowledge are actually ideas and wrong ideas at that.

No one wants to fail, yet many companies fail to get off the ground and many companies that get off the ground fail to stay aloft. That's not by accident.

It's also not on purpose. We fail *despite* all our intelligence, education, experience, motivation, and aspiration. No one gets up in the morning hoping to make lousy decisions. But sometimes smart, eager, confident, dedicated people fail. Simply being smart, eager, confident, and dedicated is not enough to protect you.

Humility will not prevent all failures, but it may help you prevent some and learn from the rest.

Humility is not the same as indecision, moral equivalence, or self-deprecation. Humility is not putting yourself down or putting yourself last. Humility is not the opposite of confidence. Humility is the opposite of *overconfidence* and arrogance.

You can be confident without being certain. You can be confident and be willing to listen. You can be confident while acknowledging you might learn something from one of the 7,599,999,999 people on Earth who are not you. We, the authors, have done exactly that by writing this book: Each of us, with our fancy educations and decades of experience, has listened and learned from the other and come away better than we began.

Confidence comes from thinking things through from making high-quality decisions.

If you want to outperform your competitors, you've got to do something your competitors aren't doing. We have discouraged formulas and imitation throughout our book because they lead you to do the same things your competitors are doing. We have encouraged stress-testing and war games, which test and simulate why you might be *wrong* not to irritate your ego but to help you make high-quality decisions and build your skill at competing.

We've talked about metaphors in this book, especially sports and war. Sports and war help because they remind us we have competition.

They hurt, though, because they call for the metaphorical or literal destruction of others.

We suggest another metaphor: an organism. Businesses (and markets) are astoundingly complex with wildly disparate parts that have different needs and make different contributions. Anyone who's been married or raised a child knows it's hard enough (and sometimes impossible) to please a single person. Now imagine tens, hundreds, thousands, or hundreds of thousands of people, each with an opinion and each with an agenda. Imagine managing them and leading them while everyone and everything is in motion. It's like operating your body atom by atom. There's no app for that.

Wisdom does not mean perfection. We—that means the whole multitude, not just Ben and Mark—wouldn't know perfection even if we saw it. Wisdom does not guarantee that everyone, or even anyone, will be happy with the outcome. Wisdom means making decisions well. And we hope we've helped you do that through this book.

A theme runs through the ideas in this book. We can sum up the theme in seven words:

Pay attention, and don't be too sure.

Pay attention. Are the bushes rustling in the wind, or is that a predator coming toward you? You know you ought to act if it's a predator. Consider whether the wind also merits action.

Don't be too sure. We're not saying you're wrong, but no one (including us) is always right. Listening takes courage and commitment to excellence—and humility.

The consequence of not listening can be dire, as imagined below.

Recruiter: Mr. Noah, I see here in your resume that you request an office with a window. Why is that?

Noah: It helps me see the flood coming.

Recruiter: So you can predict floods, is that it?

Noah: I think so. My rheumatism acts up before they come.

Recruiter: And you think you are better at it than our meteorologists?

Noah: Hmm . . . I am not sure. I guess I just pay attention.

Recruiter: Don't be ridiculous. I was assured our meteorologists do the same, and they are the best in the world.

Noah: OK. I need to go to my boat now. My bones ache. (He leaves.)

Recruiter: What a strange man. Who lives in a boat these days?

ADVICE TO THE MAVERICK, THE ASPIRING MANAGER, AND THE NEWLY MINTED GRADUATE

This book is about your career. Whether you are working your way through college, starting your own company, joining a large corporation, or have worked in one for decades, you need to be able to identify and avoid obstacles to good decisions, plus identify and *survive* dysfunctions that you can't change yet. We remind you of the major obstacles/dysfunctions you are likely to encounter in capital-C Corporate:

- Across-the-board cost-cutting is hardly ever effective at rejuvenating a declining business, but you are very likely to go through some of those mindless cuts at least once in your career. You can't do anything about the Corporate waste of billions on silly acquisitions and consultants, but you can help a bit by making positive suggestions about cutting *waste* at, and contributing ideas from, your corner of the Corporate floor.
- People are not your company's number-one asset, so don't believe that hokum. *Strategy* is your company's number-one asset. If you want the company to keep paying you, do whatever you can in your cubicle to sharpen, strengthen, and focus the strategy of your team, department, unit, or company.

Make suggestions. At the outset, no one will listen. But if you persist, and if your suggestions are about opportunities for improvements, not about complaints, eventually someone might take note.

- Expect the vast majority of your wonderful recommendations and insights never to reach the top. This is just reality. You can't expect the boss of 30,000 employees to know you. But if you think your boss, and your boss' boss, etc., puts more effort into blocking inconvenient truths from reaching the top than into discovering truths about the playing field, consider arranging new interviews soon.

- "Customer experience" is a hot buzzword backed by Big Data. At times, in large companies, it is small data and minor activities that make customers say, "screw them, I am moving to Zappos." If you have experienced the ease of doing business with Zappos, you know what we mean. The terms used in the popular press for Zappos' customer service range from "bending backward" to "legendary." That's why Amazon, not a slouch itself in "customer experience," acquired Zappos for a reported $850 million. Remember that Big Data is just small data from the past, only bigger, Capitalized (like Corporate), and accorded disturbingly big trust.

- Business is well known for relying on numbers and quantitative facts to guide strategy and for good reason. It is when the line is crossed into absurd reliance with no basis in reality that it all goes awry. The hype over millions of observations is a case in point. One of the earlier users of Big Data? Sears. That said, you can never expect to impress executives unless you back your analysis with *some* numbers. Back-of-the-envelope analysis can work: A few stated assumptions and a quick P&L calculation (assuming P&L analysis is appropriate and correct only to four decimal places instead of the Corporate-standard 12) will open more doors to communicate with the upper echelon than a mountain of PowerPoint slides. In the face of relentless pressure to include every little detail in a presentation and fill the screen with 100,000 bullet points, insist on a few major insights and take a bullet for them.

- Few good tools have done so much wrong as benchmarking. What started as trying to learn from the best turned into a race to look alike and abandon strategy. But you can't beat powerful consultants if they get entrenched with their "industry studies." Your counter-strategy? Join the consultants, at a starting salary of $140,000. That's also a way to get your (former) boss to listen to you.

- What worked for social sites and Millennial-oriented services—offering free access—has turned a whole generation against paying for services. Corporate hasn't heard about it yet. It pays a fortune for old tricks. It doesn't learn from failure. You get what you invest in and they won't invest in you, so you have to take responsibility for your skill of competing. Put yourself out there as a cautious expert on a competitor and wait for the opportunity to say something insightful about it. Don't be cocky. Just state, "If we look at it from their perspective, I believe that . . . "

- The pressure to be nice turns competent managers into cheerleaders who are afraid of confronting reality. A culture of constructive negativity is more effective than unbridled optimism, which is empirically bad for companies. If you are an unbridled optimist by nature, why the heck are you reading this book? If you are not, keep the negativity to a minimum until you establish some credibility, but never ever fall for the contagious Corporate rose-colored glasses. Be bridled.

- Slogans like, "We are obsessed with quality," sound good. It is when Corporate becomes obsessed with the wrong *rituals* that you can smell rot. Cases in point: Growth at all costs, reorganization after reorganization, and using consultants even if they just make you look exactly like their other clients. What can you do as a maverick? Nothing. Keep cool. Remember the health benefits. Breathe. Recall the advice in the previous bullet. Repeat.

the NEW employee manual

- The public is turning more cynical about corporations by the day. Eventually this will yield a much less favorable environment for business. You can't blame the public; their cynicism comes from paying attention to some companies, executives, and PR departments. GE crusaded against climate change while its former CEO, Jeff Immelt, used two aircrafts on his trips to ensure one is "on hand" at all times, according to a 2017 report by CNBC. When "game changing" means two more pixels in the camera, hype is the norm. Mavericks should develop thick skins lest they start to believe the hype. Keeping some sense of sarcasm in private is good for your health. Just don't be *seen* as overtly cynical; that's a no-no. But funny, slightly sarcastic comments once every three months (put it on your Outlook calendar!) may be OK. It may even make you look a bit less naive as long as your quips do not point any fingers at your direct boss. Blame the "system."
- It is better to under-promise, take some heat initially, and delight with better-than-expected delivery. Case to remember: UPS, FedEx, and holiday deliveries. Case to forget: The exploding Galaxy Note 7.
- Being a schlimazel means having bad luck. Bad luck happens, and by definition, it's not your fault. Being a schlemiel means doing sloppy, overconfident work. Do your due diligence on every task you undertake. Use your spellchecker if English is not your mother tongue. If you are put in the fantastic position of working with a strategy team, remember strategic due diligence: Technology and people are not the same as competitive strategy. If you elect to become an entrepreneur, never forget: Strategy means providing something to customers that others don't, even if it is just a more convenient location for furry-looking-animal soaps. Strategy means always asking what others are doing so you can *stand out*. A horde of (formerly) large, rich, famous companies have forgotten this basic lesson.
- *Sicut non hodie.* Just not worst conditioning of Corporate managers. It's the enemy of built-in resilience. If you keep

a somewhat paranoid attitude of "today," you may become Andy Grove (would be a good thing). Tie your paranoia to exciting strategy alternatives, and you might have a positive impact. More likely, though, everyone will hate your pessimism. Look around to make sure no one sees you when you practice the mentality of *today*.

- Studying individuals' behavior can provide clues as to the state of the companies they work for. Identifying uncompetitive cultures may start with small clues. Sending people to conferences where they learn nothing is one. If you are lucky enough to go to a conference, count which company seems to send most people and how many of them end up at the bar.[3]

- *The quality of decisions is the only measurement companies should use in judging their state of competing.* Ignore the Magic Quadrant's hype, but do use our 2x2 (Chapter 18) to plan ahead what you want from your career. Remember: *Every* 2x2 matrix has magic built-in if you stare at it long enough.

- No company is beyond hope of salvation, but at times, salvation comes from unexpected or unpleasant sources. The future of capitalism rides on these change drivers as the public turns against business and decision-quality declines. When you research a potential employer, look for an activist on the board. Companies under activist campaigns are pressure cookers. You are better off investing in them than working for them. However, if the company has already settled with the activist, or actually invited him in voluntarily, this is a great place to work.

Maverick, we are in your corner. Any time you feel lonely with your unorthodox, nagging questions, unsure about your job or

---

[3] It gets a little tricky when you go to conferences to see which other companies send people to conferences. Are they there to see whether your company is sending people to conferences? That might explain the 7 million people cramming the trade show halls in Las Vegas every year.

your boss or the lure of health benefits, read a passage in this book. Make it your Zen place. Know that you are not alone. If you are happy being swept by the crowd, don't let us stand in your way. But if at times, you swim against the current, remember we are your personal career consultants and, fortunately for you, our advice is tailored specifically to you. Can't you tell? We even gave you a 2x2 in Chapter 19!

If you implement just 10 percent of our ideas, you may survive Corporate. If you implement all our ideas, come work with us. We don't pay well, and we have no health insurance, but boy do we have fun.

FINAL THOUGHTS FROM BEN

There are some things that are wrong with our current economic system, even though I still consider it the best in the world. Some people think China will overtake America as the number-one economy because of the way a central authoritarian government can funnel resources into a few endeavors it deems long-term "winners" (e.g., solar energy). The same pundits probably thought Japan would be number one by now when they admired its "industrial policy" in the '70s. That didn't happen. And, naturally, being a free market advocate, I think it never will. There are much better ways to increase competitiveness and long-term thinking without having a few old bureaucrats in a politburo or ministry of trade decide who wins. One easy way is to abolish mandatory quarterly reporting. Another is to favorably treat long-term equity holders, both for taxes and corporate voting. Both require changing the regulatory and legal regime under which corporations operate so they can choose what to offer and investors can choose what to buy, but if politicians haven't listened to Warren Buffet when he suggested it, I doubt they'd listen to me. Too many powerful interests benefit from *mandatory* quarterly reporting being enforced by government.

I am worried about America's maverick status but not because of lack of central planning.

The other day, I was watching *America's Got Talent* with my family on TV. One of the acts was a most amazing number about nothing. A young Israeli actor created a whole routine around mind control and magic by doing neither. He just performed the most mundane tasks (taking out a tissue from a box, focusing hard on a spoon and, when it fails to bend, using it to eat yogurt, etc.) with the flare of a magic act.[4] It was the cleverest act—dare I say the most maverick act—on the set that day (if not ever). It takes huge talent to pull off an act like this. There is no physical skill or genetic advantage as in acrobatics, dancing, or singing. Did this act advance to the next stage? No. Mere talent doesn't always win.

If you watch several of the shows, you form a perspective. The acts that advanced to the final competition by consensus had one thing in common: The talent has been secondary to the emotional background. A semiblind singer, a homeless guy, a painfully shy young man, a choir singing in Swahili and showing incredible diversity among the members, a young woman who overcame severe disability, artists who came from disadvantaged or hardship background . . . if I were a betting man, I could have put money on which artists the judges would advance based more on the heartbreaking introduction than the talent in the act. These artists were all talented to a degree, like thousands of other artists, or maybe less than other artists, but they all rang the emotional bell of the panel's decision- makers.

The show should actually be called *America Gets Emotional*.

There is one place where emotions should not play a role: business decisions. That doesn't mean one doesn't need passion. Mark and I are very passionate about what we do. But when we make decisions or help companies make better decisions, we store the emotions away: We use logic. We use System 2 thinking, and a deliberate, calculative, reasoning process. We look at other perspectives. We validate or eliminate hunches with available data. That's where artificial intelligence can be useful to humans—no

---

[4] https://www.youtube.com/watch?v=lHBml4Nwc0s

biases, no emotional clouding of judgment, only pure cleverness (of the algorithm writers).

What's the lesson here? As a maverick, you have clever ideas, raw talent, and unconventional thinking, but you need to sell them to people who might be emotionally and mentally tied to the status quo and formulaic thinking. In other words, communication is as important as the talent/idea itself.

Mavericks, find ways to communicate as mavericks. We found one. That's why you are reading *this line*.

FINAL THOUGHTS FROM MARK

I want to tell you three things. I must start with Ben.

I find Ben fascinating, exasperating (completely unlike me), hilarious, and—one of the best compliments I can give—always worth listening to. Sharing this book with him was fascinating, exasperating, hilarious, and always worth pursuing.

The first of the three things I want to tell you, maverick, is to find your Ben. Fellowship with another maverick is mentally invigorating. The fellowship of the zing is not about an echo chamber of agreement; it is about sharing open minds. You will grow, as I hope I have.

I remember the first time I went on stage with ideas similar to those in this book. It was at some conference I was addressing or maybe a corporate workshop on strategic thinking I was facilitating. I don't remember. I was about to tell them how wrong they were to believe what I, too, had believed. There *had* to be a flaw in my reasoning, and there were so many of them vs. so few of me. I feared my enraged audience would storm the stage with torches and epithets. I thought they'd try to get my MBA revoked. But I made my argument, all the while conscious that they were seated between me and the door.

I braced myself when I was done. Sure enough, people streamed toward me. They opened their mouths to speak. And they spoke music to my ears: *I never thought of it that way before.*

The second thing I want to tell you, maverick, is to do your maverick homework and think some maverick thing through and then have the courage to share what you created. You may have doubts. *Does everyone else know this already? Am I clinically bonkers? Can I reach the door faster than my audience?* But you may hear someone speak that music to you. And if you don't, have the courage to persist.

About 20 years ago, I participated in a self-awareness seminar. In one exercise, each person in a group of five would speak for one minute to the rest of the group about the things they were proud of about themselves. The rest of the group would listen without comment. It was an exercise in acknowledging your positive points. For various reasons, it is difficult for many people, but it wasn't for me. I had no trouble filling my minute with my Ivy League degrees, my publications, the company I'd founded, my work advising Fortune 500 companies around the world. Frankly, I felt pretty good.

At the end of each person's minute, they'd be silent while the other members of the group provided positive, and *only* positive, feedback. That, too, is difficult for many people. When it was my turn, I listened as one person said impressive this, another person said cool that. Then a young man, 15 years old, turned to me, smiled, and said two words: nice start.

Remember, I was supposed to be silent. Outwardly, I was. Inwardly, I was not. Nice *start???* Are you nuts? (And much, much more in that vein.) Nice *START?!?*

Then, for once, I did something smart. I paused and asked myself: What did he mean by that? I realized I didn't know. He might have been teasing me or congratulating me. He might have blurted out the first thing that came to his mind. He was 15 years old; maybe he didn't even know what a Fortune 500 company is.

I asked myself another question: What did I say that might have made him respond so (seemingly) oddly? I reviewed what I'd said, and I realized that everything, *everything*, I'd talked about was about my career. I'd said nothing about volunteer work, nothing about helping people, nothing about the people I love, nothing about the people who love me.

There's nothing wrong with talking about careers. But I wondered whether that's really all I am. I'm passionate about my work, but I am not *only* my work. So I made some changes. For example, I published a book about self-awareness. I had the perfect title: *Nice Start*.

You don't have a business life and a personal life. You have a life.

And here's the third thing I want to tell you: Nice start, maverick.

acknowledgments

We thank Vanessa Campos of Entrepreneur Press for having the sharp maverick eye to spot our diamond in the rough. We thank Jennifer Dorsey, our editor, for taking the rough out. We naturally thank all our loved ones for the patience they displayed as we became obsessed, obsessed, and obsessed with this project, and we thank Corporate for giving us so much material for this sitcom.

Mark expresses special thanks to Sidney Schoeffler, the brilliant founder of the Strategic Planning Institute (The PIMS Program), and to Ruth G. Newman of HBS and SPI, who taught him how to write (e.g., that the passive voice should be avoided).

about
the
authors

BENJAMIN GILAD is a *former* strategy professor at Rutgers University's School of Management, a *current* war-gaming trainer for the Fortune 500, and a *future* bestselling author. He is the president of two companies, www.giladwargames.com and www.academyci. com, but not the boss at home (wife and kids rule). The rest is uninteresting, pompous hype, and too Corporate to list here. He can be reached at ben@giladwargames.com or at bgilad@academyci.com, and he actually answers emails unless they are from OOPs.

MARK CHUSSIL is the founder of Advanced Competitive Strategies Inc. (https://whatifyourstrategy.com), an adjunct instructor at the Pamplin School of Business at the University of Portland, a four-decade veteran of competitive strategy, and a lifelong maverick. He has conducted business war games, run strategy simulations, led workshops on strategic thinking, and spoken at conferences on six continents. He wrote two previous books, *Strategy Analysis with ValueWar* (with Professor David J. Reibstein of the Wharton School) and *Nice Start: Questions Only You Can Answer to Create the Life Only You Can Live* (https://nicestart.ws), chapters or case studies for five other books, and numerous articles for the *Harvard Business Review* online and elsewhere. He can run a billion simulations before breakfast and has a BA from Yale (in political science, of all things) and an MBA from Harvard.

You can contact Mark at mchussil@whatifyourstrategy.com and via LinkedIn.

Mark is married to Bridget, the love of his life. It just keeps getting better.

index